ALSO BY TED KOPPEL

In the National Interest (with Marvin Kalb)

Nightline: History in the Making and the Making of Television
(with Kyle Gibson)

Off Camera

Off Camera

Private Thoughts Made Public

Ted Koppel

Alfred A. Knopf *New York* 2000

THIS IS A BORZOI BOOK
PUBLISHED BY ALFRED A. KNOPF

Copyright © 2000 by Ted Koppel

All rights reserved under International and Pan-American
Copyright Conventions. Published in the United States
by Alfred A. Knopf, a division of Random House, Inc.,
New York, and simultaneously in Canada by Random House of
Canada Limited, Toronto. Distributed by Random House, Inc.,
New York.
www.aaknopf.com

Knopf, Borzoi Books, and the colophon
are registered trademarks of Random House, Inc.

Portions of this work were originally published in
Brill's Content.

Library of Congress Cataloging-in-Publication Data
Koppel, Ted, 1940–
    Off camera : private thoughts made public / by Ted
    Koppel.—1st ed.
        p.   cm.
    ISBN 0-375-41077-5 (alk. paper)
        1. Koppel, Ted, 1940– —Diaries.   2. Television
journalists—United States—Diaries.   3. United States—
Civilization—1970–   I. Title.

PN4874.K66   A3 2000
070'.92—dc21
    [B]   00-034919

Manufactured in the United States of America
First Edition

For Grace Anne,
who for forty years has made all the
good things in my life possible.

Introduction

Many people are mildly surprised when they meet me in or around Washington, D.C. The exchanges in which I am involved tend to follow this sort of pattern:

> VIEWER: "What brings you to Washington?"
> TK: "This is where we do *Nightline*. I've been doing *Nightline* out of Washington for more than twenty years now."
> VIEWER (incredulous): "I thought you did the show out of New York."

Depending on how much time I have, I sometimes use such occasions to underscore the fallibility of television as a medium of communication. I am, after all, introduced on each program by *Nightline* announcer Bill Rice, who intones: "... and now, reporting from Washington, Ted Koppel." I end each program by saying, "... for all of us here at ABC News in Washington, good night." For many years there was also a sign behind me identifying the location as ABC NEWS WASHINGTON. Roughly speaking, then, over the course of five thousand programs, the information has been conveyed some fifteen thousand times—without much effect, it seems.

My unsought barrage of information slows people down a little, but usually leads to a less debatable observation:

> VIEWER: "You're shorter than you look on TV."
> TK: "So are you."

VIEWER (slightly embarrassed, perhaps trying to make
amends): "You're better-looking in person, though."

I mumble something about the cruelties of studio lighting, and we continue along our separate ways.

Television, it is true, is an illusory medium. It conveys the impression of intimacy without the substance. In early March 2000, millions of Americans journeyed (as the result of Katie Couric's altogether admirable campaign against colon cancer) via television and a fiber-optic camera into the innermost recesses of the *Today* show star's privacy. Viewers saw more of Katie than they had ever seen of their significant others. How could they not believe themselves intimately connected to this complete stranger?

I have been appearing on television for nearly forty years. People older than I have watched me mature and age. Younger people, now themselves in their thirties, forties and fifties, remember me from their childhood. I have attended them in their kitchens and dens and, as several hundred women (reveling in the naughtiness and originality of the observation) have told me, they go to bed with me every night. How could they not presume to know me?

They presume to know my politics, my views on such matters as abortion and gun control. They draw their inferences from a raised eyebrow or a tone of voice. If my questions are nonconfrontational, they presume my sympathy for the person being interviewed. They appear to have a hard time believing that I would ask a tough question of someone I like. It occurs to surprisingly few people that I am principally concerned with extracting information from a guest, and that my tone or apparent mood or facial expression has little or nothing to do with what I really think.

This book may resolve some of that confusion, but not, I trust, all of it. Each of us has several layers of opinion, passion and intimacy. The stylized role of a television news anchor is designed to reveal as few of these as humanly possible. A journal is a much more subjective medium.

The title of this book is intended to suggest that it contains opinions I would never express on the air. Often these opinions deal with stories I covered for ABC News. Sometimes the entries are unrelated to my work altogether. In all instances, observations were recorded daily. A few have been deleted, but only because my new friend and editor, Jonathan Segal, found them too labored or trivial to merit inclusion. That standard might well have been applied to several more. But part of a journal's value rests in an author's willingness to leave contemporaneous observations as they were at the time they were made. Some judgments, reached at the end of a long day, betray the weariness of the writer. Others would clearly have been modified had information, available now, been known to me then. In essence, though, whatever its flaws or virtues, this book is a journal of subjective snapshots of the twentieth century's final year, and some memories and observations it triggered.

January

January 1 / Captiva, Florida

Hope and foreboding. Not necessarily in equal measure, either. What every new year has that recommends it over the old one is the promise of uncertainty. We know what happened last year. There is always the possibility that we will learn from our mistakes, tighten our abdominals, stop smoking, exercise greater patience and dedicate our lives to the selfless pursuit of Man's greater good. There is also the off chance that pigs will fly.

What makes the prospect of 1999 particularly gloomy is that the year begins perched on the detritus of 1998. What punishment, short of removal from office, will the U.S. Senate cobble together for William Jefferson Clinton? Surely someone will find an eighteenth-century solution in the delphic mutterings of the Federalist Papers. Actually, the twentieth century has already formulated its own equivalent to the pillory and stocks: Letterman, Leno, Imus and the various front pages of a hundred newspapers and magazines, together with the daily flaying on radio talk shows and television news programs, have already delivered their populist punishment, without having undermined "the will of the people" or, at least, the will of those millions of civic souls who dragged themselves to the polls to vote for Clinton in 1996.

Whichever way it goes, it will leave a nasty aftertaste. The president and First Lady will speak piously of national reconciliation, while their loyalists ram the rockets' red glare up the tailpipes of the right-wing fanatics, who have confused low morals with high crimes. The right-wing fanatics, meanwhile, will speak piously of having made television newscasts safe for viewing by their children again (as though anyone without dentures even watches the news anymore), and then they will encourage Lucianne Goldberg to collaborate with Howard Stern in the drafting of "A Moral Compass for the New Millennium."

It can safely be predicted, meanwhile, that we are all destined to become wholeheartedly sick and tired of the new millenium before it even gets under way. The term "wretched excess" was coined for the American experience during a year such as this. Has the product been designed that will not presume some benefit of association with the new millenium? Is there a family so removed from the sense of the moment that it has not yet felt the first uneasy stirrings of being insufficiently prepared for next New Year's Eve, even as it shakes off the aftermath of last night? It may yet prove to be a perfectly glorious year, in which decency, civility and good taste prevail.

Or pork chops may sprout wings.

January 2 / Captiva

One more note on the millenium: The *New York Times* editorial board must be acutely conscious of its responsibilities to point us all in the right direction. Sometimes, though, mere opining or editorializing is not enough; a declaration is required. Yesterday the *Times* declared that it was all right to take the new millenium seriously. It wasn't altogether clear whether that makes it simply permissible, or if it's now obligatory. The newspaper's finest minds will probably express themselves on the subject again.

So far this year the weather here in Captiva has been nothing short of spectacular. That's worthy of brief note, if only because most of the rest of the country is in a miserable deep freeze. Somehow that makes our weather feel even more delicious. Symbolically, that comes close to summarizing America's attitude toward the rest of the world: The weather's just fine here and don't bother us with your whining about crumbling Asian economies, corroding Russian infrastructure, pandemic disease in Africa and the growing likelihood that someone in Isfahan is packing an overnight bag with the wherewithal to pop Cleveland with a biological weapon.

I have the uneasy feeling that a few decades from now people will look back at this year and say: Oh yes, '99. That was one of the last prewar years.

Think about it. The rest of the world holds a significantly more jaundiced view of how wonderful we are than we do. We are so busy promoting our virtues to one another that we occasionally confuse the advertisement with the product. George Soros, who describes himself as amoral in the conduct of his business affairs, nevertheless contributed more to Russia in at least one recent year than did the United States of America. He, at least, recognizes that well-directed charity can have enormous practical and positive consequences for the donor. The platform of generous foreign aid, however, is not one on which any American politicican would like to run.

Americans appear to have forgotten the generosity and foresight of the Marshall Plan and how it led to the reconstruction of a vibrant West German economy. The rebirth of postwar Japan was only possible because the United States helped the Japanese back onto their feet. In Asia and in Europe the careful calibration of an unambiguous projection of force and a generous policy of foreign aid combined, ultimately, to achieve the erosion of communist power in Asia and its near elimination in Europe. Foreign aid tends to be cheaper and significantly more effective than our when-in-doubt-lob-a-cruise-missile parody of a foreign policy, but casualty-free military action plays well in the polls.

How strange that we wouldn't dream of tolerating the captain of a cruise liner setting his course by surveying the passengers, but that we have become quite comfortable watching the ship of state being steered by polls.

Anyway, the world's in a mess, weapons of mass destruction abound and we haven't a clue how we would respond to a chemical or biological attack against one or more of our cities.

God, it's beautiful outside. I think I'll go sailing.

January 3 / Captiva

The weather is gloomy. The Jacksonville Jaguars are manhandling the soon-to-be Hartford Patriots and I wonder if I'm the only football fan who doesn't care. I have yet to grow accustomed to the notion that Jacksonville has a football team, and, while the name Boston Patriots made some sense and New England Patriots could at least be justified on regional grounds, the Hartford Patriots is just silly. How about the Hartford Adjustors? The Hartford Actuarial Risk? At four the Packers play the 49ers. OK, I know that free agency has reduced us all to rooting for uniforms, but I have my standards. I'll root for a uniform with a little bit of history.

My friend, the executive producer of *Nightline*, Tom Bettag, has sent me a couple of pages of notes by a historian friend of his, responding to a reckless suggestion of mine a few months ago that *Nightline* do a series of programs on this last millenium. That, in turn, was prompted by the observations of a Stanford professor friend. My wife, Grace Anne, and I were participating in a Stanford-sponsored hike through Tuscany. Our friend was ruminating on the lifestyle of the Medicis and how they, probably the most powerful and privileged family of their age, lived in conditions that fell far short of those in which an average, middle-class American lives today. Set aside the notion that the Medicis had Michelangelo, da Vinci and Botticelli as house painters and interior decorators; they had lousy heating and cooling, primitive medical care, no electricity, information resources that would be rejected as inadequate by any late-twentieth-century American and no access to fresh fruit in the winter.

In some respects, then, mankind has made significant progress. Unbelievable progress in the areas of longevity, health, communication, travel; even social justice, in some places. But as George Bernard Shaw observed early on in this century (before we'd really gotten the hang of it), where man excels is in the science of killing.

I see by this morning's *Times* that the North Koreans may already have spirited away a few nuclear warheads. The *Times* points out that U.S.–North Korean negotiations have been stymied, that Pyongyang is making increasingly bellicose noises and that the North Koreans have shown they have the capacity to deliver such warheads to Japan, Hawaii and Alaska.

As I said, we may well be living through what we will soon recall as one of the last of the prewar years.

January 4 / Captiva

The northern chill has finally insinuated itself into central Florida. Only Canadian tourists and "snowbirds" from Michigan and Minnesota and "this reporter" (as my old friend Danny Meehan, who wet-nursed me through my first job as a copyboy at WMCA, used to say) are walking around in shorts. My excuse is that I never made it past third form at Abbotsholme School in Staffordshire, England, and consequently never reached that exalted status that would have permitted me to wear long pants in winter. This has inured me, from the thighs down, to any temperatures above 20°F.

The spartan rigors of a British boarding school in the early fifties deserve their own footnote as we come to the end of this century.

I rather doubt that my parents (German Jews who fled to England just prior to World War II) would have sent me to boarding school at age eleven had there been any other option. They, however, were back in Frankfurt, fighting for reparations in the newly reestablished German court system. They didn't want me going to school in Germany, and there were no relatives with whom to leave me in England. Hence, Abbotsholme.

One or two flush toilets may have existed at Abbotsholme in 1952, but if so, they would have been for the private and exclusive use of the headmaster and senior members of his staff. The rest of us used outdoor latrines. These were so utterly lacking in twentieth-century complexity that they cannot have differed much from whatever the ancient Saxons used. Two wooden footrests above a pit constituted pretty much the entire works.

I lie.

Generations of Anglo-Saxons, perhaps with a little help from the Picts up north, had contrived certain additional conveniences adopted at Abbotsholme: a bucket with some sand (civilized people do not leave their waste uncovered by at least a handful or two of sand), and there had to have been some toilet paper, although memory does not serve.

I do remember that "lights out" was at 8 p.m. On those occasions when a coal delivery had been made, our housemaster would creep through the corridors listening at the door of each room for the sound of boys talking. No sooner had such a group of miscreants been detected than the housemaster would launch into his favorite tirade about how "a bunch of juvenile delinquents like you are all going to end up in Borstal" (a juvenile detention center immortalized in *Borstal Boy*). He always seemed quite pleased to have uncovered our wrongdoing. He would order us to put on our Plimsolls (a crude and early ancestor of Nikes) and then lead us to the courtyard where two tons of coal waited to be shoveled into the coal cellar. Suffice it to say that when we were through with that chore, we were encouraged to take a cold bath. (I'm not altogether sure how the coal was employed, since it was not to produce hot water or heat in our rooms. Indeed, not only were our rooms not heated in the winter, we were required to leave the windows open.)

When there was no coal delivery, boys requiring some form of immediate justice would be sent on a late-evening cross-country run. The various "houses" in which we slept were scattered in a rough circle at some distance around the cluster of school buildings. The complete circuit covered approximately five miles. We would be required to run from one "house" to the next, acquiring at each a signed note from the housemaster indicating our times of arrival and departure. It was actually better than shoveling coal.

Back to the frigid North tomorrow.

January 5 / Washington, D.C.

It is an act of will to become reengaged in the impeachment morass. It now looks as though the trial will get under way on Thursday and, if there are those who know what form it will take, they're doing a brilliant job of keeping that from the rest of us. The White House is lofting trial balloons suggesting that the meek faces the president's lawyers showed before the House Judiciary Committee will be replaced (in the event of a full-blown trial) by a more combative stance. I am infected by a rampant case of beyond-the-Beltway "Who gives a crap?" Bill Clinton may yet convince me, as he seems to have convinced much of the rest of the country, that if you appear not to care, you can be impeached by the House and tried by the Senate, and it won't matter. Of course it will matter if he's convicted, but no one seems to believe that likely.

It seems to me that the Senate is desperately looking for some form of Goldilocks solution. The Constitution has left the senators with the option of doing nothing (too mild), or throwing the president out of office (too harsh). What's needed is a "just right" option. In analogous situations at the local level, juries reluctant to sentence an eighteen-year-old to ten years of hard time for a third possession of marijuana engage in the process of jury nullification. They simply refuse to convict. They, however, don't have to run for reelection.

We in the media are, at the moment, in the awkward position of knowing nothing and interviewing smart people who also know nothing; but we are confronting a story that, on the face of it, is so important we can't ignore it.

January 6 / Washington

What a mess! Our (and NPR's) crackerjack legal correspondent Nina Totenberg tells us that Chief Justice Rehnquist is like a young swain waiting to be called for a date. He's supposed to preside (starting tomorrow) over the Senate trial of the president, but, even though he's written a book on the subject of impeachment, he doesn't know what the rules are going to be this time around and he's waiting for someone to tell him. The Senate, by a simple majority, can, in effect, dictate the procedures as they go along; however, even the chieftains of the Senate, Majority Leader Trent Lott and Minority Leader Tom Daschle, are playing it by ear at the moment. Each is uncertain—especially in Lott's case—what he can get his own membership to accept. The Republicans seem determined to have a full-fledged trial, complete with witnesses. The Democrats are equally determined not to let that happen. Some sort of compromise will, eventually, be worked out, but it looks less and less like it will be of the quick and clean variety. All of this is worthy of note only in the sense that, sometimes, when history has had a chance to clean up reality and make everything nice and neat, we forget how messy reality is in its day-by-day incarnation. In retrospect, for example, Richard Nixon's departure from the White House seems to have been inevitable, when in fact the struggle to make a case sufficient to convince Nixon to leave was protracted and ugly.

Members of the Establishment (the Senate, the chief justice, the White House, the media) are trundling along, with no option but to treat all of this as though it were really important, while the public-at-large couldn't be more apathetic.

I'm off for a meeting with Bill Bradley. It's at his request, which is a clear signal that he is running for the presidency. We require all our serious candidates first to humble themselves by kissing the rings of the college of media cardinals. Lyndon Johnson raised that sort of courting of the press to a new level. Audiotapes of his Oval Office phone conversations are now available through the Johnson Library.

C-SPAN radio plays them on Saturday afternoons, and I often listen to them when I'm jogging along the C&O Canal. A few weeks ago we were treated to the then-president of the United States shamelessly stroking Walter Lippman (one of the most important—and self-important—columnists of his time).

I tried to reach you, Walter, before I issued my statement, says Johnson, *but I couldn't get to you in time. I'd like to read it to you now, if you've got the time.*

Oh, yes, Mr. President, says Lippman. (Not precise quotes, but close enough.)

Since I was only listening to an audiotape I couldn't see Lippman's tail wagging, but I'd swear I could hear it. Bradley's not that shameless. In fact, he's a really smart and decent man; it's just the way the game is played. Stroke my ego now, and maybe I'll be unintentionally helpful somewhere along the line.

Does it actually work out that way? We're all human. If someone treats us (reporters) well, we're inclined to give that person the benefit of the doubt somewhere down the road.

Later in the afternoon. I met with Bradley for ninety minutes. Nothing earth-shattering. He is, in fact, determined to run for the White House, citing his conviction that the time is right for him, though he's enjoyed the relative tranquillity of the last couple of years. His daughter is twenty-two and therefore wouldn't have to go through the "child in the White House" trauma; his wife, after more than ten years, has just finished a book on how postwar German fiction writers have treated or ignored the subject of the Holocaust.

Bradley believes that he will be able to tap into the many thousands of people whose net worth is half a million dollars or more and persuade a significant number of these folks to give $1,000 to his campaign for president. I came away from our meeting liking him enormously, wishing that someone as smart and decent could become president—and pretty much convinced that, in his case at least, it will never happen. I hope I'm wrong.

He was a little late to our meeting, so I took the opportunity to go to the bathroom. A small plaque on top of the toilet paper container read: PRESS BUTTON ON TOP VALVE TO OVERRIDE AUTO FLUSH. To think that in only one lifetime I've gone from dumping sand in an outdoor latrine to having the option of overriding an auto flush is almost more than I can absorb.

January 7 / Washington

Cold and clear, which is more than can be said of Clinton's Senate trial. There's a Rashomon-like feeling to this case. Many of the Republicans plainly see his crime as encouraging Monica Lewinsky to submit a false affidavit to thwart justice in Paula Jones's sexual harassment lawsuit. Most of the Democrats see the case just as clearly as being about nothing more than a horny philanderer lying in order to keep a semblance of peace at home. Nobody questions the latter, and there probably isn't even a whole lot of disagreement over the former. The problem is that the Constitution appears to offer only the political equivalent of the death penalty if the Senate finds him guilty.

I think most Americans would be surprised to discover how many of the senators, now grappling with what form this trial should take, are quite genuinely torn about trying to do the right thing. The ultimate irony is that we wouldn't be where we are today were it not for the unanimous decision of the Supreme Court that Jones's civil case against the president should proceed, and that it would have no undue impact on Clinton's ability to carry out his responsibilities as president. Now, Chief Justice Rehnquist is presiding over the legal pageant that proves just how wrong he and his eight colleagues were.

The president could, of course, save the country from the distress of these next few weeks, but resignation would be a remarkably selfless act, and some of those who have worked, or are working closely, with him tell me they don't think it's in his character. No, we will all have to witness this trashy spectacle so that Clinton can spend the rest of his life speculating on everything he might have achieved if his political enemies had not taken such shameless advantage of his open fly. In the final analysis, it is true that the right wing in this country has taken every opportunity that Clinton has given them to bring him down. It is also true that he has given them almost every opportunity that they have taken.

January 8 / Washington

A couple inches of snow today and it all comes a little more clearly into focus: Is that guy I talked to back in early December actually going to come by today to plow the driveway and the parking lot? Grace Anne calls to say that there are several young men banging around outside the house with shovels, while someone with a truck and a blade is clearing the driveway. There's my answer. The point is that a couple inches of snow puts my priorities more in line with those of the American public. That's the problem with those of us in the mainstream media: We ruminate about larger issues, like the Constitution's stance on oral sex, while the rest of the country worries about bursting radiators and whether the old Chevy will make it up the hill to the Wal-Mart.

In truth, the public's take on the impeachment trial is rather encouraging. There aren't many countries in the world where you could put the president, chairman of the revolutionary council, prime minister or king on trial and provoke as much apathy as we've mustered here in America. There's something quite wholesome about the country's clear conviction that Washington has gone nuts, but that in the overall scheme of their lives the trial probably won't make a whole lot of difference anyway.

January 9 / Potomac, Maryland

The roads are still icy and a little nasty, so I picked up my father-in-law with our four-wheel-drive vehicle and took him for his checkup at Holy Cross Hospital. He and my mother-in-law are planning a few weeks in the sun down at Captiva, and it's better that "Pop" get his medical ticket punched first.

It's a good day to take a step back and at least try to frame the intent of this journal. At its simplest level it's a "bread crumbs in the woods" sort of thing: You don't know where you're going or how it's all going to turn out, and by the time things get really interesting (when you're inside the witch's gingerbread house, for example) it's too late to start figuring it out. This, then, falls in the category of marking the trail of how we got to wherever it is we are at the end of this year. (And giving myself the luxury of personal comments along the way—things that wouldn't be appropriate on *Nightline*.)

Then, of course, there tends to be a natural evolution, over time, of the mundane into the interesting. Check out any old magazine, a *Look* or *Collier's* from the forties or fifties. What we once took for granted has become fascinating, even if it's only the changing cost of things: A Studebaker cost how much?

Contemporaneous observations, once the outcome of a series of events is known, also bestow on the reader a delicious sense of superiority. (You really didn't think he'd be convicted? You thought the Broncos would win the Super Bowl? You didn't know the market was going to crash?)

And then, of course, there is the simple fact that you will know what kind of a year it turned out to be. As I write these words, I do not. That's the pathos or drama or humor of surveying my ignorance from your vantage point in the future.

Arthur C. Clarke is quoted in this morning's *Washington Post* as bemoaning the near-universal ignorance that causes us to anticipate the year 2000 as the first year of the third millennium when, in fact, it is really the end of the second. After all, we attain our first birthdays at the *end* of our first year of life, not at the beginning of it (except in some Asian cultures; but that's another matter). This, though, as I'm sure Clarke understands, is an emotional phenomenon, not an historic or scientific one. The *New York Times* the other day took note of the fact that some medieval monk actually screwed up the Western calendar by several years. By his calculation, the birth of Jesus would have taken place three or four years after the death of Herod, when the New Testament account clearly indicates that Jesus was born during Herod's reign. Historically, then, the new millennium began unnoticed and unheralded several years ago. Does anybody care? It's even sillier than we think. Jerry Falwell and some of the other evangelical preachers are preparing their followers for the "rapture," the "apocalypse," as though it were a calendar event.

January 10 / Potomac

I'm sitting in the addition to the house we've lived in since 1971. Our youngest daughter, Tara, was born on the day our offer on this house was accepted. We built the addition when we learned that Grace, my late mother-in-law, had cancer. The idea was that Grace Anne's parents would move in with us, and, if the cancer proved fatal (as it did), my wife's father, Gene, would continue to live with us. My mother-in-law died here in the house, but long before the addition was completed. Gene did move in with us for a couple of years but then met and married Penny, another wonderful woman, and moved into her house. So now it's just the two of us, occupying a house that's significantly larger than the one in which we raised four children.

We are fortunate in that three of our kids live in New York and the fourth lives down the road, in Washington. They visit regularly, and it's good to have the space when they all descend at once. Still, there is something out of kilter in the way we modern suburbanites relate to our living space. Since our children tend to move according to the locus of their work, our homes empty out just about the time we've expanded them to their maximum size.

We allow ourselves to become confused these days between what is in our interest and what we are interested in. I have half an eye on the playoff game between the Jets and the Jaguars. It's not an issue, but it occurred to me that if the president's trial were taking place today, it would take a stouthearted network executive to interrupt the game even with bulletins. The thought of replacing game coverage with live coverage of the trial would be unthinkable. The air is thick these days with feigned concern that this trial may get in the way of the important business of the nation. Hell, it won't even get in the way of a football game. Never mind all this hyperventilating over deferring the State of the Union Address. How about deferring the Super Bowl until the trial's done? That would get it over with in a hurry.

January 11 / Potomac

Let me try to make sense of this one more time before the Senate and the White House turn everyone's brains to mush. Is this about privacy and sexual relations between consenting adults? Well, is it?

If we're going to accept Clinton's tortured definition, it's certainly not about sexual relations. Granted, that's a nit-picking technicality, but, for good or ill, it's his. If we're going to give any credence to Paula Jones, there was nothing consensual about her encounter. She was a state employee. He was the governor. She says he asked her to perform fellatio, which, she says, she rejected. If that account is true, that would seem to constitute sexual harassment. The political motives of those who plucked Jones from obscurity may not rise to the level of pond scum, but if, unbidden and unsought, the governor presented his Johnson for use as a Popsicle, his rights to privacy do not seem like an appropriate concern.

Monica Lewinsky says she performed oral sex on Clinton for the first time while she was still an intern at the White House. That information could have been helpful to Jones in her sexual harassment lawsuit against the president, but Lewinsky filed a false affidavit. She and the president had, she testified, previously agreed on a cover story to conceal their relationship. Did he tell her to lie? No, she says. But what is a cover story that's fabricated in order to conceal a relationship if not a lie?

The truth would certainly have been an embarrassment to the president and humiliating to his family. It could also have made Jones's lawsuit more convincing in court. Was Lewinsky offered a variety of jobs to keep her from embarrassing the president or to keep him from losing a sexual harassment lawsuit? The answer is probably both. But this case is not about privacy, and it's not about consensual sex. Both of those came later. This is about a gawky, not terribly impressive young woman who probably did reject the chance to service the governor of Arkansas in a Little Rock hotel room. That made her a convenient political pawn for Clinton's enemies and a lying piece of trailer trash to his allies.

What bothers me to this day, though, is how Jones knew what kind of sex Clinton would ask for (he insists, after all, that he neither did nor said anything inappropriate to her in that Arkansas hotel room) years before any of the public revelations made it common knowledge.

January 12 / Washington

Newsweek has a cover story on Don Imus this week: "How the King of Irreverent Radio Turns Politics into Entertainment." Also on the cover: "PLUS 20 STARS OF THE NEW NEWS." Inside, in an accompanying article on "The New Powers That Be" (everything is capitalized in magazines these days. It must be the equivalent of networks turning the sound up on commercials), I learn that I'm a transitional figure. There's a twenty-year-old picture of me, in the middle of a row of photographs that begins with Walter Cronkite's, moves on to David Brinkley's and Dan Rather's (then mine) and then Larry King's, Rush

Limbaugh's and Geraldo Rivera's. I feel like *Homo erectus* on an evolutionary chart, except we're moving in the wrong direction. That appears to be the point of the author, Jonathan Alter: "With class and insight, Ted Koppel and *Nightline* bridged the old world of serious political reporting with the new kingdom of talk."

Well, I like the "class and insight" bit, but I'm not sure I'm ready to cede the entire battlefield just yet.

January 13 / Washington

Michael Jordan retired today. It's nice to see someone pull out while he's still at (or at least near) the top of his game. It will be hard for him. Obviously, he's got all the money he or his family will ever need, and there is hardly a company out there that wouldn't pay an additional fortune to have Michael shilling for their product, should he need to replenish the supply. Still, I have a hard time imagining what it must be like for a man in his mid-thirties to acknowledge that the activity that has been the central focus of his life is suddenly over. The "used up" American athlete is often ill-prepared for much else than his sport. But Jordan seems to be a multifaceted man. He could become, as so many other star athletes have done, an actor, a social activist or a color commentator for one of the sports networks. As successful as some ex-athletes are in another field, however, it is only the rarest among them (Bill Bradley and Byron "Whizzer" White come to mind) whose later activities surpass their athletic achievements. Jordan was, arguably, the greatest basketball player of all time. Now he is the greatest *former* player of all time.

A touching moment with Congressman Henry Hyde earlier this evening. I had just finished interviewing him for tonight's program. Tomorrow, he opens the prosecution's case against the president in the Senate. I asked Hyde whether he planned to attend the State of the Union Address if the president goes ahead with his plan to come before the Joint Session of Congress. No, he said, he thought he would watch it on television from home. It would be difficult for him to keep getting up and down, and people might misunderstand if he remained seated. He clearly believed that television viewers of the State of the Union Address might assume that he was expressing a lack of respect for the president. I concluded that he would rather stay home than be thought a hypocrite for applauding the man he had helped impeach, and I must have conveyed that sense to him in one of my follow-up questions. After the interview was over, he leaned in and whispered that he was incontinent following his prostate surgery, and that getting up and down created problems for him.

Here he is, seventy-four years old, having lost his wife a few years ago. He's had the embarrassment of a thirty-year-old affair recently becoming public knowledge. His role as chairman of the House Judiciary Committee has, perhaps, won him some new admirers; but his critics are more vociferous, and now he has to move around town with a security detail because there have been threats on his life. And he has to worry about soiling himself. I can imagine that he anticipated an easier conclusion to his career.

I forgot about the ball. Mark McGwire's seventieth home run ball went for a tidy sum at auction last night: $2.7 million, plus the 10 percent commission the buyer has to pay. Sammy Sosa's sixty-second home run ball brought in something between $125,000 and $150,000. That's the difference between coming in first and second. Who was it who said Americans know the price of everything and the value of nothing?

The tendency is hardly unique to Americans. But I wonder why it is that so many rich people seem to feel the need to validate their wealth by accumulating the material evidence of someone else's accomplishment.

January 14 / Washington

Most of the House managers of the case against "William Jefferson Clinton" (as they keep intoning) are in grave danger of being indicted themselves for terminal tediousness. They're battling years of conditioning on television that keep moving us in the direction of bright brevity. All right, no one should expect that Henry Hyde, Jim Sensenbrenner (the substitute high school English teacher whom everyone hated, as one of my colleagues suggested earlier today) et al. should apply the six-and-a-half-second sound-bite rule that seems to prevail on television newscasts these days. But it's strange that all these politicians, who have internalized the importance of brevity and pith in their various campaigns, are now reduced to endless oratorical flailing. The U.S. Senate is unaccustomed to sitting silently on its hundred duffs listening to lectures about its constitutional duty. The House prosecutors must know they are only going through the motions, but seem incapable of reigning in their rhetoric.

The president pops up relentlessly in newspapers and on television in a series of civic photo ops (in the company of the elderly, high school teachers, cops) pushing his programs for rescuing Social Security, improving education, focusing on safety on the streets, while Sensenbrenner quotes the old Teddy Roosevelt chestnut about no one being above or below the law. (Thank you, Congressman. Would the chief justice mind if we all took a fifteen-minute comfort stop? There being no objection . . .)

Last night, CBS premiered its much anticipated *60 Minutes II*. It's a slavish imitation of *60 Minutes*, which is to say, it's very good, but I don't think it will prosper on prime time in midweek. Twenty years from now, a hundred-year-old Mike Wallace and a ninety-something Don Hewitt will still reign supreme on Sunday nights at seven. But Wednesdays at nine requires, I believe, something a little zippier.

January 15 / Washington

I listened on the car radio to Bill McCullum of Florida, one of the House managers in the president's trial, summarize the case against Clinton. It was very clearly and powerfully done. For all the talk of following consciences, setting examples for our children and a standard for history, I have yet to see one genuine profile in courage. I so yearn to hear one senator change his or her mind out of principle, no matter how he or she votes. McCullum, as I say, was awfully good, but I think that once again we are witnessing a dialogue of the deaf. There are political imperatives that have to be met and satisfied on both sides of the aisle. The Republicans are meeting their obligation to their conservative constituents, pressing forward with this trial to the bitter end, no matter what the lack of public appetite. The Democrats are being equally partisan and true to their constituents in maintaining to the bitter end that this is all about sex and lying about sex—everybody does it; nobody cares.

The president continues to maintain the public illusion that he is above all of this, that he doesn't watch the proceedings on television, isn't paying much attention to the process and remains single-mindedly devoted to the people's business. We have seen him grow old in this job. That seems to happen to all presidents; but Clinton, not surprisingly, has become visibly careworn in this last year. He has, at the worst of times, always had the ability to convey a sparkle, a cheerfulness, in his public appearances. Even that, for the moment, has dulled, although he puts up a better front than I could manage under the circumstances.

January 16 / Potomac

Ice everywhere. The weight of it has pushed even the president's trial to the *Washington Post*'s "off-lead" left column. "Region Iced Over and Blacked Out" is the headline over the lead story. Mercifully (and uncharacteristically for a neighborhood that tends to lose power in every summer thunderstorm) we had no interruption of electrical or phone service.

Before going to work yesterday, I left Grace Anne with a battery-operated radio and a small battery-operated television. How helpless we late-twentieth-century Americans feel when our umbilical cord to radio and television is cut. Certainly we curse the triviality and shallowness of most of what the electronic media shovel out every day, but in an era when contact with family and neighbors is far reduced from what it once was, the reassuring murmur of a radio or television is our link to the rest of society. We would feel disoriented without it. Perhaps in rural areas, where farmers still depend on one another, where churches provide much of the social glue that holds communities together, there is less need for the electronic media. But in and around our cities it is our barometer, in the literal and figurative sense. Particularly when I watch CNN these days, I'm made aware of television's multidirectional function.

One House manager finishes his presentation in the trial; the Senate takes a short break. Commentators critique the congressman's failure to mesh his presentation with those of his colleagues. The break ends and the next congressman up before the Senate references the criticism he's just heard on television and seeks, immediately, to address it. The trial is simultaneously operating on at least two levels, with participants calibrating their performances to meet the shifting reactions of public opinion and the one hundred members of the Senate.

January 17 / Potomac

The Sunday-morning talk shows have, predictably, found their common political denominator. Democrats depict the president as a knave who should be censured (severely) but certainly not driven from office. Republicans think he should be held to at least the same standard as federal judges, several of whom have been removed from office for what would seem to be no greater crimes than those Clinton is accused of. Democrats argue that federal judges, appointed for life, serve "during good behavior." The president, elected by a national constituency, serves a fixed term, which must not be terminated lightly.

Tim Russert on *Meet the Press* asked Democratic senator Bob Kerry whether the charges against Clinton were sufficient to remove him from office "were he a federal judge." Kerry squirmed and obfuscated but never answered the question.

But let's get to the serious stuff.

The Giant has a sale on Cap'n Crunch cereal today—$1.84 (half price) for a "13–16 oz." box (13–16 ounces? That's an interesting twist). Are we now selling goods within a weight range? You may be getting a full pound of cereal or maybe not. I come across another instance: Hamburger Helper—half price—$1.12 for a "6.75–8.4 oz." box. And Quaker Instant Oatmeal—half price at $1.74 for a "10.2–16.2 oz." box. That's almost a 60 percent range. I'm going to have to check the ads on a more regular basis. This is a neat little scam. Bring your own scale and calculator to figure some of these out. "Parkay $1.29 SAVE 40 cents 16 oz. Package" (OK so far). And now, in smaller print below that: "Parkay Soft Spread—Regular, Light, Squeeze or Spray 10–16 oz. Package, 2 for $3, SAVE 78 cents to $1.18 on 2." (Say what?) "DiGiorno Rising Crust Pizza $4.99, 29.43–34.98 oz. Package." (Not even 30–35 ounces—that might be too easy to calculate.)

I'll have to talk to my buddy Ed, the manager.

January 18 / Potomac

Got up before 7 a.m. to watch the "new and improved" *Good Morning America*. As Charlie Gibson, one of the cohosts, put it, it's a little bit of "back to the future." Given the success of the new VW bug and Ford's new/old Thunderbird (with its late-fifties portholes), this may be the right move for ABC. It is, without question, one small step for mankind, one giant step for our morning television show. For me, the most effective segment was the one triggered by the firing of the *Journal of the American Medical Association*'s editor. He had authorized publication of a study that shows that 60 percent of our college students do not believe that oral sex constitutes "sexual relations." His firing came because the article was timed for release to coincide with the president's trial and that, said the AMA, was a "political" decision. As the Claude Rains character said in *Casablanca:* "I am shocked." The AMA and politics? God forbid!

Still, I *am* shocked by the numbers in the study. Have we become so legalistic in our language that nothing is measured by the simple standard of common sense anymore? It's not too much of a stretch to analogize between the oral sex definition and the 29.43–34.98 oz. Rising Crust Pizza pricing charade. The same Old Testament that spelled out a code for our sexual behavior in simple and unambiguous terms also called on merchants to provide clear and fair measure in the sale of their goods. It was all part of an overall moral code. These days we seek to find excuses for everything in loopholes.

Society at large is not likely to tolerate so many smothering legalisms for long. My fear is that the misuse of the law and plain language will lead, eventually, to the discarding of essential safeguards under the law.

There are many things that we will tolerate as a society when times are good. We are at peace now. Unemployment and inflation are at historic lows. The economy continues to prosper. But let the wind go out of all of those sails and the pendulum will swing wildly back from general permissiveness and an exaggerated sense of tolerance to an inflexible fundamentalism.

January 19 / Washington

It has been a good day for the president. His lawyer, Charles Ruff, did a first-class job of raising questions about the facts underlying the case made by House managers. So the president remembers it one way and Monica Lewinsky remembers it another (as to who touched whom where and how). Are you going to throw the president out of office on the basis of a "he-said-she-said" difference of opinion? He also demonstrated, with a time-line chart, that while the president's good friend Vernon Jordan did intensify his job search for Lewinsky on the day that a federal court judge in Little Rock ruled that "other women" in Clinton's life would be allowed to testify in the Paula Jones lawsuit, the ruling was not transmitted to the various lawyers in the case until late afternoon, by which time Jordan was already on a plane to Amsterdam. He had made his calls in Monica's behalf before the judge's ruling was handed down. The fact is that the president's lawyers had already known for about five days that the ruling was coming down and that it would probably go against them, but Ruff was effective, nevertheless.

Tonight the president delivers his State of the Union Address. He has demonstrated on many previous occasions that he can deliver under pressure.

Back to the more mundane. I stopped by the Giant to check on the prices and weights in the ads. Fascinating. It depends, for example, on what kind of pizza it is: plain or pepperoni. Now, as it was explained to me, the pizza with pepperoni (which is more expensive) might be at the lighter end of the weight scale. So you have a smaller pizza, but *with* pepperoni, for the same price as a larger pizza, without pepperoni. So, too, with the cereals. Some have blueberries in them. That's more expensive. So that would come in a smaller package. (Is all of this clear?) Why not, I asked, put all the cereals or pizzas in the same-sized box or container and simply charge a little more for the ones with blueberries or pepperoni? Wouldn't that be a lot clearer to the consumer? Yes, allowed my source at the Giant (Ed, the manager, was off, and my other source doesn't want to be identified), it might be clearer, but it would take up more space in the ads. Am I the only person so far who has raised questions about the language in these ads? Yup, it appears I am.

January 20 / Washington

I've been watching Cheryl Mills, an attractive young black woman who is deputy White House counsel, deliver her defense of the president on the floor of the Senate this afternoon. It is her task to contradict the charges of obstruction of justice. I find her performance pretty banal. Later, at the elevator, I run into my colleague Dave Marash. He's beaming. "A star is born," he says. I think, at first, that he's being sarcastic, but, no, he thinks Mills was just brilliant, as does Larry Drum, the makeup artist. When I come back upstairs, I feel that I should warn Tom Bettag that perhaps my poor opinion of Mills's performance is not universally shared. It turns out I'm essentially alone in my view.

I have to be careful to find the proper balance between being too judgmental and walking around with a wetted finger in the air trying to find consensus. After thirty-six years at ABC News I can no longer count myself among the young turks. These days, when I express an opinion here at the *Nightline* offices, there's a tendency for it to be taken as an edict. Bettag and I work hard at setting standards, but we don't want to stifle initiative or honest expressions of opinion.

It was exactly one year ago tonight that we were in Havana covering the Pope's visit to Cuba when we got a call from Roone Arledge and a number of New York executives with word that Jackie Judd, one of our fine Washington correspondents, had learned of a bizarre new scandal. The Office of Independent Counsel claimed to have audiotapes in which a former White House intern, one Monica Lewinsky, says she had a sexual relationship with the president. Further, reported Jackie, Lewinsky claimed that the president had told her to deny their relationship, while the president's good friend Vernon Jordan promised to get her a job, telling her that people didn't go to jail for lying in a civil action.

It was after 10 p.m. by the time we got word of the story. Bettag and I were extremely reluctant to try to piece together such a sensitive program on short notice and from Cuba to boot. I resisted the idea of trying to integrate the story into what was clearly a program about the Pope's visit to Cuba. In retrospect, I still think it was the right thing to do that night, but Jackie's story held up remarkably well. We all returned to Washington the next morning, and it has been pretty much the Monica story, on and off, ever since.

January 21 / Washington

The air seems to be going out of the impeachment balloon. I truly don't believe it has anything to do with the quality of the president's legal defenders. As noted yesterday, I haven't been terribly impressed by either the force or the eloquence of their arguments, although I do believe Ruff was excellent. The simple fact is that most people want this over with. Pat Robertson, the sometime politician, sometime television entrepreneur, sometime televangelist and full-time conservative, gave cover to Republicans yesterday when he told his 700 Club audience that he thought the president hit a home run with his State of the Union Address and that it was probably time to give up any expectation that he would be forced from office. Washington is abuzz now with speculation on how quickly the trial can be wrapped up.

That would be an enormous relief, but we will live to regret our addiction to public opinion. Having set the impeachment process in motion, there has to be a rational, even deliberate, solution. We are trapped between the near-certain knowledge that the president cannot be convicted by this Senate and the wish to see the process through to a dignified conclusion. There is no clear way that twelve Democrats can be found to join the fifty-five Republicans. Anticipation of the verdict may be inevitable, but if you allow it to govern the outcome, you undermine the process.

The goal line keeps shifting, depending on who has the floor. The House managers, acting as prosecutors, insist on their right and need to call witnesses (which would lengthen the process by at least several weeks). They clearly hope that some alchemy in deposing or hearing witnesses will strengthen their case. The president's defenders (eloquently represented today by Clinton's old Arkansas friend, former senator Dale Bumpers) are quite prepared to roundly denounce the president's behavior: "Indefensible, outrageous, shameless," said Senator Bumpers today. But I wonder how often, if at all, those words will be used by the president's allies once this impeachment trial is over. Then, I fear, all we will ever hear again is how this entire scandal was a put-up job by the president's right-wing enemies.

January 22 / Washington

I came to work early today in order to go up to the Hill. The president's trial gets under way each day at 1 p.m., in part because the chief justice is busy with Supreme Court business until after lunch. In any event, it means that senators tend to be free for interviews in the morning. The plan today was that I would raise with a few senators and with Mario Cuomo, who happens to be in town today for an appearance at the National Press Club, the disconnect between high approval ratings for Bill Clinton in terms of his performance as president and the dismal poll results when questions turn to his honesty, trustworthiness and ethical standards. How did people respond to the statement that "he is honest and trustworthy"? Twenty-four percent say he is, 73 percent do not. "He has high personal moral and ethical standards." Twenty percent agree with that statement; 77 percent do not. "He's a positive role model for young people." Eighteen percent agree, 79 percent do not. These kinds of reactions (positive and negative) come from the same people who give him high marks for the job he's doing as president. I'm not surprised; but it's worth taking note of the fact that in early 1999 the majority of the American people are perfectly content to have a president whom they regard as having low moral and ethical standards, who is not a positive role model for young people and who is neither honest nor trustworthy, but who appears, figuratively speaking, to be bringing home the bacon. Cuomo said, "Yeah, I wouldn't trust this guy in church and I wouldn't let him date my sister, but he's a terrific president." He then proceeded to explain that developing social programs helpful to the American public goes a long way toward explaining his continuing popularity, and that the other half of the equation is the "unpopularity of the effort" against him (he was talking about Kenneth Starr, et al.)

I have similar conversations with Senator Dianne Feinstein of California and Senator Tom Harkin of Iowa. They are perfectly willing to express their personal disgust with the president's personal behavior, but what, they both ask rhetorically, does that have to do with what kind of a president he is?

All of the president's supporters keep hammering away at the mantra that James Carville first introduced several months ago: "This is all about sex." Carville, though, has been replaced by H. L. Mencken now, who was quoted yesterday by Senator Bumpers: "If somebody tells you, 'It's not about the money,' it's about the money." To which Bumpers then made his own 1999 addendum: "If someone tells you it's not about the sex, it's about the sex." Paula Jones is destined to become nothing more than a footnote, just another of the many women who have engaged in consensual sex with the president, or wished they had, or made up some imaginary story on the subject.

The Republicans are pissing up a rope. Today, somewhat belatedly, I think they're almost ready to throw in the towel. What's sad is that good people like Cuomo and Harkin feel obliged to make the argument that it doesn't matter whether the president of the United States is a person of high morals and ethical standards.

I realize we've had presidents before whose personal behavior was no better than Clinton's. By all accounts, John Kennedy was just as randy and even more reckless. He, after all, shared the favors of Judith Campbell Exner with Sam Giancana, one of the nation's more notorious mob bosses. Kennedy even had a brief fling with a young woman who turned out to be an East German spy. The difference between his actions and Clinton's, between then and now, is that Kennedy's extramarital affairs were neither reported on contemporaneously, nor did they become a matter of public knowledge in any other way at the time. Now, the media have done their job, the public does know and the news is being dismissed as essentially irrelevant.

January 23 / Potomac

I watched a six-year-old *Nightline* special this morning: "72 Hours to Victory." All of the principals, Bill Clinton, Hillary, George Stephanopoulos, James Carville, Paul Begala, Mandy Grunwald and Stan Greenberg, were captured in a moment of exhausted rapture, that sweetest of all moments, when you've expended every last ounce of energy to bring about a personal dream and success is assured.

There is some poignancy in viewing those events through the prism of hindsight. Carville is choking up as he tries to summarize, dispassionately, the role of a "hired gun" like himself when the campaign is over; his admiration for his then-girlfriend, Mary Matalin, and her staunch loyalty and support for George Bush; his contempt for the "rats" who jumped Bush's ship. Hillary is rejecting my suggestion that what little privacy she had enjoyed until then was likely to evaporate. The president-elect, sitting with me in the garden of the Governor's Mansion in Little Rock, makes an unintended double entendre when he speaks of his intention (now as president-elect) to "reach out and touch people." What also comes through, however, is his determination (as he put it during that interview in the garden) to "focus like a laser on the economy." He has done a good job of restoring and bolstering the American economy and, to the degree that any president has the right to take personal credit for the collective actions of his cabinet and staff, the chairman of the Federal Bank and the actions of Congress, Clinton has earned that right.

It helps explain why a grateful (or superstitious) public is willing simultaneously to condemn his ethical credentials and hold on to him as president.

January 24 / Potomac

Monica is back! It is an unanticipated detour in the endgame, but part of the endgame nevertheless. Henry Hyde and his House managers turned to Kenneth Starr last Friday and asked him to require that Monica give an interview to the managers. Starr passed the ball to Federal District judge Norma Holloway Johnson, and she ordered that it happen. The Democrats are outraged, the Senate threatens to fracture along the same partisan lines that divided the House and six months from now it will all seem as stale as Iran-Contra.

About a year ago, I proposed to the network brass that we create a series called *American Obsession*, predicated on our national tendency to suck the marrow out of a current fixation and then toss it aside, rarely to be visited again, except as an historical curiosity or a question on *Jeopardy*. It's amazing how little we care about the issues that once riveted our attention—the Berlin Wall, Iran, Vietnam, Cuba, Nicaragua, Watergate, the Soviet Union—or, for that matter, how little we care to hear from the players in these and other dramas whose utterances we once sought so avidly: Mikhail Gorbachev, Gary Hart, Jim and Tammy Faye Bakker, Fawn Hall, Oliver North. They couldn't get arrested on television now, except for a possible guest appearance on *Hollywood Squares*. When news traveled by sailing ship or on horseback, consumers had to make it last. It would be a long time before the next information "fix" arrived. Now, satellite technology and twenty-four-hour cable networks inundate us with every latest development, even as it unfolds. We chew them up and spit them out and, almost immediately, reach for the next morsel.

Like Jim and Tammy Faye, like O. J. Simpson, Monica had an unusually long run, but her road from banner headline to crossword puzzle clue will be surprisingly short.

Meanwhile, Russia continues to unravel at an alarming rate, NATO "views with alarm" the horrific events in Kosovo, and neither, on this Sunday morning, merits front-page attention from either the *New York Times* or the *Washington Post.*

January 25 / Potomac

Two weeks ago the price of a regular letter stamp was raised a penny, from thirty-two cents to thirty-three cents. The post office has issued a one-cent stamp for people who have a stash of otherwise useless thirty-two-cent stamps. The problem with the one-cent stamps is that they're so cheap the stickum on the back doesn't work; they keep falling off the envelopes. So, I took a batch of our thirty-two-cent stamps to the post office this morning, hoping to trade them in on an equal number of thirty-threes and just pay the difference. Of course, I expected an argument.

There was a long line, as there has been every day since the price hike went into effect. Standing on line, I had a chance to ruminate on the changing face of post offices. They used to be as gray and unimaginative as most government offices, but not anymore. The clerks have small pots of flowers on their counters, one today still adorned with Christmas decorations. The walls are festooned with large, colorful, bustling ads for stamps: "Collect Our Greatest Hits." There's Babe Ruth slugging one out of the park and, just below, a smaller picture of Jack Dempsey loading up for another kind of "hit." There's Louis Armstrong, among pictures of a series of other great jazz musicians. Another wall is covered with "gifts and collectibles." I'm drawn to the "static cling Superman 32-cent collectibles." Thirty-two cents? Damn, that means I'll have to add one of those defective one-cent stamps.

"Classic Monster Stamps." Boris Karloff (in his most famous role as Frankenstein's monster) would be pleased. Behind the clerks, high on the wall like a relentless, electronic hourglass, the liquid silicone sands of time are expiring a hundredth of a second at a time. "2000 Time Is Running Out." The words "Three-hundred-forty" over the word "days" and then the boxes and numbers for hours, minutes, seconds and hundredths of seconds. I feel a slight sense of panic. That's my life leaking away while I wait for a bunch of goddamn stamps.

Where's the FBI's most-wanted list? Where are all those front and profile photographs of the baddest of the bad? These days, caught up in the mercantile competitiveness that oozes into every aspect of our lives, the post office is reduced to warning me that "Time Is Running Out" for me to "Collect the Century in Stamps."

By the time I get to the counter (changing the thirty-two-cent rolls for thirty-three-cent rolls is no problem) about 90,000 ticks of the hundredths of a second counter have passed. A friendly word to the post office: An ordinary clock would leave your customers with a greater sense of your clerks' efficiency. Waiting fifteen minutes is one thing, but ninety thousand hundredths of a second . . .

January 26 / Washington

The Pope is looking very frail. He can barely raise his head. The Parkinson's disease from which he suffers causes serious tremors in his left hand. Still, he is an impressive-looking man. I don't know whether his impassive expression is a result of the Parkinson's, but it serves him well. Unlike the politicians who flock around him on occasions like his current visit to Saint Louis, he does not change his mask from cheerful smile to serious attention, matching whatever it is that is being said to him or about him. President Clinton, sitting on a stage listening to the Pope, is an absolute master of facial calibration. It is impossible to know what he is thinking simply by looking at the expression on his face. In that sense, at least, his defense lawyers are right. Those who believe they can know whether or not he was paying attention during the Paula Jones deposition as his lawyer, Bob Bennett, made certain assertions in his behalf don't know what they're talking about. Clinton's facial expressions are the least revealing thing about him.

CNN employs the "split screen" as an alternative to the exercise of editorial judgment. There is Clinton greeting the Pope. There is David Kendall making the case against witnesses in the impeachment trial. The Clinton-Pope segment of the picture is larger than the Kendall "box," so for the moment we must believe the Pope's visit takes priority. But what we're really saying here is that the president's temporary association with the Holy Father bestows upon him a fleeting touch of virtue, even as those "vultures" in the Senate trial try to bring him down. Question: Absent the impeachment trial, would the president have flown out to Saint Louis for this photo op?

It's beginning to look as though the House managers will get to call (or at least depose) three witnesses—Monica, Vernon Jordan and former columnist, now White House aide, Sidney Blumenthal. The White House is hinting at a scorched-earth policy. They will have to call untold witnesses. Deposition and preparation will take weeks, maybe months. Nonsense. They will end this as fast as they possibly can. Anyway, that's what press secretaries and $400-an-hour lawyers are supposed to do—act like thugs while the boss's fingerprints are nowhere to be found.

All of this is like the baptism scene in *The Godfather,* where Michael Corleone is prominently visible in church while all of his enemies are being methodically assassinated. Clinton has an even better alibi: He's with the Pope.

January 27 / Washington

There is a current advertising campaign for the milk industry that relies on photographs of important (or at least well-known) people sporting milk moustaches. I just saw a piece of videotape of John Elway, the great quarterback for the Super Bowl–bound Denver Broncos, at a photo shoot. He was having the "milk" moustache painted onto his upper lip as he stood under the lights in his football regalia, looking foolish. We are only a few days away from the Super Bowl, so getting a few hours of Elway's time must be costing the milk industry major bucks. It's interesting, because a piece in the *Wall Street Journal* the other day took note of this campaign, citing its popularity (and enormous expense), but pointing out that the milk industry has seen its sales decline.

I think that perhaps the main reason so few people are paying attention to the *trial* is that nobody feels threatened by its outcome. As I said earlier, whether or not the president is dumped is perceived as having no direct impact on the lives of most Americans. True, when asked, most people express the opinion that they don't want to see Clinton convicted and removed from office. But it's an opinion, not a passion. When people do feel passionately on the subject, it seems to have more to do with the unpopularity of the president's enemies. Most people just don't want to see the Republican right wing, or Kenneth Starr, or Linda Tripp or the *American Spectator* win this battle. But if, by some fluke, the president were removed from office, it would cause barely a flutter in the national pulse. Al Gore would ascend to the presidency, assert his continuing faith in Alan Greenspan, and, after a hiccup or two, the Dow Jones Average and particularly the NASDAQ would continue their upward climb.

January 28 / Washington

At a given point every year (I forget when) some organization (I forget which one) pokes its finger in the eye(s) of the major media establishment by publishing a list of the most important news stories that never got covered. This should be a banner year. Programs like *Nightline* are especially vulnerable to this sort of criticism in that we cover only one story a day. And since the network has been opting out of gavel-to-gavel coverage, we're carrying some of the corporate responsibility for making sure that the trial is given appropriate attention. On one level that's the right thing to do. The charges against the president are serious, and, even if they weren't, this has risen to the level of an impeachment trial. Still, Washington's obsession with this event has diminished the visibility of so much else, including the real importance of the Whitewater–Travelgate–FBI files–Paula Jones–campaign contributions–Monica Lewinsky epic. It has demonstrated, for one thing, how dangerous it is to assign to any one man the budget and the powers that go with being an independent counsel. Kenneth Starr does not strike me as being a bad man in any sense of the word, but the genius of the American system of government lies in its checks and balances. In the final analysis, Starr was brought low by mudslinging and character assassination, not by an appropriate balance of powers.

I am even more concerned, though, about the culture war that is being waged throughout the country. The Clinton story is simply our national Rorschach test. I've been plodding through the Old Testament for much of the last year and have found myself floundering in Leviticus. I don't know how Moses was taking notes up there on Mount Sinai, but the good Lord certainly didn't believe in keeping His directions simple. Fortunately for me, the text that I'm reading is replete with scholarly notes on the text. This morning's reading threw me headlong into the subject of sex, it being largely an enumeration of all the family members one is not supposed to sleep with. There were clearly a lot of bad examples around, and the Lord warned Moses not to follow that of the Egyptians (whose hospitality the Israelites had just left behind) or the Canaanites (which is where they were headed). The overarching message, however, had to do with the sort of moral rot that sets in when a society loses its sexual inhibitions—that seems to describe us pretty well—and the prognosis for what happens to nations when they lose their moral compass (even when it's just about sex) is not encouraging.

January 29 / Washington

I have a natural affinity for the Luddites. Their suspicions about and hostility toward the "new machinery" of the industrial age was, I think, well founded. But it was as nothing compared to the damage we are capable of inflicting on ourselves in this age of microchips, gigabytes and CD-ROMs. Grace Anne's hard drive crashed a couple of days ago. "Not to worry," cooed the cognoscenti, "all that stuff can be retrieved." We hustled the hard drive off to some company that has the confidence of the CIA. They took it into a "clean room" where it was dissected, sliced, diced and cored—and pronounced dead at about 10:30 this morning.

Most, if not all, of Grace Anne's family tree research is gone. Bank records, gone. A legal brief she was working on, gone. It's not a fatal disease. It's not the loss of a loved one. But for a piece of equipment that is supposed to make life so much easier, it certainly does have a way of clubbing its users into submission.

I really do feel best with a legal pad and a #2 pencil.

Last night we got off the impeachment trial for the first time in weeks and did a very nice piece on a nurse down in Birmingham, Alabama. She had been working at a clinic that, among other services, performed abortions. One year ago today a bomb exploded in front of the clinic. An off-duty policeman who had been moonlighting at the clinic was killed instantly. The nurse was terribly mutilated. Almost from the first, her husband began recording her recovery on videotape. It made for an extraordinary story of courage and resilience. The husband has been a rock. At the end of the program, I made reference to the suspect in this case, a man who has been evading capture by the FBI for a year now. He's something of a will-o'-the-wisp and has even engendered some admiration for his survival skills. I was making the point that the bomber is anything but a hero. If you're looking for heroes, I suggested, how about this woman or her husband, for that matter. This morning, in my E-mail, I received an anonymous suggestion that we go to a particular site on the Internet where, sure enough, one of my "heroes," the husband, is listed as a convicted child molester.

Another reason I don't like computers.

January 30 / Potomac

Flashback. Boarding school, 1951. Eight or ten of us are in the playroom and someone has filled the blackboard with nasty one-liners about a classmate whom we all know only as "Septic." Septic is afflicted with an early case of hormones, which manifests itself in facial eruptions—boils, pimples, acne. I don't recall being particularly amused by anything that has been chalked onto the blackboard, but neither am I moved to sympathy, let alone outrage, in Septic's behalf. Now, almost fifty years later, I have no memory of the boy's actual name, only that his face and his nickname seemed, if not fair, then at least reasonable.

Suddenly, without warning, one of the boys goes to the blackboard, erases all the references to Septic and substitutes the name "Koppel." The nasty one-liners instantly become customized darts, specially designed and sharpened for me. When I protest, I discover that what was evolving has been prearranged by common agreement. I have been put "in Coventry," which means no one will initiate a conversation with me or respond to anything I say. It lasted for two weeks, during which time I was left to infer the nature of my crime against my fellow eleven- and twelve-year-olds.

We had recently returned from our Christmas holiday. Since I was one of only two Jews in the school, it never occurred to me to think of them as anything but "Christmas" holidays. The fact that Chanukah might occur during the same time period was a happy coincidence but did not, in any way, factor into the school's planning. My religion was of no particular interest to anyone at Abbotsholme. The other Jewish boy and I were simply expected to attend Church of England services on Sunday mornings with all the other boys, and "chapel" all other evenings. This seemed reasonable enough to us at the time. It never occurred to me that there was any anti-Semitism at work here. Nor do I think there was now. It was simply a private matter that I was expected to deal with on my own.

Certainly, as the child of German Jews, I was doubly an outsider. (The war was only six years past.) But to expect the school to modify its rules for one or two of "us" would have been a form of political correctness that was still a couple of generations off.

In any event, I had brought back with me to school, that January of 1951, a collection of Schuco toy cars from Germany, where my parents were engaged in search of reparations. The cars must have been a Chanukah present. I thought they were hot stuff and clearly conveyed that. (I still have a few of them and they're quite wonderful, far better than their British equivalents, which, if memory serves, were called "Dinkys.") Suffice it to say that boasting about the superior quality of German toys so soon after World War II was not smart. I was judged to be a show-off, and so I found myself in Coventry, a form of loneliness that is both painful and conducive to introspection.

I am convinced that whatever my abilities at listening, at detecting subtle changes in mood and attitude and tone, they were first shaped in that particular cauldron.

January 31 / Potomac

Born in England of German parents, I was, when we came to this country in 1953, quickly and irrevocably Americanized. All immigrants experience the assimilation process differently, but I embraced it eagerly. Language, of course, was not a problem, although my English accent and certain linguistic peculiarities subjected me to a certain amount of teasing. A "rubber," I quickly learned, may be used for erasing pencil mistakes in England, but in America it has a somewhat more interesting use. Whatever this place is, quilt or melting pot, its peculiar strength lies not just in its diversity, but in the conviction (sometimes loudly expressed, more often secretly held) of each group that its own origins are at least the equal of, more likely superior to, those of every other group. In reality, it is the pungent brew that is superior to any of its individual ingredients. Having said that, the spirit of cultural diversity and political correctness is turning sour. We are in danger, in our efforts to be fair, of acceding to some wrongheaded positions, simply because they are held by someone in a minority group. Genuine equality entails ensuring and enforcing the rights of all Americans, but sometimes even minorities can be wrong.

The District of Columbia has a new mayor, Anthony Williams. He is a light-skinned African American, well educated and somewhat nerdy in appearance and demeanor. The other day, David Howard, a staff aide to Williams, used the word "niggardly" at a meeting with other staff members. Howard is white. His use of the word was perfectly correct, in terms of context and definition, but a black staff member (apparently not familiar with the word, but believing it to be related to the word "nigger") protested. Howard, I gather, tried to explain, apologized and then tendered his resignation to Williams—who accepted it.

This incident has become a paradigm for the unease that still marks race relations in our country. Mayor Williams is, as I understand things, concerned that he may not be perceived, in predominantly black D.C., as black enough. Howard (who, the newspapers now inform us, is gay) seems to be the classic sensitive liberal, all too ready to don the mantle of guilt for the unintended consequences of a perfectly correct but perhaps ill-chosen word. And what of the black staffer whose outrage fueled and set in motion subsequent events? I understand him best of all. He thought "niggardly" was derivative of that other N-word which blacks have heard all too often. Then, when he found out he was wrong, he felt doubly humiliated.

Here are three insecure men, each of whom has been damaged because common sense was surrendered in the face of what was presumed to be politically correct.

February

February 1 / Potomac

Denver won the Super Bowl last night.

Now begins the darkest month of the year for American sports fans. Football is over. Basketball (in this lockout-shortened season) is about to get under way, but with half the season lost and the retirement of Michael Jordan, it's hard to get interested in this season. The glory of March Madness, when sixty-four of the best teams in college basketball fight their way through the sweet sixteen to the final four and, ultimately, the NCAA championship game—is six weeks or more away. So, too, is spring training for baseball. The Stanley Cup playoffs seem to take place in June these days.

If we are ever going to turn America into a truly literate society again, I recommend beginning in February.

February 2 / Washington

There was an earthquake in Colombia last week, in which nearly a thousand people were killed; as many as two hundred thousand are said to be homeless. We did not cover the story on *Nightline*. I have no doubt that if Tom Bettag and I had flown to Colombia we could have produced some extraordinary broadcasts. When we flew to Honduras to cover the damage caused by Hurricane Mitch late last year, we did some of the best work we've produced in a while. So, why didn't we go to Colombia? Monica and money.

It is not a bad thing that the corporation wants the news division to be sensitive to a relationship between what is earned and what is spent.

Still, I think we are in danger of becoming overly concerned, to the point that it will have a negative impact on the coverage we air. Americans are already too inclined to ignore anything that doesn't have a direct and immediate impact on our own lives. That also explains why the rest of the country doesn't give a damn about the impeachment story (beyond wanting to know when it will end).

February 3 / Washington

We've been talking about putting together a broadcast that would be a reprise of the past twelve months. One of our producers, Dan Green, proposed the notion that, in many respects, the unfolding of the Clinton-Lewinsky affair has the elements of a Greek tragedy. He has spoken to a number of experts at universities around the country who encouraged him in this idea. To me, there is one major missing element: the tragedy. In some respects this is more like vaudeville, and Clinton more appropriately fits the role of Harry Houdini. He's cuffed, he has manacles around his ankles, he's submerged, head down, in a barrel of water, and a lid has been nailed over the top. He can't possibly escape. Wait a second! Isn't that Harry in the balcony? How the hell did he get up there?

If there are aspects of a tragedy to all of this they lie in what Daniel Patrick Moynihan calls "the defining down of deviancy." There are things we now routinely discuss in public that we wouldn't have dreamed of saying openly only thirteen months ago. We have lowered the standards of public discourse. We have become far more partisan than we were (or, at least, we have revealed the intensity of our partisanship). We have raised hypocrisy to the level of a national anthem. Who cares about the president's ethical or moral level? Who cares if the president is no longer a role model? The economy's still doing fine.

I wonder if, a year or so ago, we had seen this profile of ourselves we would have believed such a rapid descent into national cynicism and an open discussion of semen stains, oral sex and the use of cigars as sexual toys would have been possible in so relatively brief a period of time.

February 4 / Washington

I just got off the phone with Leon Wieseltier, literary editor of *The New Republic*, having failed to convince him that he should come on the broadcast tonight. I've known Leon for a number of years. He's extraordinarily bright, one of the few original thinkers and genuine wits among the ranks of Washington journalists. Long before the Lewinsky story broke, Leon described Bill Clinton as believing in serial monogamy. He was also quoted as having said (although he claims not to remember), "CNN is where ABC correspondents go to die."

Leon is not allergic to television cameras, but today, he tells me, he's got absolutely nothing to say. He finds the story so dull, at this stage, that he can't think of anything he wants to add to the conversation. One of the advantages of being literary editor of *The New Republic* is that he doesn't have to. Perhaps, on national television, we still lack the necessary confidence to avoid the story simply because the presidency could be at stake.

February 5 / Washington

My colleague Barry Serafin did a really nice spot on *World News Tonight* yesterday on the fact that we are currently enjoying the lowest gasoline prices in history. He showed some gas stations where "Regular" was selling for 67 cents a gallon. Everything is based, of course, on the adjusted value of a dollar. I remember buying gas for 25 cents a gallon in the early seventies. But given how much the value of a dollar has depreciated over the past twenty-five years or so, 67 cents a gallon may be as cheap as it has ever been.

Barry closed the piece with a terrific object lesson. Even at its average price of 98 cents a gallon, gasoline in America is now selling for two-thirds the price of bottled water, the cheaper brands of which are available at $1.49 a gallon. That's another reason to treat the predictions of "experts" with great caution. During and following the oil crisis of 1973, when the Organization of Oil Producing and Exporting Countries (OPEC) clamped down on supply and prices soared, we were warned that the world's oil supply would be largely exhausted

shortly after the turn of the century. It was that spectre that induced
the development of smaller cars in the United States, that led to the
development of alternate energy sources, that encouraged conserva-
tion. Prices, we were told, would never fall again. The experts were
wrong on that count. The problem, however, is that, these days, we are
encouraged to believe that they were wrong across the board, which, of
course, they were not. Oil prices will inevitably rise again, but when we
are treated to a string of Indian summer days in late October, we like to
pretend that winter will never come. This economic bubble of ours is
going to burst one of these days. That's the easy prediction. The
tougher truth to remember (when the next recessionary and/or infla-
tionary times descend on us) will be the notion that good times are also
a part of that endlessly repetitive cycle.

King Hussein of Jordan is, effectively, dead. The poor man was rushed
from Jordan to the Mayo Clinic in Rochester, Minnesota, for an emergency bone marrow transplant, but it failed. Last night his doctors flew
him back to Jordan. It appears they have had him on life support since
he left the hospital, and that the question of when Hussein "dies" is
now more of a formality, having to do with when the crowned heads
and other dignitaries can make it to Amman for the state funeral.

I wish I could be privy to the conversations and reminiscences
about Hussein among the old spooks, generals, diplomats and foreign
correspondents who interacted with the king during his colorful life.
All anybody talks about these days is the king getting out of his sickbed
(during what does now turn out to have been the last months of his
life) to breathe a little energy into the Wye peace conference. There
were many times when U.S. policymakers cursed the king, referring
disparagingly to him behind his back as "His Tiny Highness," especially when he sided with Saddam Hussein before Desert Storm. At
other times, when Hussein believed it in Jordan's interest to assist the
United States in the Middle East, he became "the plucky, little king."
He was physically small, but he was tough. We forget that the Black
September Organization was so called by Palestinians after Hussein's
crackdown on Palestinian forces in Jordan during that month in 1970,
and that most militant Palestinians loathed him.

I liked him a lot. He showed real courage in his dealings with
Israeli leaders, even though for many years they occurred behind a veil
of secrecy. Jordan has few, if any, natural assets, and Hussein could ill

afford to alienate his richer and more powerful Arab neighbors. Still, after 1967, I think it's fair to say that he did what he could to normalize relations with Israel, while doing what he had to to maintain Jordan's place at the Arab table.

His extraordinary politeness could be a little disconcerting. He was so deferential, calling his male interviewers "sir," for example, that I found myself bending over backward to match his courtesy. It made for excruciatingly boring interviews. From what I understand, he was a little less formal and considerably more intimate with a number of his female interviewers, although, initially and on camera at least, he called all of them "madam."

I remember being in a group of reporters around then-Secretary of State Henry Kissinger, who had just returned to Amman airport from a helicopter ride, piloted by Hussein. "How was it?" we asked. "If it weren't for the great honor," said Kissinger, "I would just as soon have walked."

February 6 / En route to Atlanta

I will have a hard time dealing with anonymity when it comes again. The folks at the United Express counter in the airport are as nice as can be but flutter helplessly on the flypaper of corporate policy. They have apparently been instructed to say that "the computer has overbooked" my flight. I argue that computers still depend on humans for their input and that I intend to reason with a human to find a remedy for what the agent thoughtfully points out is "my problem." Agent #1 retreats briefly to consult with agent #2. He comes back and amends his preliminary argument. The computer did overbook, but that happened only because I was not at the counter twenty minutes before departure time. I point out that I was at the counter, but was standing behind the customer ahead of me, whose seat had also been double booked. We were both in time (I can hear my voice taking on an edge similar to that creeping into the voices of the House managers, whose case is also hopeless), but while we're arguing the plane is "boarding" and I am not. I want to talk to a "supervisor." ("Just one more witness . . . you need to look into Monica's eyes.") "He's on his way," I'm told. The flight is now six or seven minutes from departure. I can see the supervisor ambling toward me from five or six gates away. He relishes this opportunity to talk with me as much as Trent Lott looks forward to another conversation with Henry Hyde.

He is Indian (not Native American—Indian), and his voice has that soft Welsh-sounding lilt. "I'm sorry, sir, but there's absolutely nothing I can do."

"Wrong," I snarl. "You can pay someone a lot of money to take a later flight."

"We already tried that," says agent #2.

"How much?" asks the supervisor.

She holds up three fingers. He sighs and walks out to the plane.

I know this isn't going to work. I think of Henry Hyde and his bitter riposte to Senate Republicans who were ready to throw in the towel days ago. "It's a good thing they weren't at Valley Forge."

The supervisor returns, defeated but amazed at his own boldness. "I offered $350 and an upgrade . . . ," he says.

I am shameless. I start muttering about calling the president of United. (Who is the president of United? For that matter, does United Express have anything to do with United Airlines?)

My plane takes off. Monica's videotaped deposition is playing in the background. I am offered $300 in flight coupons. I don't want any coupons. Congressman Rogan, battling electronically nearby, doesn't want a censure resolution. He wants a conviction.

I want to get to Fort Myers. My wife, inbound on another flight, will be waiting for me at the airport. The next direct flight from Dulles will be in eight hours, from National in six hours.

Agent #2 is working the computer. U.S. Air has a flight to Atlanta leaving in twenty minutes, connecting to a flight for Fort Myers that gets me in two and a half hours after I was originally scheduled to arrive.

"Let me see that censure resolution one more time."

Why did I cut it so short this morning? Our new SUV, which had a nasty tendency to leap forward when put into gear on a cold morning, had to have its transmission replaced. This morning, as a result, the engine was racing wildly as I pulled out of the driveway. I thought it would settle down, and it did—permanently into first gear. By the time I realized it wasn't going to self-adjust, I was three miles from home. I nursed it back and took Grace Anne's car to the airport.

Late.

February 7 / Captiva

King Hussein died today. I would not be surprised to learn that he actually died a few days ago at the Mayo Clinic, or aboard the private plane that flew him back to Amman. It is not hard to understand why his family would want to go through the charade of having him "live" for a day or two after his return to Jordan so that he could "die" at home.

May his soul rest in peace.

What, if anything, is the difference between Hussein (who certainly had his share of adulterous relationships) and Clinton? Maybe I'm doing the president a great injustice, but I am hard-pressed to think of a single act of his, throughout what I guess will come to be known as the Lewinsky matter, in which he put the nation's welfare ahead of his own.

February 8 / Captiva

I turned fifty-nine today. I began the day with a swim in the Gulf of Mexico and then biked five miles to pick up the papers. There's a good, gentle southerly breeze, and I plan to go sailing later. This afternoon, at four, tennis. This evening, I will see a movie and have dinner with Grace Anne. She is my other half, and I have been blessed by her companionship. We have loved each other since we met at Stanford in 1960, and we are sufficiently different that there has always been a constructive tension between us that allows nothing to be taken for granted. We have never and will never become bored with each other. I am blessed also with the love of four good, smart and decent children, a fine son-in-law and a grandson whose existence alone, at this stage of his life, guarantees universal adoration within the family.

My job has always been totally satisfying to me, and I am surrounded by fine colleagues. Beyond the normal vicissitudes of life among those I love, then, there are no external factors to account for the regular visits of (as Churchill put it) "the black dog." And yet, I believe that even depression, in moderate doses, is an essential element of my life. It forces empathy on me, and without empathy, Man is a hollow vessel indeed.

This year I've asked the kids to give something to a charity they like, instead of sending me a gift. It is certainly no sacrifice on my part, but it could become a wonderful family tradition, one that, I would like to think, will survive me.

February 9 / En route to Washington

Our nation is moving, simultaneously, in opposite directions on the perceived value of precise language. Paradoxically, both camps are demonstrating a measure of contempt for the power of words. The president and his lawyers take full advantage of precision of language whenever it best suits their purpose. The definition of perjury is so narrow, so dependent upon the intent of the accused perjurer, they argue, that while he may have deliberately misled his interrogators while under oath, the charge to tell "the truth, the whole truth and nothing but the truth" did not require the president to be "particularly helpful" to his questioners. He could, therefore, with a clear conscience assert that since he and Monica were not engaging in any improper behavior or relationship on the day of his deposition (or perhaps even more narrowly, *during* the deposition itself) "that it all depends on what the meaning of 'is' is."

Wow! you think. What a boost for the study of advanced English. Fool your friends, confuse your parents, evade accountability. You, too, can use the English language to avoid the consequences of your behavior.

Instead, throughout the land, there seems to be general disgust for anything but the most fundamental use of words. The reliance on correct grammar is seen as pedantic; precision in language (except as it relates to defining sex, lying about sex or engaging in sex) is regarded as effete. The distinction between whether someone *may* or *might* have done something has disappeared. These days when someone tells you that "the president *may* have told the truth," they could be leaving open the possibility that he lied; but, more likely, they are suggesting that he would have told the truth, if only . . .

We are devaluing the currency of language, both in using it too cleverly and too carelessly. While it is true that language can be used to cloud meaning and to evade responsibility, its primary purposes should still be clarity and communication.

English is the richest language in the world. How sad that we seem resigned to driving it around in first gear, except for those rare occasions on which we're trying to evade arrest.

February 10 / Washington

It occurs to me that, if anything, the endless machinations of this last year prove quite the opposite of what everyone is saying about the Office of Independent Counsel. There is a great deal of wailing and gnashing of teeth over the uncontrolled power that the OIC has exhibited. There are certainly arguments to be made that Kenneth Starr overreached. Certainly his expenditure of $40 million to $50 million and the years that he and his predecessor have spent on following up on the original Whitewater allegations seem to make the point that the powers of the OIC need to be curbed, if not eliminated altogether. And yet, if this ongoing battle between the president and the OIC proves anything, it is how difficult it can be to corner a sitting president of the United States. Judge Walsh, in his investigation of Iran-Contra and President Reagan, also spent more than $40 million, and his investigation lasted seven years. In the final analysis, the ability of a White House staff to stonewall any investigation is almost limitless.

Had Richard Nixon not recorded his own conversations and had those conversations not contained the "smoking gun" that ultimately condemned him out of his own mouth, he, too, would have completed his term of office.

We may well come to the conclusion that the only high crime that requires Congress to impeach, convict and remove a president from office is that of trying to hold on to office beyond his elected term. In all other matters we are likely to conclude either that the crime does not rise to the level of an impeachable offense, or that it is simply too difficult to pry a sitting president out of the Oval Office if he is determined to remain.

February 11 / Washington

I just barely got to know Gerry Laybourne before she left the comfortable nest of the Disney corporation and went off to find real fame and fortune on her own, but I think I can fairly refer to her as a friend. In any event, my friend Gerry and my old buddy Oprah (I knew Oprah when she did a local show in Baltimore) are on the cover of *Forbes* magazine with Marcy Carsey, whom I don't know. The three of them are creating a media empire based on the assumption that what the world really wants is interactive television. They are targeting women as their principal audience. They have lots of funding (about $750 million, according to the article) and, in a few years, this item will be of interest because (a) Oxygen Media—the name of the new enterprise— will be one of the first great communications industry success stories of the twenty-first century, or (b) Gerry and Oprah and Marcy will have pissed away well over a billion dollars by then, and people still won't have figured out why they want to watch something on TV, order it on their computer and receive it on their fax machine.

This is actually the big nut of the moment. Whoever cracks this one will create a new era in entertainment, sales, information and product delivery. The premise is easy enough to understand, but television has had a couple of generations now to condition its viewers to watch passively. One of the underlying reasons that television has been so successful is precisely because it requires so little of its audience. In the early days (that is, before the remote control) the viewer might occasionally rise to change a channel or, more likely, to adjust the rabbit ears (the antenna) or the vertical or horizontal hold. Pictures were always rolling or flipping or dissolving into electronic fuzz. Since more recent improvements on televisions and antennae and the development of the aforementioned remote control, however, one of the joys of television viewing is that it can be accomplished while in a state of torpor.

The problem with interactive television is that there was never meant to be anything active about the activity of watching the tube. I'm with you, Gerry, but I have my doubts.

February 12 / Washington

It's over. Clinton has been acquitted and the Dow is down over a hundred points. Go figure.

He came into the Rose Garden, looking appropriately chastened, and apologized once more for causing so much pain. It was brief, to the point and hit just the right note. He wasn't going to answer any questions, but Sam Donaldson tossed him one he couldn't resist: "Are you prepared to forgive and forget?" The president hesitated for a moment, realized he had a good answer and didn't want to waste it: "I believe any person who asks for forgiveness has to be prepared to give it." Not bad. This morning on the *Today* show, James Carville was asked whether he's ready to bury the hatchet with Ken Starr. James gave his old Cajun skull snort and allowed as how he knew where he wanted to bury that hatchet.

What I found particularly interesting about that interview was James saying how proud he was to have been able to help the president when he asked for it. He said it twice. I could've sworn the White House had taken the position that Carville was an unguided missile, that he'd never been asked to do anything and that whatever he was doing or saying about Starr in particular was just James being James.

He's probably backing the truck up to the ammo store right now, chuckling over that nice "any person who asks for forgiveness has to be prepared to forgive" line.

February 13 / En route to Fort Myers, Florida

I admire those who keep going in the face of adversity, those who refuse to quit no matter how overwhelming the odds arrayed against them. Again, I think of the three hundred Spartans who gave their lives blocking Xerxes' gigantic army at Thermopylae. I think of Churchill in the days of his political isolation in the 1930s, and then, as prime minister, rallying his countrymen after Dunkirk. I think of Nelson Mandela and Natan Sharansky and John McCain. I marvel at that incredible fusion of stubbornness and courage, and then I think of Bill Clinton and wonder. He is clearly a proud and stubborn man who refused to cave in, even when his political survival seemed unlikely in the extreme. He put on a good face and gave every appearance of continuing to focus on his job, despite the humiliation, despite the distractions, despite the chorus of voices calling for his resignation. Throughout it all, he battled on.

But beyond the ignoble, self-inflicted nature of his adversity, why do I have such trouble admiring Clinton? Perhaps because, while it is clear that he will fight tenaciously to protect himself, I doubt that he would ever sacrifice himself for the rest of us.

February 14 / Captiva

Valentine's Day. Grace Anne and I bought cards for each other but left them in Maryland. She gave me a beautiful pecten shell that she had found on the beach. I was delighted to find a large fragment of a spectacular lion's paw, which I knew would please her. A pristine lion's paw comes close to being the Holy Grail among shellers. Grace Anne is enough of a collector that she values even a good fragment of one. There is something enormously satisfying about being able to exchange noncommercial tokens of affection.

The cold-blooded commercialization of our most tender moments is one of the least admirable aspects of our culture. Hell, it goes way beyond just commercializing the natural milestones of our lives. Hallmark, the floral industry and balloons "R" us have not been satisfied with requiring tens of millions of us to memorialize one another's birthdays, weddings, anniversaries, graduations, first communions and circumcisions with cards, flowers and lighter-than-air sentiments that float over our heads until all the gas escapes. They have invented a slop bucket of occasions, each brimming over with phony sentimentality: Valentine's Day, Mother's Day, Father's Day, Secretary's Day, Grandmother's Day.

The national bloodstream is on a permanent intravenous drip of artificial sweeteners. We celebrate our employees of the week, of the month, of the year, not so much for their achievements, as for being less obnoxious than the rest of us. We award each other plaques under the same logic that caused Monica to show up the other week as #5 on a list of most-admired Americans. When we say "most admired," we really mean most visible or best known. We have dinners for one another. Not "You come to my house, I'll come to your house" kind of dinners: *dinners!*—$50-, $250-, $1,000-a-plate dinners, devices with which we raise money for causes and candidates. And if you don't come to my dinner to raise money for cerebral palsy, I sure as hell won't come to your "Let's raise money to find a cure for AIDS" dinner.

Half the mail I get at home is identifiable by the fact that one of the numbers in our street address is consistently and uniformly incorrect. There must be some organization out there that has publicized my home address but got one number wrong. Every one of these letters contains a request for a signed piece of memorabilia that can be sold at a charity auction. Many of them don't even bother with maintaining the illusion that it's *my* piece of autographed memorabilia that is so important to them: "Dear Celebrity," these letters begin.

> Dear Charitable Organizations,
> If you're reading this, please know that I no longer even open your envelopes before pitching them.
>   Sincerely,
>   Anonymous celebrity

February 15 / Captiva

Grace Anne gave me a copy of Anne Morrow Lindbergh's book *Gift from the Sea*. She writes of life's different rhythms: "Rollers on the beach, wind in the pines, the slow flapping of herons across sand dunes"; and how they "drown out the hectic rhythms of city and suburb, timetables and schedules." She wrote the book in the mid-fifties when the memory of her kidnapped and murdered baby boy must have receded into a permanent, dull ache.

This has long been a place for the wealthy and the famous to find a way of retreating back into nature comfortably. "One never knows what chance treasures these easy unconscious rollers may toss up on the smooth white sand of the conscious mind; what perfectly rounded stone, what rare shell from the ocean floor. Perhaps a channeled whelk, a moon shell, or even an argonaut," she wrote in 1955. When I think of Lindbergh walking along this same stretch of beach, scanning the sand just above the waterline, I feel the sort of continuity that Walt Whitman wrote about in his poem "Crossing Brooklyn Ferry." Our discoveries in nature and the emotions they awaken in us connect us to generations past and future.

It's calm out in the gulf today, but a couple of days ago when big breakers were crashing in I jotted down a line that captured the moment for me: "The beach daisies are bobbing and weaving and the wind is tearing lace curtains of foam from the waves as they collapse on the beach."

February 16 / Captiva

Sailing is wonderfully instructive in Man's subordinate role to Nature. When there is no wind, you cannot sail. When the wind is too powerful, it is foolish to sail. You cannot sail directly into the wind, but by tacking patiently back and forth you can arrive at the point from which the wind is coming. Never take the wind for granted. It can change force and direction without apparent notice. But if you can read the signs, there will always be a few seconds to prepare. When you are sailing as close to the wind as you can, you feel as though you are moving faster than when that same wind is directly at your back. When the wind *is* at your back (a following wind), it is at its most treacherous.

I cannot imagine a sailor so competent or confident that he has not, at one time or another, whispered the mariner's prayer to himself: "Oh, God. Your sea is so great and my boat is so small."

February 17 / Captiva

I've been trying to plod through a *New York Times* series by Jeff Gerth and a number of other *Times* reporters on the world economy. I don't get it. On one level, this is indisputably a reflection of my ignorance on the subject of economics. If there is a single theme that runs throughout the series, however, it appears to be the inability of the world's smartest economists and businesspeople to fully grasp what is happening. The dollar seems to be at the heart of everything, an international will-o'-the-wisp that bestows prosperity where it stays and financial disaster when it leaves. Or is it the other way around? Prosperous economies attract dollars; failing economies drive them out.

Either way, the name of the game is attracting dollars back. Strong economies have flourishing businesses, and flourishing businesses attract investment. But failing economies are short on flourishing businesses, so they have to raise interest rates to attract dollars. The worse the economy, the higher the interest rate; the higher the interest rate, the more expensive it is for local businesses to get loans. Therefore, local businesses either fail, or their products are so expensive that no one at home can afford them and no one overseas wants them. As businesses fail, commodities like oil and steel are less and less in demand, sending their prices to historic lows. That's great for thriving economies like our own, but disastrous for failing economies like Russia's (oil and gas) or South Korea's (steel). Actually, it's not altogether great for our economy either. American steel companies, for example, are being forced to compete with incredibly low prices from overseas. The only way they can do that is by laying off workers, cutting costs.

It seems inevitable that our own economy will eventually contract, but instead, the market keeps thriving. That's the part I don't understand—that and how to restore the economies of Asia, Russia and Latin America, and how to keep investor greed from upsetting whatever balance the IMF and the treasury secretary, Bob Rubin, impose.

February 18 / Captiva

We have a team at work in New York City gathering material for a program about a young African man, Amadou Diallo, a street vendor, who was mistaken for a rape suspect by four New York cops and then shot to death. Just how the attempted arrest actually went down is now the subject of an investigation, but the cops apparently thought the suspect was armed (he wasn't), and all of them opened fire on him. Forty-one shots were fired; I believe he was hit twenty-one times. He died, of course. His family has taken the body back to Africa.

New Yorkers are uncharacteristically content these days. Mayor Giuliani has done a terrific job of cracking down on street crime. He likes to call it his "broken window" approach. Giuliani's theory is that if a house has a few broken windows and they're not fixed, the house becomes a target. Fix the windows, maintain the property and you give notice that the house is important to you, and the petty criminals, at least, will stay away. That's at the root of the mayor's various campaigns to keep street vendors off the street, and to get rid of the so-called "squeegee men" who used to harass motorists by wiping their windshields at red lights and then hitting them up for a buck or two. But Giuliani has also empowered the police to get tough. By and large, the public has responded very favorably to that. My sense, though, is that we're only hearing the reaction of New York's white community. I'm interested in learning whether that sense of things getting better has also spread into the black and Hispanic communities.

I've requested an interview with the mayor. His press person is complaining that the only time *Nightline* wants an interview is when something is perceived as wrong in New York. She says we haven't responded when they've come to us with story proposals. Actually, I can't recall any occasion on which they have done so; but, to tell the truth, I also prefer that we be the ones initiating the stories that we cover.

February 19 / Captiva

Our two youngest children, Drew and Tara, are with us for the weekend. Dinner conversation meanders until the subject of last night's TV program *ER* comes up. None of us has seen it. I wanted to see the last episode of the Stephen King miniseries on ABC. Grace Anne had found that unpleasant to watch and gone to bed early. Tara and Drew were flying down here from New York. But Grace Anne had seen a segment of *ER* on the *Today* show this morning. Tara had heard that the George Clooney character was moving to Seattle, and I (who had seen the last ten minutes of last week's episode) was able to explain the car accident scene in which the physician's assistant who is HIV positive receives a number of facial cuts. Drew has heard that she may now also have hepatitis C. At this point it occurs to me that we are talking about all of these people as though they existed. We have fallen, however briefly, into the soap opera zone.

February 20 / Captiva

I forget who it was but some comedian used to joke that his wife took care of all the trivial things, like shopping, cooking, getting the kids off to school, the family's medical care and paying the insurance premium, and he took care of the major issues, like peace in the Middle East.

A major Kurdish leader was captured by Turkish commandos in Kenya a couple of days ago. It appears that U.S. intelligence was helpful in tracking him down. He seems to have been a pretty brutal character, ordering many who opposed him to be tortured to death. Still, I can't help wondering what's happening to him now. U.S. foreign policy may have achieved the impossible, in that we are now hated equally by the Iraqis and the Kurds. Add Osama bin Laden to the equation, and a major terrorist action against an American target must be inevitable.

I was thinking about that today when reality intervened. Rosafina, our elder cat, had escaped and was playing hide-and-seek with my wife and daughter under the house. Drew and I joined the hunt, and for the next ninety minutes catching that damned cat was the only thing on any of our minds. That's life. We may think about the big picture from time to time, but, for the most part, it's the little things that occupy us.

February 21 / Captiva

Just as words have the power to imbue things with meaning, so, too, names can bestow human qualities on creatures and vice versa.

A couple of years ago, a seagull hung around my deck chair whenever I was sitting on the beach. He would sometimes stand there for an hour or more, until I went inside and brought back some bread or crackers. We called him Stanley. Ever since then our family has maintained the conceit that Stanley remembers us. The fact is that if you start throwing bread around on the beach, you will instantly attract a dozen or more seagulls. We like to think that the first to come or the last to leave is Stanley. Just having given him a name distinguishes him from all other seagulls, makes him smarter, more sensitive. More like us.

It works the other way around, too. Those New York cops who so easily refer to blacks and Hispanics as animals effectively dehumanize them. It's a lot easier to pull a gun on an animal than someone who shares the same qualities you have. Call a cop a pig and you achieve the same end. It's only a word, just a name, but the power of words and names is greater than we think. Both are distilled thoughts.

February 22 / Captiva

I'll be heading back to work tomorrow. I spoke to Mayor Giuliani today. He *is* pissed. He wonders why the only two programs that *Nightline* has done on New York City in the last five and a half years (is that how long he's been in office?) were about police brutality, and now here we are back again doing another program about police brutality (or, at least, excessive force). Come to think of it, the only programs I can remember doing in or about Los Angeles over the last half dozen years were about police brutality, riots or the O. J. trial. But that's beside the point. The mayor would like some credit for all the good that he's done. I explained that he will indeed get credit on this upcoming program. It is quite possible for him to have done a superb job curbing crime, making New York a more livable place, and, at the same time, have permitted (or even encouraged) a mind-set among New York's finest that makes people of color fearful every time they encounter a policeman. Anyway, he's agreed to an interview.

February 23 / Washington

A jury found John King guilty. He and two other white men were charged with wrapping a chain around the ankles of James Byrd Jr., a black man, hitching the chain to the back of their pickup truck and dragging the man to his death in Jasper, Texas. The jury consisted of eleven whites and one black juror who was chosen as their foreman. They found King guilty in two and a half hours.

This is a century that began with black men being lynched on a fairly routine basis in this country, especially in the South and Southwest. In those days King would not have been found guilty, there would not have been a black man on the jury and the citizens of Jasper would have been unlikely to engage in the sort of soul-searching that's under way now.

That is of scant consolation to Byrd's family, but, on that score, America is moving in the right direction.

February 24 / Omaha, Nebraska

I've been pestering Warren Buffett (the second wealthiest man in America, behind Bill Gates) to do an interview for the past six years or so. He agreed late last fall but impeachment got in the way. Now our schedules have finally intersected.

Buffet met me at the airport shortly after noon so that he could drive me around town for half an hour or so before we recorded our interview at the Dairy Queen. (He was driving, and there was nothing memorable about the car.) Berkshire Hathaway, his holding company, bought Dairy Queen a short time ago for the same reason that Buffett buys almost every one of his investments: Simple logic convinces him that people are going to be munching burgers and slurping milk shakes fifty years from now, just as they'll be buying insurance (Geico), drinking sodas (Coca-Cola) and shaving (Gillette).

Buffett is a complex man hiding behind a plain demeanor. The "tour" is all part of the mask. Five generations of Buffetts have attended the local high school (although Warren went to high school in Washington, D.C., where his father, Howard, served in Congress). His grandfather ran a local grocery store, paid his help $2 cash for a day's labor but insisted that they give him 2 cents to pay the Social Security tax. He wanted them to grasp the evils of socialism firsthand.

We drive past the house where Warren has lived for forty years. It is large, pleasant, unpretentious. The office building in which Warren works—he tends to answer his own phone—is nondescript.

We lunch at the Dairy Queen. Warren has the Super Saver and a cherry Coke. He presents a simple story line: Multibillionaire as just plain folks! "It may," as Henry Kissinger likes to say, "have the additional virtue of being true."

Anyway, Buffett's investment policy is disarmingly simple and sensible. He puts his money only into businesses he understands (no technology stocks) run by a management he respects and likes. Then he tends to stick with the investment for the indefinite future. Never buy on margin! He is not a fan of the gambling style of Internet investors. He thinks the bubble may be about to burst.

Let's see how Wall Street reacts to that.

February 25 / New York

John King has been sentenced to death for the murder of James Byrd Jr. In New York City today Rudy Giuliani expressed anger at demonstrators who carry signs that read NYPD=KKK. He's right: That's wrong. But he doesn't want to acknowledge the level of alienation that New York blacks and Hispanics feel from what is, after all, *their* police force, too. When I told him that almost every black we'd interviewed said he'd been stopped at one time or another by the police, Giuliani said he'd been stopped several times, too—before he was mayor. It turned out he was talking about traffic stops or sobriety roadblocks.

He's much too smart not to get it, but with a 63 percent approval rating among New York whites and only 13 percent approval among blacks, he knows where his support lies.

America is changing, but not fast enough.

February 26 / Washington

ABC has dropped another bomb. Without warning, they've announced that they're implementing their contract with NABET (the National Association of Broadcast Engineers and Technicians), which includes our videotape editors and camerapeople. There was a union walkout a few months back, which precipitated a company lockout. The National Labor Relations Board confirmed the company's right to lock out the workers, but it was painful nevertheless. The economics of our business dictate a redefinition of roles and responsibilities, and Wall Street is notoriously unsentimental. Broadcasting is still an enormously profitable industry, but not as much as it once was. When I joined ABC in 1963, I was a radio reporter. When I went on assignment, I had to take an engineer with me to run the tape recorder. Television camera crews in those days consisted of cameraman, soundman, and electrician. Crews almost never include electricians anymore. Local television stations frequently send out camerapeople who also do their own sound. Before too much longer, TV reporters will cover stories alone, using small, handheld video cameras, just as radio reporters now carry their own tape recorders.

Still, these men and women have worked for this company for a long time. Their membership voted to reject the "final" contract offer from the company, and now the company is implementing that contract. I don't know whether this means that folks will be heading out to the picket line again.

It's important to remember days such as this. We tend, over a period of years, to develop close relations with the people for whom and with whom we work. But large corporations are rarely influenced by friendship. Their boards and shareholders demand that their top executives do what is in the corporations' best economic interests, and, at times like these, personal relationships count for very little.

February 27 / Potomac

We are living in an era in which the imperatives of the achievable goal have taken priority over the goal of great achievement. Whether it's Giuliani in New York or Clinton in Washington, the emphasis in politics (and, by extension, throughout our lives) is on setting the bar knee-high: the "broken window" theory in New York, "100,000 cops on the streets" nationally. These are concepts designed to be easily understood by the electorate, easily achieved by the politicians and easily recalled on Election Day. There's nothing fundamentally wrong with setting achievable goals, except that it seems to discourage breadth of vision, boldness and the far more difficult task of a leadership that can convince the public to move in a direction it was not prepared to go.

I thought, at the beginning of the Clinton administration, that the president was willing to show some of that vision and boldness in his policy toward gays in the military, for example; or that he would expand his undeniable sympathy for African Americans into real policies that would help eliminate the lingering remnants of racism in this country. Instead, he issues an apology for slavery. Like most of us, I suppose, Clinton finds it easier to apologize for what he did not do than for what he did.

February 28 / Captiva

If you want to know what Americans fear or crave (they are essentially two sides of the same coin) as we reach the end of the twentieth century, look at our television ads. One health center, clearly catering to women going through or emerging from menopause, has an actress/doctor referring sympathetically to "vaginal dryness" and what can be done about it. Moments later, you may see Bob Dole, Republican presidential nominee in 1996, retired Senate Majority Leader, wounded World War II veteran, speaking on behalf of the Pfizer chemical company putatively on the subject of courage. It's a winding path (but in the context of a one-minute commercial, quickly navigated) from war to prostate cancer to "erectile dysfunction." Pfizer's gift to the departing century, Viagra, is never specifically mentioned in Dole's ad, but the connection will be made clear to Pfizer stockholders.

Nature's message to men and women "of a certain age" would seem to have a certain harmonious foundation. After all, vaginal dryness and erectile dysfunction are clearly intended to comfortably coexist. But Americans deal badly with all signs of aging. Other commercials will quickly sketch a composite profile of our vanities, promising, as they do, the restoration of hair, the elimination of facial lines, the tightening of thighs and buttocks. There's nothing new about Man's quest for eternal youth, but the American mercantile drive has intensified it in unprecedented fashion.

March

March 1 / Captiva

Suggestion: Let's combine all the awards ceremonies for the communications and entertainment industries and name that one event after the
single piece of equipment used by all of us—the microphone. I suggest
calling the occasion "the Phonies." The record industry, which picked
the less descriptive part of the word "gramophone" for its self-
congratulatory orgy, celebrated its event the other night. Lauryn Hill
was nominated seven times and won five Grammies. The next morning,
a Washington disc jockey by the name of Doug Tracht, whose nom de
micro is The Greaseman, played one of Hill's records and then said,
"No wonder people drag them behind trucks." He was summarily fired.

The Greaseman is what is known as a "shock jock," precisely
because he specializes in saying outrageous things on the air. The most
famous practitioner of the art is Howard Stern. He and the radio
group that puts him on the air have been fined well over a million dollars for the outrageous things Stern has said. Advertisers, however,
have compensated the group with that much more money, which is to
say, his program is so successful that Stern is no longer fired. (He was
when he was younger and not so profitable.) What makes The Greaseman's offense fireable, in other words, is not so much what he said as
that he doesn't bring in enough revenue doing it.

March 2 / En route to New York

We may have passed through what will come to be known as the
golden age of information. The nature of commercial broadcasting

was such that on radio and on television competition existed only within a remarkably small circle. The three major networks essentially comprised it. There was plenty of money to go around, and it was produced exclusively by entertainment programming. News and public affairs were not expected to generate revenue, and so there was little pressure to cater to the lowest common denominator. The Federal Communications Commission (FCC) was hardly fierce in enforcing the edict that the networks operate in "the public interest, necessity and convenience," but there was no question that there were obligations to be filled in that area, if only because no other entity could do so in as sweeping a fashion.

Now there is a plethora of media outlets. Literally millions will soon be able to "broadcast" over the Internet, should they choose to do so. The networks, increasingly desperate to draw money out of a shrinking pool of viewers (the pool is actually growing larger, but those in it have an ever increasing number of options), have turned to their news divisions to make money. Instead of expanding, though, the news divisions are being cut back. Instead of broadening the range of subjects, these divisions are reproducing mass appeal newsmagazines that are essentially parroting one another's format, style and subject matter.

Those with the inclination can find everything they want and need in print, on NPR or on the Internet. But the networks, which still reach the largest audiences, are cutting back on stories they might once have felt an obligation to cover—especially foreign news. The most accessible media are devolving into the least useful and daring. The educationally and economically deprived in our society, who used to receive at least some exposure to information they might not have selected for themselves, but from which they might have received some benefit, are now reduced to watching only what we believe they want; and we have little confidence in their appetite or range.

March 3 / Washington

What *will* people watch? Monica. This is Barbara Walters's big day. (She's had many of them, but this one will stick in people's memories.) I watched an advance copy of her much anticipated interview with Lewinsky. Barbara is amazing. She has perfected a look that is simultaneously encouraging, sympathetic, slightly incredulous, and modestly disapproving but not judgmental—all in one expression, mind you.

Monica was clearly having a good time. After she got her apology to the nation out of the way, it was clear that she relished her affair (yes, it was an affair, she says, even though they never had intercourse and therefore it doesn't count as sex) and would do it again in a heartbeat. She is, however, a very sad and troubled young woman, and it makes me think even less of Clinton that he succumbed to her thong flashing.

March 4 / Washington

The Monica interview exceeded ABC's fondest expectations, achieving a 48 percent share of audience. Somewhere in the neighborhood of seventy-five million people are believed to have watched one or another part of the two hours.

We are in the middle of watching the establishment of a contrition industry. After Monica's little apologia at the beginning she launched cheerfully into selling her rehabilitation: her ghostwritten book (450,000-copy first printing), a major interview on the BBC, an interview with *Time*, European photo shoots. She is now her own industry.

This evening I interviewed Doug Tracht, a.k.a. The Greaseman. He's on his own contrition tour, going from radio station to radio station, television station to television station, spinning out his mea culpa to all listeners. Part of the tour will involve a visit to Jasper, Texas, where he plans to apologize personally to the family of the man who was dragged to death behind the truck. "My people have been having a hard time reaching the mother," he told me. I suggested that perhaps this was a call he should be making himself. Earlier today former Georgetown coach John Thompson (who now has his own radio show) told Tracht that he needs counseling. Fine. No problem. If that's what it takes to get back on the air again, counseling it will be. And why not? Isn't this in keeping with the template created by the president? What else should it take but a sincere apology, well delivered? As the late George Burns liked to say: "If you can fake sincerity, you got it made."

March 5 / Washington

There was a memorial service today for Jack Carmody, for twenty years the television columnist for the *Washington Post*. Dubbed "Captain Airwaves" by his *Post* associate and friend Tom Shales, Carmody evoked the term "curmudgeon." The word, once purely perjorative, has somehow come to suggest someone who only seems rough and ill-tempered, but who is really a pussycat, and that was Carmody. The occasion today was notable for the fact that the three major network anchors, Peter Jennings, Dan Rather and Tom Brokaw, spoke, and very well, too. It's nice, every once in a while, to confirm that these three men (indeed, most of the network anchors) are intelligent, literate people who take their jobs seriously.

Carmody would, I think, have been astonished to hear how beloved he was. It prompted me to suggest to former *Post* editor Ben Bradlee and his wife, the writer Sally Quinn, that we have Ben's memorial service while he's still alive. The only ground rule would be that Ben, lying in state on a table, would not be permitted to interrupt or respond. It's somehow such a waste to expend all this admiration and affection on someone who is no longer around to hear it, and who, as in Carmody's case, had no immediate family to benefit from it.

March 6 / Potomac

I don't know the etymology of the word "gay" insofar as it relates to homosexuals, but if it is supposed to evoke any of its former meaning—bright, cheerful, happy—it is doomed in this time and place to evoke only irony.

The *New York Times* this morning recounts the murder of thirty-nine-year-old Billy Jack Gaither of Sylacauga, Alabama. He was clubbed to death and then his corpse was burned on a pile of tires. Police say the two men charged with the crime became enraged after Gaither made a sexual advance toward one of them.

Gaither, it appears, would have left town for some other part of the country in which he could have lived an openly gay lifestyle had he not been caring for his disabled parents. His room, the *Times* reports, was filled with artifacts from *Gone With the Wind;* Scarlett O'Hara dolls and the like. His father is still in denial over his son's homosexuality.

Gay? Certainly not in Sylacauga, Alabama.

March 7 / Potomac

The aftershocks from the Monica earthquake continue to rumble even if their force on the social Richter scale keeps diminishing. Andrew Morton, the British journalist who became Princess Diana's confidant/biographer, was on *Meet the Press* this morning talking about his newly released book written "with" Monica. Linda Tripp was on *This Week with Sam Donaldson and Cokie Roberts* (featuring George Will), giving her response to the Monica interview with Barbara Walters. Each subsequent event seems to have half the impact of the one preceding it, which means, I suppose, that we will never achieve complete silence on the subject ever again.

I've just finished a wonderful, small book (physically small) by Alan Lightman, *Einstein's Dreams.* It is a series of novelistic reflections on the nature of time and the ways in which our differing perceptions of it affect our lives and the way we conduct them.

Perhaps the disconnect between American journalism and the American people, these days, is a function of that differing perception. We journalists, after all, tend to operate within the confines of a deadline. Truth itself becomes a shifting target, depending on our access to information and sources before that deadline expires.

Much of American journalism has become a sort of competitive screeching: What is trivial but noisy and *immediate* tends to take precedence over important matters that develop quietly over time. Nor is it simply the fault of journalists. The degree to which the public avidly consumes journalism as entertainment and ignores it when it appears as social cartography makes the sensational nature of what we do almost inevitable.

Our consumers think in terms of long-term goals and imperatives: their children's education, how to take care of their aging parents, their own retirement. Maybe there's always been that disconnect between journalism and the actual lives that people lead. But it does seem to me that more and more we are read and watched for fun, and then people worry about their daily existence.

March 8 / Potomac

You can tell when nothing much is going on. The *New York Times* and the *Washington Post* have only one front-page story in common today, and that one is below the fold: the death of Stanley Kubrick, director of *2001: A Space Odyssey*, *A Clockwork Orange*, *Dr. Strangelove*, *Lolita*, *Full Metal Jacket* and *Spartacus*.

Other than the Kubrick piece, though, the *Times* and the *Post* had nothing in common on their front pages. That rarely happens.

Actually, no more or less than usual is going on in the world. We are simply without a story of such common interest or importance that the editors of our two most important newspapers can agree.

There will be no such problem tomorrow morning. Joe DiMaggio died today.

March 9 / En route to Boston

We are doing a program on schizophrenia. I'm traveling to Boston to meet a man named Moe Armstrong, himself a schizophrenic, who counsels others with mental illness. Moe is a Vietnam veteran, a former medical corpsman with the Marines. His bouts of madness began after one too many long-range patrols, and after he was prevented from treating wounded Vietcong prisoners, some of whom subsequently died. ("Fuck 'em," said the Marine officer in charge, according to Moe, "they're only gooks. Let 'em die.")

We are working on this story at the initiative of an old friend and *Nightline* producer, Joe O'Conner. His mother died last year after a lifelong battle with schizophrenia. Joe remembers being dragged out of his house, as a young boy, by his terrified mother who was running from her own internal demons in the middle of the night.

There are millions of such people in America, and while we avoid terms like "mad" and "crazy" these days, our attitudes toward those suffering from acute mental illness have not much improved. Joe and I are hoping that Moe will help bridge the gap. It is no help that television dramas and movies in general tend to portray the mentally ill (especially schizophrenics) as violent and dangerous.

Many of America's violent and dangerous may be mentally ill, but most of our mentally ill are neither violent nor dangerous.

March 10 / En route to Washington

I got trapped in Boston last night by the heavy snow in Washington. ABC booked a suite for me at a perfectly nice hotel in Cambridge, on Harvard Square. It was what I suspect many people dream of when they imagine a suite in a fine hotel—huge. There was a gigantic dining room cum living room cum den (there was a baby grand piano in an alcove off the living room part), with a full bathroom and kitchenette adjoining. There was also the master bedroom, another bathroom and a walk-in closet.

I invited my friend Peter, an architect who works in Cambridge, to join Joe and me for dinner in the suite (it seemed a shame to waste all that space). Peter took one look, laughed, and said it reminded him of three motel rooms tacked together.

The space was, essentially, pointless. None of it was designed to be used. It was designed to make jaws drop, to provoke an Omigod, this is so big! reaction.

This morning I was treated to the room designer's idea of a luxury shower: one regular shower head, flanked by two vertical shower "bars." In theory, you can see how it's supposed to work: the entire body surrounded by steaming jets of hot water. In reality, the water pressure was so diffused that it simply dribbled out.

The shower and the room are symptomatic of our times. We tend to confuse big and garish with luxurious and tasteful.

March 11 / Washington

My dear friend Sam Donaldson is sixty-five today and not liking it one bit. He has terrorized his staff into avoiding any mention of the event, let alone a celebration; but I think he was pleased, nevertheless, to have a contemporary stop by to commiserate. There are all these terrible associations with turning sixty-five in our culture. It's the age at which most people retire. It's just five years away from our biblically allotted three score and ten. It's absolute nonsense, of course. Some people are truly old at sixty-five. Sam is not among them.

I had occasion this afternoon to do a final interview with a young man who wants to become my assistant here at *Nightline*. He's bright, ambitious and refreshingly eager. He'll be taking the place of George Griffin, a young man who has become a dear friend over the years. I promised George that I would plant my foot in his butt and kick him out the door if he was still with me after three years. It's been almost six. But George didn't want to leave until he could be promoted within *Nightline*, and we're finally in a position to do that.

It doesn't seem all that long ago since Sam and I were young reporters here at ABC News, watching the old veterans with a mixture of awe and amusement, wondering how long it would take before they realized they had not merely lost a step but were tripping over their own feet.

I hope that he and I have the good sense and grace to leave before that happens to us.

March 12 / Washington

How ugly and how predictable this town can be.

There's been what is clearly a major security violation. The Chinese have developed a miniaturized, multiple warhead weapons system that bears a striking resemblance to the U.S. W-88. Exactly how the Chinese got it is unclear, but once the *New York Times* broke the story last weekend, it was clear that someone had to be thrown to the wolves. A Chinese American computer scientist has been fired, with some considerable fanfare. What's interesting about his firing is that it took place a couple of days after the *Times* story, though no charges have been brought against the man. He hasn't been arrested, and our FBI sources are telling us that he probably won't be.

On the other side of the ledger, a gaggle of Republican presidential candidates—Buchanan, Alexander, Forbes—have called on the president's national security advisor, Sandy Berger, to resign.

Whenever something like this happens, there's a political gag reflex. Whoever is in the opposition first looks for someone to blame and fire, and then demands that we stop coddling the Chinese (or the

Soviets, or whoever happen to be the bad boys of the moment). What totally escapes people at times like these is that maintaining bilateral relations with an unfriendly country, like China, is not some sort of unilateral favor that we bestow. It's something we do because it is in our national interest to do so. If the day ever comes that there is no benefit whatsoever to be gained from having diplomatic relations with China, we'll break them.

March 13 / New York

Bob Iger, ABC's CEO and a friend of many years' standing, invited me to join him; Michael Eisner, the head of Disney; and Senator John McCain for dinner and the Evander Holyfield–Lennox Lewis fight at Madison Square Garden. I have never been to a boxing match in my life. I've watched a few on TV over the years and enjoy a well-matched fight. Still, it always counts as a guilty pleasure. I'm as curious about the carnival at ringside as I am about the fight itself. I can't pretend feverish excitement about even a championship bout between two fighters, only one of whom (Holyfield) I know at all, and neither of whom has any of the aura generated by Joe Louis or Jack Dempsey or Archie Moore or either of the Sugar Rays (Robinson or Leonard) or Muhammed Ali. But it is a heavyweight-championship fight.

March 14 / En route to Washington

It looked to me as though Lewis was robbed. The fight was declared a draw, which neither pleased nor outraged anyone (in the sense that no chairs were flung into the ring, since most bets were simply voided), and considering that this was a world-championship bout, it may even have been fair. Lewis had the upper hand more of the time than Holyfield, but when the ultimate title(s) in boxing are at stake, perhaps a fight should be convincingly won.

The setting was the thing. The Garden was packed. Forty-five hundred seats were designated "ringside" and sold for $500–$1,500 apiece. We were "ringside"; actually, five rows back. Senator McCain ended up sitting next to Rolling Stones guitarist Keith Richards, who looks as though one more joint or Budweiser would finish him off once and for all. But then, he has looked like that for twenty years. He and the senator hit it off famously.

The producers of the event, obviously committed to leaving no tacky stone unturned, had the ring announcer call for ten seconds of silence, tapped off with chimes from the ringside bell, in memory of Joe DiMaggio. Some of the British fans, untouched by the pop gravitas of the moment, yelled obscenities. They had been doing that all along, but now we could hear them. A gray-haired, florid-faced, sprightly little man in a red blazer sang "God Save the Queen." He was blown out of the Garden by a young black man in a leather jacket and sporting an elaborate "do" who made each note of our national anthem into a personal rebuttal of all things English.

Present, in no particular order, were: Don King, Rupert Murdoch, Al Sharpton, Patrick Ewing, "Magic" Johnson, Michael Douglas, Kweisi Mfume, Jack Nicholson, Spike Lee, about seventy-five hundred Brits and several serious-looking gentlemen in $5,000 Italian suits and an attitude.

I'm glad I went. But I think I'll skip the rematch.

March 15 / Potomac

Postscript to the fight: It turns out that the "experts" see it much as I did—Lewis "wuz robbed!" The presidents of the International Boxing Federation and the World Boxing Association (Holyfield holds those two titles) and the president of the World Boxing Council (whose title Lewis holds) have ordered a rematch within six months.

So let's see if I have this straight: After getting $20 million and $10 million respectively, Holyfield and Lewis are being "ordered" to do it again, although this time each of them will probably ask for and get *more* money.

On the other world stage, it seems we cannot be sure of even getting the Kosovar Albanians to sign a U.S.-sponsored deal that would have had NATO (read the United States) launch bombing attacks against Serbian-Yugoslav targets, should the Serbs reject the deal, as they've indicated they will do. Actually, the Albanians may be doing the United States a huge favor. I cannot imagine why the Clinton administration (abetted by Bob Dole) is so eager to embark on a road that will put twenty-six thousand NATO troops (five thousand of them American) on the ground, indefinitely, in Kosovo without an exit strategy. The Serbs have the military power; the Albanians have the numbers; and we have the debatable privilege of interposing ourselves and all the other NATO nations between the two sides to keep two NATO nations, the Turks and the Greeks, from taking sides if the fighting spreads.

March 16 / Washington

We have just completed a disturbing couple of broadcasts that will air tonight and tomorrow night. At their heart is the question of what to do about a convicted pedophile who has served his five-and-a-half-year sentence and has now moved to a small community on the outskirts of Portland, Oregon. His mother bought a small house in one community. Her new neighbors put it to her this way: "Either we buy you out or we burn you out." She sold that house.

Mother and son then moved to another small community, their present home, only a few miles down the road. The neighbors there are no happier about having the young pedophile (he's in his late twenties) in their neighborhood. They would prefer his going back to prison for the rest of his life. They are afraid for their children.

The pedophile is restricted by dozens of regulations, the violation of any of which would result in his going to jail for a couple of days. He cannot be on the road in his car heading to work at the time that the school bus is on the road. He cannot leave the country without special permission. His parole lasts for another twenty years. He must consult during this time with a psychologist who will tell him when he can have sex with his girlfriend.

Unlike a kidnapper, bank robber or even a murderer, he will be identified for what he did wherever he goes, and while he insists that what he is is no longer what he was, no one believes him.

March 17 / Washington

It got into the sixties today—sunny, beautiful, springlike. It's amazing how rejuvenating a day such as this one can feel, even after a relatively mild winter. It helps that it snowed like hell all day Sunday, so that the transition is particularly abrupt and clear. One day we're slogging through the slush and now we can look forward to six or seven months of T-shirts and shorts and being out on the water. The contrast, though, is an essential part of the joy. I'd go nuts living in Florida all year. To have a proper appreciation of warmth, you need to have been cold. A great meal is one of life's great joys, but it pales into insignificance compared to a heel of bread and chunk of cheese when you haven't eaten for a day or so. Sleep is always good, but when you're thoroughly exhausted, when you've worked for two or three days and nights straight, the act of lying down is one of the most exquisite feelings in the world.

I'm happy that winter is over, but I'm glad there's another one coming.

March 18 / Washington

You never know how and when you're going to have an impact. Back on January 17 I took note in these pages of the confusing nature of certain Giant ads in the *Washington Post*, products listed at one price but covering a range of weights.

I discussed the issue with an assistant manager at our local supermarket, and then, a few days later, with the manager. He, it now turns out, raised the issue with Odonna Mathews, the vice president of consumer affairs for Giant Food, Inc. Damned if they haven't changed the ads. They now clearly list the exact weight and price of each product. We'll see how long the changes remain in place. But I'm tickled.

March 19 / En route to Fort Myers

We are headed for trouble, if not disaster, over Kosovo. It's one thing when the country at large is resistant to, or even apathetic about, a foreign policy initiative involving the use of force. The most important initiatives are often those whose importance is not immediately visible to the public. I'm not even overly concerned about the military's lack of enthusiasm. Despite conventional wisdom to the contrary, it is usually the State Department, not the Pentagon, that favors military options. In this instance, though, it's hard to detect enthusiasm or confidence on the part of either the White House or the State Department for the proposal to bomb Serbian targets in Yugoslavia. It is the Serbs who seem confident and determined and convinced of the righteousness of their cause. The Kosovar Albanians have finally signed the U.S.-sponsored "peace" plan, but they had to be bullied into doing so. Apparently, they are not altogether convinced that this policy is in their interest. The United States, meanwhile, is publicly cringing at the possibility that Yugoslav air defenses could shoot down an American warplane. We seem to have reached a point at which war is tenable only if we are confident that casualties will be limited to *their* side. We are much too quick to opt for cruise missiles and air attacks and far too deficient in discussing and explaining why a given military action is essential to our national interest.

If any U.S. pilots are lost over Yugoslavia, not one American in a million will be able to explain why it was allowed to happen.

March 20 / Captiva

Down here, especially when, as now, Grace Anne and I are in a brief vacation mode (a long weekend) and in the company of friends, the threat of military action over Kosovo seems especially distant and irrelevant to our lives. It is only when American lives are actually lost that the dreadful nature of war intrudes into the consciousness of most people living in a land at peace. There is, after all, not a hint of war to be detected here. There is no rationing, nor are there any shortages connected with our presence in Bosnia, in Haiti or in South Korea. Our regular air strikes over Iraq have not, as yet, resulted in a single American casualty. It's dangerous when so many fuses are lit and we are unaware as a people that all of them are attached to potential bombs.

A Huey helicopter just flew by over the Gulf of Mexico. It has been thirty years since I listened for that sound in Vietnam, thirty years since it meant the imminent arrival of food and water and, often, safety. The sound and the memory of what it once meant still makes me salivate, literally.

March 21 / Captiva

Grace Anne and I often analogize our lives to the performance of an acrobat/juggler who keeps twenty or more plates spinning on the tips of an equal number of twelve-foot-long flexible wands. No sooner does he have the plates at one end of the line spinning merrily and safely away than one or more of the plates at the other end threatens to fall and smash. Life is made up of running from one plate to another, keeping them all aloft.

As children, totally absorbed in the solipsistic cocoon that a safe childhood bestows, we are unaware of any pressing needs other than our own. Marriage, parenthood, professional responsibilities multiply the demands on us until there is rarely a moment when all the plates are spinning securely.

I'm not altogether convinced that this is such a moment, but I am temporarily unaware of any pressing needs or emergencies. Ignorance is almost as good as genuine stability. After all, what else is a happy childhood but ignorance of adult pressures and problems?

March 22 / Captiva

We stayed up until 12:30 in the morning to watch the Academy Awards, although I can't for the life of me explain why. The production was cheesy, Whoopi Goldberg was unfunny and so deliberately crude that she must have decided she doesn't want to do this anymore; and it is difficult to understand why so many creative people are reduced to embarrassing gibberish when all they really have to do is say, Thank you, I've wanted one of these for most of my life.

It's like eating Cheetos: Your fingers and tongue are bright orange early on, but damned if you can stop before finishing the bag. And then you feel silly.

March 23 / En route to Washington

Since two of our daughters and our son-in-law are Duke graduates, it is with some satisfaction that I watch both the men's and women's basketball teams advance to the final four of the NCAA tournament this year.

Hillary Clinton is touring North Africa with Chelsea. The First Lady is being studied for signs, hints and portents: Will she run for the U.S. Senate seat being vacated by Daniel Patrick Moynihan? She shouldn't, but she probably will. It's likely to be a brutal campaign in which her role in the Whitewater real estate deal, the Travel Office fiasco and the secretive health plan will be dug up and reexamined. She's not accustomed to taking direct hits in a campaign (although the carom shots that have bounced off her husband have been difficult and given her useful experience). Her marriage appears shot, and I can understand the mind-set that "It's time to see what I can do in my own behalf."

March 24 / Washington

Nightline is nineteen years old today. It doesn't seem that long ago when the first executive producer, Bill Lord, and I agonized over what, if any, changes to make in the format of "America Held Hostage," which focused entirely on the fate of fifty-two Americans being held at the U.S. embassy in Tehran. For the first few months we made sure there would be an Iran update every night; eventually, the transition was made to focus on whatever story captured our interest that day. It took us a long time to take off the training wheels.

What is difficult for me to accept is that some of the interns now working at *Nightline* were only two or three years old when the program began. I'm beginning to sink into old-fartism.

NATO planes (most of them American) and cruise missiles (all of them American) have been unleashed today on Serb targets in Yugoslavia and Kosovo. American television has slipped into its now customary role of providing maps, meaningless pictures (little explosions of brightness against the grainy green of nighttime lenses) and marginally informative babble. Those who truly know what's going on aren't talking or, if they are talking, are in full spin cycle. Television is awash in "formers"—former secretaries of state and defense, former national security advisors, former generals and admirals. They are trapped, for the most part, between remembering their own resentment at being second-guessed by a previous generation of "formers," and pique at not having been consulted on the current crisis. (If they are being consulted, they usually won't appear on television.) But very few television programs are focused on substance, anyway. There is temporary interest in "exit strategies" and "endgames"—the "formers" are close to unanimous in concluding that the Clinton administration has paid insufficient attention to either. But when you consider that the attention span of the average American television viewer has been pared down to considerably less than a minute—if surveys are to be believed—the administration would be fully justified in believing that, before long, some juicy little murder or sex scandal will combine with apathy to overtake the public's fleeting interest in Serbs and Kosovar Albanians.

Many years ago, Milton Berle joked that the way to end the war in Vietnam was to book it on ABC. "That way," he said, "it'll be canceled in thirteen weeks."

If American soldiers start dying in any number, no U.S. president could possibly sustain a war for that long in this day and age.

March 25 / Washington

Cabinet officers and senior representatives of the administration are everywhere, blanketing television, from the morning shows to *Nightline*, as though fearful that silence on their part might be filled with the voices of skeptics. They don't have the stomach for this thing. They're already beginning to retreat a little from the initial demands they made on President Milošević of Yugoslavia. He was going to have to sign the agreement hammered out at Rambouillet. Now they want him to "embrace the framework" (read: We can still renegotiate some of this stuff).

The president and his senior cabinet officers speak vaguely of being able to end the bombing when they have "degraded and diminished" the Serbian military capability. Well, technically, they could make that call after the first tank is destroyed. Who decides *how* degraded or diminished, before they can declare victory? The president does; and trying to keep the other eighteen members of NATO on board while this campaign goes into week two or three or, God forbid, a second month, is not something he wants hanging over him as

NATO begins its fiftieth-anniversary celebration here in Washington a few weeks hence.

About thirty-five years ago, the late Senator George Aiken of Vermont proposed that the United States declare victory in Vietnam and get out. I think Bill Clinton remembers that advice and is ready to heed it now. As for the Kosovar Albanians, I think Milošević is going to destroy their little army, whatever it costs him. He knows damned well that NATO won't send in ground troops to protect them, and he seems to believe that he can ride out the bombing raids.

March 26 / Washington

It is as though someone had created a handbook for "How to Handle a Crisis." Indeed, in a sense, a succession of White House "handlers" has. We interviewed a number of presidential advisors of recent years, ranging from Hodding Carter III, who was State Department spokesman during the Jimmy Carter administration, to Ken Duberstein, who was Reagan's chief of staff during his later years in the White House. We also spoke to George Stephanopoulos, David Gergen and Dee Dee Meyers, each of whom put in time at the Clinton White House. They have it down to a fine art: Try to get out ahead of the crisis. Prepare Congress and the American people for what's coming. (Clinton gets low marks on this.) Lay out your reasons for putting American lives at risk. The president has to do this repeatedly, and all of his top foreign policy advisors have to appear on the various TV programs as sort of a Greek chorus.

(They have. William Cohen, the secretary of defense, made ten "exclusive" appearances on television yesterday.)

Here's where it gets a little tacky. Americans tend to be moved by humanitarian issues. So, hammer away at the atrocities—fathers and sons being shot on their knees, side by side; villages being torched. And, indeed, you can hear every one of the administration's spokespeople using the same words, pushing the humanitarian theme. We put about ten such proclamations of outrage together, and edited videotape of them, one to another. They don't look all that sincere when you put them back-to-back.

Gergen talked cheerfully about the impact of those cruise missile pictures from Desert Storm, the ones that show a missile slamming down the elevator shaft of some building in Baghdad. We need some of that, David suggested. Today, courtesy of NATO headquarters in Brussels, the networks got their first batch of gun camera videos. David also recommends that the administration encourage the Air Force to take reporters along on B-52 missions over Kosovo. Two of our staff just went through altitude training yesterday for precisely that purpose. The Pentagon is already scheduling rides like Disneyland.

Call me old-fashioned. I'd still like to know how our national interest is so deeply invested in Kosovo as to justify this undeclared war. It's infuriating to hear the analogies to World War I and the Holocaust. The atrocities are real enough; but those alone have never drawn the United States into any war, and the notion that the Balkans are a powder keg (that phrase is actually being used) threatening to ignite the rest of Europe is pure nonsense.

March 27 / Potomac

The Serbs have shot down a U.S. jet. The pilot was rescued in a matter of hours, but until he was extracted, CNN reports, his fate was the sole focus of attention at the Pentagon. It's understandable, in the sense that the loss of a single pilot could begin the process of undermining public confidence in this operation. But what the hell are we doing in a war whose outcome is of so little concern to our perceived national interest that we are not prepared to pay whatever it costs?

March 28 / Potomac

Jake, our sixteen-month-old grandson, has been visiting while his parents (our daughter Deirdre, and son-in-law, Larry) are in town for a wedding. I find myself doing all the silly sleight-of-hand tricks that would fool only a sixteen-month-old and that I found so ludicrous when my father did them to amuse our children.

Larry's parents and my wife and I have divvied up the grandparental names in civilized fashion. His parents are Pop-pop and Grandma; we are Opi and Nan.

Jake has not yet mastered "Nan," but he does a respectable "Opi." He actually thinks he's saying "open," a word with practical applications that he really does know, but he's prepared to go along with my rabid displays of enthusiasm for the word. Although I'm sure it's a little confusing for him that I cheer every time Jake wants the tray of his high chair removed or wants to get into a closed box or out of a locked room.

Deirdre is still the lovely young woman she has been for years, but like an optical illusion, I now see her more as Jake's mom and have to strain to see her in the simpler role of my little girl.

The baton gets passed, but for the most part we never see it happen. It just does.

March 29 / Potomac

ABC News launches *The Century* tonight, the first installment of what will be six two-hour programs. The series is being promoted as having been a hundred years in the making. Almost. My dear friend Lionel Chapman gave his life to the project. The tragic irony is that it was going to be something truly special. It was going to be many more hours long and intended to incorporate not only the American but also the Asian and European perspectives. Lionel simply couldn't get anyone to focus. The frustration, the endless hours that he put in, the Diet Pepsis and Marlboro Lights, finally did him in. I think he was forty-three.

Peter Jennings, who hosts the series, is a friend of many years' standing, and I wish him nothing but success. The book he wrote with Todd Brewster based on the series is, I believe, one of the most successful coffee table volumes ever. Lionel began that project, too.

I ache in his memory.

March 30 / Washington

The administration is desperately afraid of losing American lives over Kosovo. That is simultaneously admirable and pathetic. To repeat what I said earlier, you do not go to war if your principal purpose is avoiding casualties. The administration has mousetrapped themselves. It is they (not anyone else) who put the so-called credibility of NATO on the line. Having done so, they must defend it; but it is clearly not of sufficient importance that it can bear the weight of real casualties. Therefore we avoid sending ground troops at all costs (which is probably wise, in that we wouldn't get them out again for years, and we'd lose a lot of men in the process). We cannot possibly win a meaningful victory without ground troops, however. Ultimately, then, we will have to define ourselves out of this mess. We will announce that Belgrade's forces have been sufficiently "degraded" for us to stop bombing.

In the meanwhile, of course, Milošević and his Serbs have created a new reality on the ground in Kosovo. The Kosovar Albanians have been decimated, either by death, capture or by being driven into neighboring Albania, Montenegro or Macedonia. Even theoretically, the only way that we could reestablish any sort of balance in Kosovo is by arming the Albanians (which is precluded by the very Rambouillet agreement we're trying to impose on Milošević) or by putting peacekeeping forces into Kosovo indefinitely, which would very likely lead to NATO ground troops fighting the Serbs anyway.

What a mess.

March 31 / Washington

It's almost 11 p.m. and I've come back to the office after having left at 6:30 to attend a Passover seder. What obliged me to return to ABC is the news that three American servicemen who were on a training mission along the Macedonian-Kosovo border were surrounded by armed men (it's not yet clear whether they were Serb troops, special police or even local brigands) and came under fire. They were in radio contact that was broken off. Their condition and whereabouts are unknown. For an administration which has been trying to avoid any and all casualties for fear that they may undermine the fragile support that exists for the Kosovo involvement, this is the worst possible news.

April

April 1 / Washington

We seem destined to tumble helplessly from one obsession to another. A few weeks ago, *Nightline* would have been all but alone in airing a commercial network program on Kosovo. Foreign policy is not customarily a popular category on the noncable networks. Now, when I occasionally look up in the newsroom, I see every monitor—reflecting the output of CBS, NBC, FOX, MSNBC, CNN and ABC—showing something about the conflict in Kosovo. Every morning, the *Times* and the *Washington Post* display banner headlines on the subject. I shudder to think what will happen if another crisis—in Iraq or Korea, or some huge terrorist action here at home—competes for the government's attention. One is left with the impression that the president will be hard-pressed to handle much more.

It may be possible for the administration eventually to "define" its way out of Kosovo, but I don't think we will fight our way out. President Clinton understands that if he sends ground troops in to fight, the bloodshed will be enormous for both sides. The time will come when Milošević will indicate some sort of readiness to talk again. Whether that will take the form of NATO being permitted to send in peacekeepers for the maintainance of sanctuaries in which Kosovar Albanians will be allowed to live, I don't know. Whether that will ever be palatable to the United States, I don't know either. But in a few weeks Washington will be desperate to get out of this mess, and whatever emerges will be "defined" as "the best we could do," and possibly even victory.

April 2 / Washington

I wonder who is running or calibrating our propaganda war. He (or she or they) should know that, in the Serbians, he is up against people who have a long and chilling tradition of striking fear into the hearts of their enemies. Vlad the Impaler is still a legendary figure in the region, specifically in Transylvania. His memory is revered, even though he had several thousand of his own people impaled on poles in fields that were in the path of invading Turkish troops. The Turks took one look at Vlad's handiwork and drew their own inferences as to what would happen to them. If, after all, he would do that to his own people . . .

NATO planes are bombing in the heart of Belgrade tonight. By all accounts they've hit only a couple of government buildings; one of them, I believe, was the police headquarters. Apparently that building was emptied out several days ago; but it is next to a hospital, and I'm sure the Serb government will make the most of that.

The real impact of this war is being felt by hundreds of thousands of Kosovar Albanians who have been driven to the borders with Albania, Montenegro and, most especially, Macedonia. I'm haunted by the accounts of helpless Jews in the late thirties and early forties, whose reports of what was going on in Germany and later in Poland and other parts of eastern Europe were not believed; and, for that matter, our skepticism in the mid-seventies when we got our first accounts of what the Khmer Rouge were doing in Cambodia.

It's always easiest for those of us living in safety to discount reports of mass atrocities. We must maintain a healthy skepticism, without descending into cynicism.

April 3 / Potomac

The kids are down from New York, and Andrea is coming over from D.C. for the annual Easter gathering. There are daffodils in profusion—the harvest of a long, chilly fall afternoon, many years ago, when Grace Anne and I "heeled" hundreds of bulbs into the ground. The forsythia is nearing full bloom, and the pink cherry tree at the bottom of the garden is approaching its brief moment of glory. From here on in, spring is, in every sense of the word, a *living* reproach to fear and doubt.

The trees, shrubs and flowers must be beginning to bloom along the borders of Kosovo, too. I don't know whether the symbols of life and renewal have much impact when you're hungry, thirsty, cold, homeless and afraid.

NATO seems to be creeping toward some sort of intervention on the ground, prompted, in large measure, it seems, by the heartrending images of refugees hemorrhaging out of Kosovo by the tens of thousands every day.

Question: Is it the suffering or the images of suffering, or the reaction to the images of suffering, that alters policy? Or are the architects of our policy cynical enough that they have been planning intervention on the ground all along but have been waiting for public opinion to demand it?

I hope they're not that cynical. I'm afraid they're not that far-sighted.

April 4 / Potomac

Easter Sunday. We are drifting, sliding, edging and stumbling toward one of the last bitter ironies of this century. The Clintonians, children of the sixties, implacable judges of those architects of Vietnam, are repeating many of their mistakes.

They have underestimated the tenacity of the enemy. We are not an expansionist power, but we find ourselves constantly fighting on somebody else's land. It is a critical factor. We and our NATO allies have someplace else to go. Home. The Serbs do not (and ultimately, neither do the Kosovar Albanians). It would be humiliating but, in the final analysis, we can afford to lose. They cannot. We seem to believe in the effectiveness of gradualism, although it sucked us deeper and deeper into the morass of Vietnam. We even proclaim it: "Phase one, phase two . . ." And yet, publicly, we are ruling out using ground troops. We are all but telling Milošević, Hold tight, we won't take it too much farther.

Still, we are sending troops to Albania to help the refugees. How long will it be before we have to send combat troops to protect the humanitarians?

In Vietnam we built air bases and then had to send Marines to provide perimeter defense.

We are always one or two phases behind. Barry Schweid of the Associated Press used to joke about buying a Mercedes: "Just when I decide that, maybe, $20,000 isn't too much, it costs $35,000."

April 5 / Potomac

We are drowning in information and starving for knowledge. The various government spokespeople brief us to death but tell us next to nothing. Twenty-five years ago, Henry Kissinger offered me the job of State Department spokesman. One of the reasons I turned him down was the recognition that when reporters uncritically accept what spokesmen are telling them, they are not doing their jobs. When spokesmen give reporters everything they want, they are not doing theirs. I know that many of my colleagues here in Washington don't agree, but I don't believe the revolving door that permits reporters and spokespeople to exchange jobs is healthy.

NATO allies and the United States have pledged to take in a hundred thousand refugees—one giant step for humanity, one difficult precedent when the next similar crisis occurs in Rwanda or Sudan. Twenty thousand Kosovar Albanians will be brought to the United States, but where? Will they be kept in camps, or will they be allowed to move freely around the United States; and will we then set Immigration and Naturalization Service (INS) officers the task of rounding them up again when it's time to send everyone home to Kosovo?

I am glad that we are, at least, offering sanctuary. I pray that we will see the day when an American president opens the door as generously to an African exodus.

Later in the day. The refugees will apparently be given temporary shelter on Guantanamo or in Guam. That answers my question about the INS. It won't be hard to find the refugees in Guantanamo or in Guam; but it still finesses the question of what to do with those refugees who are unconvinced by NATO's assurances, and who refuse to return to Kosovo.

One problem at a time.

April 6 / Washington

The Serbs have offered a unilateral cease-fire. That is, they will stop killing Albanians over the Eastern Orthodox Easter. They may even remove a few of their troops from Kosovo. The offer has been rejected by NATO for the fraud it is. I interviewed the spokesman for the Yugoslav Foreign Ministry this afternoon and asked whether his government is prepared to accept any foreign troops as guarantors of the safety of returning refugees. "Absolutely not," he said.

Everyone is acting as though this can go on forever. It's still too early to say who will crack first.

April 7 / Washington

I just finished interviewing a spokesman for the Kosovo Liberation Army in the operational district that includes the capital of Pristina. It is his position that essentially all Kosovar Albanians have now been forced out of their homes. The ethnic cleansing is over.

Taking into account what has to be an extraordinarily high propaganda quotient, this still raises serious questions as to how NATO goals are going to be achieved. The Albanians have been dispersed or driven out of the country. The Serb military is now in a position to break up into small units and also disperse; they will be difficult to target from the air and would be unlikely to engage larger NATO units on the ground. If Milošević agrees to some sort of political settlement, NATO peacekeepers will spend the next ten years or more in Kosovo, and that would be the happiest outcome of this confrontation. If he doesn't agree to a settlement, NATO faces the unpalatable option of seizing territory through combat and creating artificial "zones of safety" for the Kosovar Albanians. Then we can face the prospect of several years of combating guerrilla attacks.

I have requested of our polling unit that, in its next survey, it ask respondents not only whether they would approve of NATO ground units going into Kosovo, but whether they would accept (a) casualties, (b) more than a hundred casualties, (c) more than a thousand. I suspect that if there are more than a hundred casualties, Americans will have very little stomach for this operation. That is understandable, even commendable, but it is no foundation on which to sustain a war that may last more than a few weeks. This is an issue we must come to terms with as a nation, for we may find ourselves in this situation often.

April 8 / Washington

We don't yet have all the polling responses, but we do have some initial results. The polling unit asked about sending ground troops in. Fifty-seven percent of the respondents think that may be necessary. Once our polling people added in the possibility of sustaining casualties, the number of people supporting ground troops drops to 45 percent. When the number of potential casualties is posited as being one hundred or more, the percentage of those supporting the introduction of ground troops falls to 32 percent.

What in heaven's name are people thinking about? There must be a sense among a significant portion of our population that sending combat troops into action doesn't require even the *consideration* of sustaining casualties. Perhaps when the president gave his little history lesson to the members of the American Federation of State, County and Municipal Employees (AFSME) he should have reminded them how many Allied troops died during World War I. Granted, the loss of a hundred American soldiers would constitute a terrible price, but if, as the president suggested, we are talking about the avoidance of something like World War I, with its hundreds of thousands of Allied casualties, a hundred lives should not be regarded as an exorbitant cost.

The public disconnect that troubles me is this: Either you believe that Kosovo isn't worth NATO involvement in the first place, or you believe that it is. But if it is, you have to get over the notion that war can ever be cost-free, even for the good guys.

April 9 / Washington

I flew up to New York yesterday afternoon to make a few introductory remarks at a dinner for the Legal Aid Society. Since our son, Andrew, works for Legal Aid, they knew I'd be happy to do it. I admire the organization enormously.

Treasury Secretary Robert Rubin was one of the honorees. He was nice enough to offer me a seat on his plane back to Washington. I asked him why the market seemed so unaffected by the "war" in Kosovo. Essentially, he said, what happens in that pocket of the Balkans is perceived to have very little impact on the rest of Europe and, therefore, on our economy—which is exactly the opposite of the rationale the president gave for getting involved there. Among other arguments—humanitarian, the need to degrade Milošević's military, the continued credibility of NATO—the president had argued specifically that the United States had to be concerned because Europe's economy was so integrally involved with ours and Europe's economy was directly threatened by instability in the Balkans.

We're doing a town meeting on Kosovo on the program tonight. The guests will be former Secretary of State Larry Eagleburger; former Defense Secretary James Schlesinger; former National Security Advisor Brent Scowcroft; former director of operations for the Joint Chiefs of Staff General Tom Kelly and former State Department spokesman Hodding Carter III. For all their combined expertise (and it's enormous) I increasingly wonder about the value of these panels of experts opining on television. They fill a vacuum, no doubt; but that's the point. They can fill it only with the expertise they acquired in other crises. The person who really needs to be seen and heard laying out the rationale for this current involvement is the president. This is when he should be leading the nation with a clear and forceful exposition of how and why our national interests are at risk. Instead, he has given a couple of lackluster speeches and leaves it to his national security advisors to fight the daily fight. The problem is that none of them has the heft or credibility of so many of the "formers" appearing all over the tube.

April 10 / Potomac

Is there any aspect of our lives so personal that we are not prepared to expose it in order to reap the potential benefits of big-time marketing?

All across America last night, couples of childbearing age were attempting to procreate (even more than usual). Forget the condoms, never mind the Pill; there were no worries about such things. Last night, young Americans (and some not so young) were copulating with a vengeance and a purpose. The aim is to come up with a "millennium baby" to be born on January 1, 2000. I suppose the really motivated are attempting to target even more precisely by having the *first* baby of the new millennium.

In any event, a number of radio stations across this great land of ours have offered prizes for millennium babies, and I'm sure that somewhere on the Internet last night you could watch some exuberant couple going for the gold.

Oh, incidentally, Boris Yeltsin threatened NATO with nuclear war yesterday if it doesn't stop bombing Yugoslavia. Everybody assumes he's kidding.

April 11 / Potomac

Somebody should take Dan Quayle aside and explain the Peter Principle to him, the tendency of people to rise to the level of their incompetence. Somehow, Quayle got elected to the U.S. Senate from Indiana, which brings to mind the late Senator Roman Hruska's famous response to a rival's jibe that he was mediocre: "Even mediocrity," said Hruska, "deserves representation."

There is no evidence that Quayle did any damage while serving in the Senate, but people are still scratching their heads and wondering what qualities he displayed that prompted George Bush to pluck him out of obscurity as his 1992 running mate. Now Quayle can point with legitimate pride to a résumé that demands respect. Unfortunately for him, he continues to evoke little more than ridicule. I've had long conversations with Quayle, and he is not stupid. He is also likable. But you would feel uncomfortable serving under him in a platoon. I cannot imagine what makes him believe that he could be commander in chief. He was on *Meet the Press* this morning, making extravagant efforts to *look* serious. He does this by scrunching up his eyes in what he must believe is a Clint Eastwood sort of squint. That may work on a campaign poster, but it's an image that is seriously undermined the moment he opens his mouth.

April 12 / Washington

Elie Wiesel and I are meeting for a cup of coffee this afternoon. He's giving a "Millennium Lecture" at the White House this evening. He put my name on a list of five friends that the White House told him he could invite. I told Elie three weeks ago that the White House would never pass that invitation on, that we have simply done too many *Nightlines* that the Clintons didn't like. Elie felt sure they wouldn't just ignore his request. They did, which is why we're meeting for coffee.

April 13 / Washington

Nightline this evening is actually the work of David Turnley, a Pulitzer Prize–winning photojournalist who has brilliantly catalogued the faces of victimhood from Northern Ireland to Rwanda. He is trying to create what amounts to a new form of photojournalism, in which he intercuts some of his black-and-white stills with color videotape. It is truly amazing how different the same scene can look, photographed by the same man, at just about the same instant. In many respects the black-and-white photograph is more instructive, perhaps because the photographer is, in effect, taking the viewer/reader by the hand and saying: Here, look at it this way. His "eye" informs the layperson about how to look at the scene, whereas the video camera, capturing the ongoing action, is much more distracting. When you put the two together, it's impressive.

Judge Susan Webber Wright has found President Clinton in civil contempt for lying in his deposition before her. Both the *Times* and the *Post* played it as a big story—right column lead; but in fact it's a story without particular political impact anymore. This is the judgment that neither the full House nor the U.S. Senate could muster the will to make. Granted, in the context of an impeachment process, the consequences would have been more draconian than the crime required. But at least now there has been a ruling, which history can place into its own context: The president lied under oath.

April 14 / Washington

A column of refugees inside Kosovo has been hit by warplanes. The Serbs say that seventy people died in the attack and immediately facilitated access to the scene for an Associated Press television crew. U.S. spokesmen are not yet in a position to confirm or deny what happened. Ken Bacon, the Pentagon spokesman, is somewhat lamely suggesting that there have been previous reports (not today) from refugee sources that Serbian planes may have deliberately strafed refugee columns. I call it a lame suggestion not because it may turn out to be untrue, nor even because it would be irrelevant today. It is irrelevant, period. We already know that there are several hundred thousand displaced Kosovar Albanians roaming around Kosovo, at the whim of Serbian forces. There is every reason to believe that these civilians have been, and will be, used as human shields. If NATO takes the position that its planes will not hit any target that has been deliberately placed next to or within a civilian environment, we may as well keep our Apache helicopters at home. American public opinion has got to be made to understand that even the smartest of "smart" bombs and the most careful pilots cannot avoid civilian casualties (and let's for the love of God stop calling them "collateral damage") when the enemy deliberately places civilians between his military forces and our aircraft. If we keep trying to fight a war in which we will neither tolerate casualties to any of our own forces nor engage the enemy when he shields himself behind civilians, we will lose.

April 15 / Washington

I just have time for a short notation this evening. I want to drop in on a farewell party for Hal Bruno, who for years was one of *Newsweek*'s top foreign and then political correspondents and then, later, was the head of ABC's political unit. Hal is a bright and delightful human being who is genuinely beloved not only by those with whom he works but also by those whom he covered. This is billed as his retirement party. What that really means is that he was perceived as being a little long in the tooth and he is being eased out. There's a lot of that going around these days. As many times as I have seen it happen to an old colleague,

I have yet to find a way of dealing with it in any fashion that isn't awkward. It's like acknowledging a fatal disease in a friend. Nothing you say is going to make the disease go away, and as sincerely as you may intend your empathy, you can see that it's essentially meaningless.

So, we will all engage in meaningless banter. A few heartfelt toasts will be offered, and Hal will have to deal with the painful reality that, in our career-oriented culture (especially when your career has been one you have loved, as Hal does), a retirement party bears uncomfortable similarities to a wake.

April 16 / Washington

Ken Bacon has just called to say that the military will open "all doors" to us if we want to go to the Balkans next week. The United States is clearly getting pummeled in the public relations war. First there was the commuter train that was hit by two missiles in Serbia, then the seventy-plus civilians killed by NATO fighter bombers in Kosovo a couple of days ago. Dan Rather has been in Belgrade this past week. While he hasn't scored either of the coups he clearly hoped for (an interview with the three U.S. prisoners or a session with Milošević), having Dan report from the heart of Yugoslavia is not the kind of publicity the administration wants right now. They can't be sure of what they'll get from us, but at the moment they're in a mood to gamble.

April 17 / Potomac

Last Thursday there was an announcement that astronomers have identified a solar system with planets that revolve around a star, just as ours do around the sun. Setting aside for a moment the fact that this news is based on observations of visual evidence that originated some forty-odd light-years away (and who knows what can happen to a solar system in forty or more years), this raises some interesting eschatological questions. Does this suggest that heaven and/or hell are even farther away than we previously thought? Or, to the contrary, does this argue that they have always been within us, and what happens out there in other solar systems is as irrelevant to the disposition of our souls as it was in days when we believed our earth to be flat? (Come to think of it, I've never heard a serious discussion, among those who believe in such places, as to the locus of either destination.)

Should this discovery of another solar system in any fashion change our outlook with regard to death and dying? What about living? I am glad that there are minds suffused with curiosity about such matters. I am even prepared to accept (on faith) that this discovery will someday affect humanity in a direct and tangible fashion. I confess, though, that I haven't a clue how.

April 18 / Potomac

One hundred years ago today, Alice, the baby who would grow up to become my mother, was born in Frankfurt. My mother's father, Moses Neu, was a coffee wholesaler. My mother had an older brother, Fritz, who would later emigrate to the United States, where he evolved from Fritz Neu into Fred New. On April 18, 1899, Man had yet to prove that he could fly, and the automobile was a recent and amusing if still impractical challenger to horse-drawn vehicles. There would have been no telephone in Alice's home, though it had been patented twenty-three years earlier by Alexander Graham Bell.

World War I was still fifteen years off. Bosnia-Herzegovina, no longer under Turkish control, would in 1908 be formally annexed by the Austrian Hapsburgs. When the Archduke Ferdinand was shot in 1914, his assassin was a Bosnian Serb. In immediate retaliation the Hapsburgs rounded up hundreds of Serb peasants and executed them before declaring war on Serbia.

Some echoes of the past seem less distant than others.

April 19 / Potomac

Yesterday there was an event of such impact that the *New York Daily News*, a tabloid, has printed its front page today in the format of the *New York Times*, so that its headline (one huge word) runs across the front page north to south. A picture runs east to west, across the tabloid fold, covering the front and back pages of the paper. "FAREWELL!" shouts the headline, and next to the picture of Wayne Gretzky are the words: "Tears flow at the Garden as the Great One plays his final game."

Wayne Gretzky is to ice hockey what Michael Jordan has been to basketball, what Babe Ruth was to baseball. Still . . .

Time, which used to be a newsmagazine, has a color photograph on the cover of three actors who portray leading characters in the Star Wars prequel, *The Phantom Menace.* It is expected to be the megahit of all time, by which we mean, loosely, the seventy or eighty years during which movies have been produced and marketed. It's certainly a big deal. Still . . .

There is a war going on, too.

April 20 / Washington

The novelty, the adrenaline rush that accompanies the first phase of every war, is beginning to wear off. Some of the difficult realities are asserting themselves. Flying attack missions at fifteen thousand feet, at four hundred knots, will protect U.S. air crews, but it will also cause civilian casualties—more than if the planes flew lower and slower. Apache helicopters, which, I believe, were intended to operate in concert with friendly ground forces, may not prove to be the ideal weapons platform for Kosovo. They do fly low and slow and have the capability of "killing" tanks and armored personnel carriers, but they are also vulnerable to shoulder-fired ground-to-air missiles. Let's hope the Serbs don't have too many of those.

The pressure to send ground troops into Kosovo is growing. But so is resistance to that notion from Greece and other countries. I don't believe the Clinton administration can form a consensus within NATO to send in a ground force of sufficient strength to defeat the Serbs. Meanwhile, the rain has created a literal quagmire in Albania, making the establishment of bases incredibly difficult. Hundreds of thousands of displaced persons (there's a term I haven't heard since just after World War II) are huddled throughout Kosovo; hundreds of thousands more are straining the hospitality of Macedonians, who don't much care for Albanians to begin with.

We are scheduled to leave for the region with a unit of the 82nd Airborne from Pope Air Force Base in North Carolina on Thursday.

April 21 / Washington

The "war" has been swept off the air. The paradox, as I said on the air last night, is that four weeks of military action against Serbian forces in Kosovo and Yugoslavia have resulted in not a single U.S. or allied casualty. But two high school students in a suburb of Denver, Colorado—Littleton—walked onto the campus of their school carrying two sawed-off shotguns, a semiautomatic rifle, a pistol and about thirty homemade bombs and in the space of only a few hours they had killed fifteen (including themselves) and injured about twenty others.

The community is understandably shocked, and, in truth, it is difficult to see how anyone could have foreseen such a totally random act of violence, but . . .

Both kids had records and belonged to a group that called itself the "Trenchcoat Mafia." Members of the group liked to draw swastikas on their clothing. Clearly, they were alienated from the rest of the class. The two killers had brought a videotape to school in which they showed off their gun collection.

I'm not suggesting that anyone could have or should have known what the boys would do, but surely someone among all those teachers and counselors should have spotted a sign or two of impending trouble.

We are terribly offended when people in other countries (foremost among them, perhaps, the French, British and Japanese) observe such incidents of violence and question American values. Perhaps we should not be. Such things do not happen as frequently among teenagers in most other countries, and it cannot be altogether coincidental that such incidents are rarer in countries where firearms are less easily available and where violence on the mass media is less ubiquitous.

April 22 / Jonesboro, Arkansas

We have just finished a two-hour town meeting in this community of fifty thousand. About 250 to 300 people assembled to talk about a shooting that took place thirteen months ago. At that time, two boys, thirteen and eleven, triggered a fire alarm at the local high school and then opened fire on the exiting students and teachers. Our assumption was that the people of Jonesboro might have some helpful things to say to the people of Littleton, Colorado. We brought a couple of dozen students, teachers and counselors together in Denver and, via satellite, the two groups could talk to each other. That worked well. I feel less good about another aspect of the program.

In the audience last night (I am writing this in the early morning hours of April 23) were relatives and friends of the shooting victims in Jonesboro. There was also the mother of one of the shooters. I talked with her yesterday afternoon and found her to be an impressive woman. The family has no money to speak of, but she has personally written to each of the three thousand or so people who wrote to her after the shooting. That's about $1,000 in stamps alone, not to mention the enormous expenditure of time and energy.

Anyway, despite some misgivings, she came last night. It did not go well. She believed that people would recognize how much courage it took for her to attend. Most did, but not the relatives of the dead. In retrospect, their reactions were understandable, predictable. I shouldn't have encouraged her to come.

April 23 / En route to Paris

I didn't have much time to unpack from the Jonesboro trip and repack for the Balkans, but I had lunch with Grace Anne and made a few phone calls. I spoke to each of the kids. Tara was a little apprehensive about this trip. She, like her mother, her sisters and her brother, is a veteran of my peripatetic lifestyle, and she couldn't explain why she felt uneasy about this assignment. When the children still lived at home, Grace Anne and I tended to make our tearful farewells in private, so as not to worry the kids; it was a huge and difficult extra burden for her. But for the past thirty-six years, whenever I have needed to leave (usually on short notice), Grace Anne has been there for me and the children. There is no way I can ever fully repay that debt.

I also made a call to the mother of that shooter in Jonesboro. I told her how sorry I was that things didn't go as well as we had both hoped. She told me how, at one point, when the husband of a teacher who had been killed got up to say he and his small son had visited the grave of his late wife the previous day, a woman in the row behind her whispered loudly: "And did you take your new wife with you, too?" He remarried less than a year after his wife was killed, and many in the community have had a hard time accepting that.

Anyway, Tom Bettag and I are bound for the Balkans. I recall the flavor of the Balkans evoked in the wonderful pre–World War II books of Eric Ambler and Graham Greene. So part of me anticipates the Balkans of the 1930s, even though I know that what awaits us is a very different setting indeed.

One of my last calls at home came from the Yugoslav ambassador to the United Nations. He has been acting as our intermediary with the foreign ministry in Belgrade. The foreign minister has OK'd visas for us. With all the other stops we have planned, I'm not sure how we will fit it all in, but these are good problems to have.

April 24 / Aviano, Italy

Our military is able to turn any corner of the world into a little piece of America. The runways and revetments are one thing; but on a sunny porch outside the room where flight gear hangs awaiting the pilots and other crewmen, steaks are being grilled on a large, brick barbeque. Armed Forces Radio variously pipes in the Rush Limbaugh program or *All Things Considered*. National Public Radio is surprisingly popular.

The married pilots commute to war. They live with their families in villages ten or twelve miles from the base. At night they play with their children. In the morning they fly across the Adriatic to drop bombs on ambiguous targets. The Serbs have camouflaged their heavy equipment, and one pilot we interviewed concedes that flying in at fifteen thousand feet (which our pilots do to avoid missiles and anti-aircraft fire) makes it even more difficult to know what is being bombed. If there were U.S. troops on the ground, he tells me, the planes would fly much lower. NATO has concluded that Kosovar Albanians do not merit such a risk.

April 25 / En route to Sarajevo, Bosnia

Brig. Gen. Dan Leaf, Aviano's base commander, is about five feet eight inches tall and has a broken nose, probably earned in a lifelong struggle to prove that short doesn't mean easy. I take him aside before our interview to let him know that one of his pilots is out on a bit of a limb. He has conceded to me that he and the other pilots would fly at lower (and, therefore, more dangerous) altitudes if they were flying close ground support for U.S. troops. Refugees, clearly, do not warrant that kind of risk. General Leaf concedes the point in private and then disputes it in the interview. This general is not forfeiting his second star to support some young major.

Clearly, though, when Leaf contends that the air war is fully accomplishing its purpose, protecting the lives of Kosovar Albanians does not enter into the calculus. He's talking about degrading the Serb military, diminishing its capacity for shooting down planes or engaging in command and control communication. When I point out that neither has anything to do with preventing Kosovar Albanians from being driven out of their homes, he agrees that the Serb army and police are still doing fine on that front.

When we arrive in Bosnia, it seems that Serbs and Muslims and Croats and even a few Albanians are living, if not in absolute comity, then at least in a state of semipermanent cease-fire. The U.S.-led peacekeeping force, which was supposed to be out of here two years ago, has settled in for the duration. This, if it can be achieved in Kosovo, will define victory.

April 26 / Aboard an SFOR helicopter flying from Sarajevo to Tuzla, Bosnia

Colonel Hockman, the chief public affairs officer for SFOR (Stabilization Force in Bosnia), vetoes a junior officer's suggestion that we grab a cup of coffee before takeoff. The weather is poor and the colonel has just spoken to the pilot. "She says we only have a fifteen-minute weather window." She. Another shovel of dirt on the residue of my male chauvinism.

Last night was fascinating. We had asked Farouk, our Bosnian "fixer," to assemble ten or twelve Sarajevans of different ethnic backgrounds. He pulled together four Muslims, three Serbs, two Croats and an Albanian for good measure. All of them agreed that SFOR must stay for the foreseeable future. One young woman was particularly adamant: "While I am alive; while my children, my grandchildren are alive." Without SFOR, they all agree, the war would begin again.

Do they think there should be U.S. ground troops in Kosovo? And how! "You have to finish what you began," said one young journalist. They are also unanimous in believing that Milošević must be removed from Serbian leadership.

America would profit from studying up on the Balkans. We're going to be here for a while.

April 27 / Tirana

We spent a good deal of yesterday flying, driving and walking around some of Bosnia's more memorable datelines: Brcko, Tuzla and Sarajevo. We flew first into Camp McGovern on the outskirts of Brcko. It is the headquarters of a batallion of the "Always Ready" 1st Cavalry Division. (I knew them in Vietnam as the 1st *Air* Cavalry Division.) Their commander, Colonel Buck Conner, is a tall, rangy bundle of hyperkinetic energy who has substituted "Always Ready" for almost all other forms of greeting. His men, when they are not patrolling, stay on base. Command doesn't want U.S. troops screwing up the local economy or the local lovelies. First and foremost, though, it's a security risk. How much so was evident when we walked through the Monday-morning market in Brcko and I stopped to talk to a local Serbian pig farmer. I introduced myself as an American reporter and never got to ask a question. He launched into a furious denunciation of America, Clinton and the cowardice that causes the United States to bomb and kill civilians. I can understand the anger, but not the blinders. He dismisses any notion that Serb troops or police have injured anyone.

Bosniacs (Muslims), whom we met later at an indoor fruit and vegetable market, are equally passionate on the other side. One man, who says he spent fourteen months in a Serb concentration camp, responds to a question about pulling SFOR out of Bosnia with a bitter, "Then you may as well kill all of us before you leave."

We were able to avoid an interminable trip to Tirana (via Ramstein Air Force Base in Germany) through the courtesy of General Monty Meigs. ABC was able to charter his personal Learjet, which, since it's flown by army pilots, is able to cross the Adriatic, go down the length of Italy, go around the boot and then fly up again to Albania. It was a four-hour trip, counting a refueling stop in Italy, but it sure beats the hell out of the alternative.

We arrive in Tirana looking forward to a quiet dinner and getting to bed. Dinner (that is, the process of placing the order and getting it served and, finally, eating it) takes three hours. Shortly before midnight, we receive word from one of our correspondents, Forrest Sawyer, who has been with a unit of Apache helicopters and their crews for the better part of the week, that one of the choppers has crashed and burned. The crew is OK; but our military has been extolling the merits of these choppers so enthusiastically that tonight's crash marks a notable setback for the military, which was just about to put the Apaches into action. It is (in the grotesque logic of journalism) a great story for us, but it means staying up all night and reworking the program. I got up at 5:30 a.m. yesterday and finally got to bed again at 6:30 a.m. today.

April 28 / Aboard an Albanian helicopter charter to the Albania-Kosovo border

The helicopter, an AS350, ABITIBI, is French, which gives us a bit of greater confidence. As we fly north, over Albania, we see concrete bunkers everywhere, like families of gray turtles. Enver Hoxha, the late and not terribly lamented dictator of Albania, had them built by the hundreds of thousands. He must have been inspired by his Chinese soul mate, Mao Zedong, who put the Chinese people through a "dig tunnels deep" anti-Soviet frenzy.

We are flying through and across a nasty mountain range where, during World War II, the Serbs on their retreat home lost many thousands of men. I'm flying with Alex and Francesca Bruckner, a fearless and superb camera team. Francie is tiny, and has an enchanting smile she employs shamelessly to deceive and disarm suspicious policemen, border guards and soldiers of sundry dictatorships. She is, in fact, tough as nails and, pound for pound, probably stronger than her bearded giant of a husband, Alex, who shoots some of the most beautiful video under the most terrible conditions.

Also flying with us is Tony Birtley, a British video journalist who used to work for ABC News, doesn't like to anymore, but makes an exception for *Nightline*. Look in any journalist's dictionary under the word "intrepid" and you will find Tony's picture. He nearly lost a leg covering the fighting in Bosnia, but he can't stay away.

A lot of us in this business have mild cases of adrenaline dependency. Tony is a hard-core addict. He just spent two weeks with the Kosovo Liberation Army (KLA), though he was supposed to be with them for only a week. We all feared he was dead. He's taking the Bruckners and me up to one of the KLA camps on the border for a quick look-see.

The weather may be a problem. It's almost May, but there's snow all over the mountains, and there are still hailstorms at this time of year.

Ten a.m., same day: The helicopter flight was quick and uneventful. We put down in an open field next to an Italian camp for Kosovo refugees. There's supposed to be a car and a "fixer" waiting for us. There aren't. Tony and I leave the Bruckners with the gear and start to hike into Kukes, about two kilometers away. Halfway in, a couple of Albanians in a car stop and give us a ride into town. The place is crawling with journalists. We stop at a local hotel, where Tony tries to borrow a satellite phone to call London, so that someone in the ABC bureau there can call Tirana. I negotiate with a local English-speaker (in the sense that he speaks a helluva lot more English than either of us speaks Albanian, but in no other sense) for a four-wheel-drive vehicle. He wants a hundred dollars for the day. We'll see what Tony comes up with.

Another British journalist stops by to chat. He spent a lot of time in Kosovo before the bombing began. He describes the NATO campaign as "genocide by inadequate assistance."

April 29 / Tirana

There is a corner of every "war zone" where life takes on a surreal quality. The Rogner Hotel in Tirana, Austrian owned and managed, is such a place. I'm sitting on a garden terrace—lemon trees, cactus, palmetto palms, lilies and a burbling fountain between me and the swimming pool. Business is flourishing here. The service is polite, cheerful and excruciatingly slow. A three-course dinner can easily take three and a half hours. The hotel management never expected full occupancy and has not hired enough staff. I've just finished writing the script describing yesterday's trip up-country with Tony and am awaiting a call to drive out to the airport, where I will debrief Forrest on his total immersion with the Apache unit. He has spent the entire week chronicling the arrival and training exercises of the U.S. Army's pride and joy. They are expected to be in action sometime this weekend. Anticipation is high. I'm not sure I understand why.

But back to the Rogner. War tends to attract the same cast of characters: the old pros (and I suppose I'm in that category now, having covered my first war more than thirty years ago), who delight in running into one another and recalling earlier disasters; the ambitious young reporters, who hope to make their reputations here; the officers and spooks from various armies and intelligence agencies; the idealistic aid workers, needing an hour or two away from the misery; and the camp followers, who wear tight jeans, formfitting T-shirts and no makeup, because this is a serious place and they wish to exhibit sobriety, along with their asses and breasts.

There are sparrows all around me. They have never seen such an abundance of crumbs.

April 30 / Tirana

Above all else, the U.S. Army is a bureaucracy, as distinguished from the lean, mean, green fighting machine that it fancies itself to be.

Forrest Sawyer has been promised total access to the Apache helicopter operation that is due to go into operation against Serb forces any day now. He and our *Nightline* crew have lived and slept with the unit for a week, and it has been a tough, dirty grind. Most of the work is done at night, when the helicopters fly. All of what has been recorded thus far is merely foreplay. The payoff was to come when Forrest and his crew were put aboard the command and control aircraft as the Apaches go into action. Two days ago, there was confusion on that point. Had the Supreme Allied Commander for Europe, Gen. Wesley Clark, really approved that? I called the Pentagon on Wednesday and received assurances that this was the case. Clark's PAO (public affairs officer) E-mailed the following message to Lt. Gen. John Hendrix, who's in charge of the Apache unit in Albania: "The CINC [commander in chief] has clarified his guidance. . . . He has no problem with giving Sawyer maximum access and information. Recommend granting the Sawyer request." General Hendrix has interpreted this message as a no. He will change his mind, we are told, only if directly ordered to do so by General Clark. It's Friday afternoon here, but I have to wait a couple of hours for the Pentagon to open for business.

Forrest is understandably crushed.

One of the army PAOs here succinctly summed up Hendrix's mind-set as "hero or zero." That is, unless you're convinced that something is a total win-win proposition, don't do it.

I'm inclined to believe that our military leadership would have been well advised to apply that theory to this whole operation. What has been assembled here, in Italy and in the Adriatic, is a logistical miracle, but it is shaping up to be a military swamp that we will wish we never entered.

May

May 1 / Budapest, Hungary

The toughest thing about traveling in the Balkans is traveling in the Balkans. The roads, especially in Albania, are terrible. We left the hotel at 6:15 yesterday morning to join Forrest at the airport/base so that I could debrief him *on* the Apaches in *front* of the Apaches. By the time we got back to the hotel, it was after noon. We are still trying to reach Belgrade today. The Air Force agreed to let us hitch a ride on one of its C-17s. We left the hotel at 8:45 p.m. and boarded at 1 a.m. These cargo planes are enormous, like a flying storage building. Tom and I were invited to fly in the cockpit, which was a kick. The plane is amazingly quick and agile and very smooth.

We got into Ramstein Air Force Base at 4 a.m., transferred our gear to a bus and drove for ninety minutes to Frankfurt airport. At 8:15 a.m. we left Frankfurt for Budapest. When we arrived, we drove to the Yugoslav embassy, which was open only from noon to 1 p.m. To our amazement, our visas were waiting, but the Yugoslav political officer at the embassy was in a mood to talk. By the time we got out of there, it was too late to make the six-to-eight-hour drive to Belgrade before dark. We were all disinclined to become "collateral damage" to one of NATO's increasingly severe after-dark bombing raids.

Tom Bettag and I are a little concerned because Alex (who has been in Belgrade many times) is worried. He thinks I might be a tasty target if the Serbs want to get even for the bombing of the TV station.

We leave for Belgrade at 6 a.m.

May 2 / At the Hungarian–Yugoslav border

We've been here since 9 a.m. and it is now 10:30 a.m. The Yugoslav army guard says he has to get word from an official in Belgrade to allow us through. The miracle of the cell phone allows us to call the foreign ministry in Belgrade. We are told that permission has been passed to the border post. But here we sit.

A stork circles lazily overhead. A Franz Lehar operetta plays on the local Hungarian radio station. A pair of owls exchange melancholy hoots. It is a perfect spring morning, clear and warm. Ideal bombing weather.

There are two well-stocked duty-free shops at this border crossing. Johnny Walker Black Label is less than $20 a fifth. Cigarettes—Rothman, Dunhill, Marlboro—are less than $10 a carton. War is hell, but that's still a few miles down the road.

May 3 / Belgrade, Serbia

We are detained for nearly three hours at a checkpoint outside Novi Sad, Yugoslavia's second largest city. The oil refinery is billowing smoke and belching fireballs. We stopped at the side of the road to do an on-camera standupper. The police at the checkpoint said we had been spotted "filming" seventeen kilometers up the road. "No," we say, "that's a mistake."

"Did you shoot anything?"

"Yes," I tell them, pulling out our little Hi-8 video camera. "I made a couple of shots at a rest-stop gas station."

"Why?" the cop wants to know.

"It's my personal camera," I tell him, "and it was my first opportunity to tape something in Yugoslavia."

We will have to wait for his commander.

Suddenly, one of the older policemen says to Alex, "You should show the world what NATO bombers are doing."

"OK," says Alex, and leisurely shoots about fifteen minutes' worth of flames and smoke and surrounding countryside. It's actually much better material than we were able to tape earlier. Alex and Francesca are old hands. They slip the cassette out of the camera while the police aren't watching and insert a blank one—which the commander, an hour later, makes him erase. It's a very minor victory, but beyond getting into the country, it's the only one we've enjoyed.

We arrive in Belgrade at 5 p.m., after eleven hours on the road. We go immediately to the military press center to pick up passes, without which we cannot operate in Belgrade. We are told that because one of their computer cables is broken we will have to pick up our passes in the morning. We will have to cancel a roundtable with half a dozen Serbs at a local café. We're through for the day, or so we think.

At dinner in the Hyatt (a surrealistic monster of a hotel built for the Arab trade), the power goes out. Half of Serbia is dark. We learn this through our local "fixer," DaDa, a thirtyish single mother from an influential Serb family. She is in cell phone contact with sources throughout Serbia. There is no electricity, no water. "Worst of all," says DaDa, "no way for government officials to charge their cell phones overnight." We shoot a candlelit standupper and, shortly after midnight, go to bed. By midmorning today, some power had been restored, but not enough to generate our passes.

The foreign minister will come to my suite for a promised interview at noon tomorrow.

May 4 / On the road to Belgrade

We are passing through Novi Sad again. It is truly an environmental disaster. The oil fires are still burning and the smoke has been pouring into the sky for two and a half days now. One of our "fixers" from Belgrade, Srejah, has accompanied us to Novi Sad in case we are stopped at another police checkpoint. We aren't; so, just past the checkpoint, he gets out to bid us all farewell and . . . locks his keys in his car. When he tries to open the door, his alarm goes off. That, of course, attracts the attention of the cops at the police checkpoint. They, fortunately, are only amused. We want to get out of the country before dark, which is when the NATO bombing raids usually take place. We desert Srejah as he prepares to break a small side window of his car with a rock.

Tom remains in the van throughout all of this, dictating my script of tonight's broadcast to Richard Harris at *Nightline* in Washington.

For some reason, cell phones seem to work more efficiently through-out Yugoslavia than anywhere I've seen. Our local support staff in Bel-grade must be spending hundreds of dollars daily on phone bills alone. But so does everybody else, it seems. Even the Yugoslav government appears to be held together by a network of cell phones. Steve Erlanger of the *New York Times* told me of a government-sponsored trip to Kosovo (to view the aftermath of a NATO bombing attack on a refugee convoy) during which he saw three reporters relieving them-selves, side by side along the shoulder of the road, simultaneously fil-ing their stories on cell phones.

I leave Yugoslavia more convinced than ever that inserting ground forces here would be an unspeakable folly. Ultimately, there will be some sort of negotiated settlement. NATO is infinitely more powerful than Yugoslavia, but the Serbs know that they are more passionate about their sovereignty over Kosovo than the United States and its allies are about the Kosovar Albanians.

May 5 / En route from London to Washington

A point of clarification on the ubiquity and efficiency of cell phones throughout the Balkans: The old East European phone system, it turns out, was such a disaster that, when the Berlin Wall came down and the Communist bloc crumbled, it was essentially bypassed with the newest and best relay system in the world. I am still sufficiently a child of the rotary dial era and have spent enough hours waiting impatiently at remote post, telegraph and telephone offices praying that a call home or to the office would finally go through, that these cell phone calls to and from London or Washington while rolling through the war-torn countryside of Yugoslavia still astound me.

A few summary thoughts on the war, while the experience of rac-ing through the region remains fresh: A democratic alliance, such as NATO, was designed to function in the face of a mortal threat to some or all of its member nations. Even in the days of the Soviet Union and its Warsaw Pact, the thought that the United States would be willing to engage in or endure a nuclear exchange for the sake of, say, France, had stretched the credibility of some. Charles de Gaulle was suffi-ciently skeptical that he ordered the creation of France's own *force de frappe*. Maybe de Gaulle was right, maybe not, but the survival of

Europe certainly fit into the category of being in the U.S. national interest. The fate of the Kosovar Albanians does not.

The human tragedy of what the Serbs have done and are doing is undeniable, but it is still significantly less terrible than the human tragedy in Sudan, where one and a half million people, most of them civilians, have died without provoking any real outrage (and certainly no military campaign) by the international community.

Must the atrocities be committed in Europe? NATO need scarcely look beyond its own charter membership—the Kurds will be only too happy to file their own bill of particulars against the Turks.

Without the actual survival of its member states at stake, NATO's cohesion will not last much longer. Milošević can do a diplomatic pirouette or two and outwait his enemies. Neither our survival nor Europe's is at stake in Kosovo. The bombing has worsened the condition of Kosovo Albanians, and NATO, for all its talk about preserving its own credibility, does not rank the survival of the Kosovars at the same level as the survival of its own troops. If we are not willing to die for a cause, then our national interest has not been sufficiently threatened in the first place.

NATO is an outdated organization looking for a new mission. Kosovo is not it.

May 6 / Washington

All the headlines today have to do with an agreement that has allegedly been hammered out between the senior NATO members and Russia (the so-called Group of Eight). Basically, it would put a peacekeeping force under a U.N. banner of some sort. It's unclear if this means that the Security Council would control the nature or mission of the force. Has it been determined that NATO forces (under what would be the U.S. interpretation) that make up the core of the peacekeeping group will actually control it? That is also unclear. Has it been decided what kinds of arms would be available to the peacekeepers? Clearly not. And somehow implied in all that has been left unsettled is the notion that the Kosovo Liberation Army will be disarmed. I wonder how the powers that be plan to go about doing that?

Still, for all the ambiguities—perhaps even because of all the ambiguities—it's beginning to look as though NATO and Milošević are warming up for a diplomatic dance that will permit each side to claim some sort of victory.

Will this maintain NATO's credibility or define its mission for the next century? I don't think so.

May 7 / Washington

America wants no part of this thing, but we are going through the motions. Those three soldiers who got themselves captured in Macedonia were awarded Purple Hearts today. Technically, it's because the Serbs beat them up; in reality, it's because the White House needs American heroes, not patsies. The first planeloads of refugees are arriving in New York and New Jersey. There are to be twenty thousand in all. They, I suppose, are the lucky ones.

The Chinese embassy in Belgrade was hit by a stray missile today. Not so lucky.

May 8 / En route to Captiva

Drew was able to get a few days off from Legal Aid, so he's been down in Captiva with his friend Annie. I'll join them for a few days and then, next week, Grace Anne flies down so that we can spend our thirty-sixth wedding anniversary together.

The papers are full of last night's bombing of the Chinese embassy in Belgrade, but the nation seems disengaged and disinterested. The aftermath of the shootings at Colombine High School in Littleton, Colorado, loom much larger in the American psyche.

We are, as is our tendency, overreacting a little. Schools across America are now suspending students for wearing dark trench coats or camouflage pants (worn by the "Trenchcoat Mafia" in Littleton), and ACLU offices are being inundated by parents complaining that their children's rights are being violated.

NATO released estimates today that forty-six hundred Kosovar Albanians have been murdered and a hundred thousand of their men have disappeared. Now *those* are violations of rights, but very far away.

May 9 / Captiva

In 1987, our daughter Deirdre was graduating from Duke, and I was invited to deliver the commencement address. I spoke, at the time, of the Vannatizing of America, referring to the extraordinary (and, since she is still at it, I should add, durable) popularity of Vanna White. She points at letters in the context of a television game show called *Wheel of Fortune*. Contestants spin a roulettelike wheel that determines how much money they can win (or, sometimes, lose) on a particular turn. Then, they pick consonants or "buy" vowels, which either are or are not reflected on a board containing a concealed name or phrase or sentence, attended by Vanna. If they pick a letter that is on the board, Vanna points at it and applauds. If it is not, Vanna shakes her pretty head and, with a rueful smile, bids the next contestant on. What Vanna rarely, if ever, does is speak. What she never does is express an opinion. This, I believe, is at the root of her popularity. We are able to project on her whatever we please, and, therefore, find her sympathetic.

George W. Bush seems to have studied at Vanna's knee, which may account for his overwhelming lead in the GOP sweepstakes these days. I wonder if he can keep it up until he's elected president.

May 10 / Captiva

We are right not to call this exercise in the Balkans a war. It is proving to be a particularly dangerous form of self-indulgence by, perhaps, the most self-indulgent generation of leaders we have known.

NATO was created as an essential military and political alliance to counterbalance that of the Soviet Union and its Warsaw Pact. Neither one exists anymore. Now we fashion a need to justify the continued existence of NATO.

We are still not tailoring our tactics to secure the safety of the Kosovar-Albanians. We continue to avoid sending in ground troops. Our pilots continue to operate under orders that have them flying at an altitude that is safer for them but dangerous for their unintended victims on the ground.

We have also adversely affected our relations with Russia and China to a degree that we have yet to grasp fully.

If we can only hold on, we may, through Russian mediation, be able to strike a deal with "the butcher of Belgrade." Whether that will ultimately be seen as having enhanced, restored or degraded NATO's credibility, I cannot say.

I am hard-pressed to believe that in Kosovo we have found a template for future NATO operations.

May 11 / Captiva

Stewart Klein has died. He was only sixty-six. Stew and Charlie Osgood and Jim Harriott and Betty Adams and Howard Hodgkins and I were hired in June 1963 to create (under the guidance of producers Frank McGuire and Ivan Ladizinsky) a radio program called *Flair Reports*. Stew was a veteran radio news writer who, at the time, was already working for ABC Radio News. Betty was the only professional reporter in the bunch. Charlie had managed a classical music station in Washington, and described himself as the world's oldest cub reporter. Howard had been a public relations type for NASA, but had just come from a recent engagement as a night clerk in a motel. Jim was a disc jockey, one of the WMCA "good guys." It was through Jim that I, then a twenty-three-year-old copyboy at WMCA, learned about the opening at ABC Radio.

Stew had a raspy voice, a New York dialect and no one with more experience than Frank and Ivan would have put him (or any of the rest of us) on network radio. Experience can be overrated.

Flair Reports didn't last all that long, but I loved it and it provided my big break. We worked long hours, sometimes ten to twelve hours a day, polishing and crafting our little three-and-a-half-minute gems.

Stew's classic was his annual (for the three years that the program lasted) tribute to Senator Everett Dirkson, Republican of Illinois, and his perennial campaign to make the marigold the national flower of the United States.

Stew would go on to become a beloved film critic in New York City.

May 12 / Captiva

I brushed off the bombing of the Chinese embassy in Belgrade the other day. I was wrong to do so.

The embassy was, it turns out, hit by three missiles that were accurate to a fault. Those targeting the strikes were using outdated maps. Even that does not explain what happened, because the old maps show an empty lot where the embassy now stands. Why would NATO target an empty lot? The American embassy in Beijing has been under more or less constant siege, pelted by angry students and other demonstrators with rocks, bottles and broken bits of paving stone. The Chinese government is making the most of our stupidity. They will use the incident to (a) distract attention from the tenth anniversary of the Tienanmen massacre, (b) distract attention from revelations of Chinese influence buying in U.S. election campaigns, (c) distract attention from espionage cases in which Chinese scientists are believed to have stolen secrets from U.S. research laboratories, (d) take back concessions made to gain entry to the World Trade Organization and (e) play havoc with diplomatic moves to end the Yugoslav war.

In 1972, just prior to the Nixon visit to China, Bob Siegenthaler, who was the network "pool" producer for the event, reluctantly agreed to Chinese demands that a Chinese chauffeur drive ABC's million-dollar remote truck. During the driver's first time out, he hit another vehicle. Bob, informed of this at the front desk of his hotel, smashed his fist on the counter in anger, cracking a piece of glass. From that moment on, whenever he raised the issue of the truck, the Chinese raised the broken piece of glass. They are experienced in getting the most bang for the buck.

May 13 / Captiva

My wife and I are involved in a lawsuit that is the outgrowth of some restrictive covenants on a piece of property, some of which is owned by a limited partnership controlled by Grace Anne and the rest of which is owned by another investment group. Our partnership bought the land on the condition that homes built on any of the lots would not exceed a certain square footage. Potomac, Maryland, is already bursting at the seams with "cluster mansions" (as a friend of ours calls them), and Grace Anne wanted to ensure that this property not become another example.

The builder, whose profit is a function of a home's size, has, we contend, repeatedly exceeded the upper limit, while refusing to provide to our partnership the plans that would prove his violation of the covenants.

Among the more frustrating aspects of this case has been dealing with our own lawyer.

May 14 / Captiva

Our son, Drew, has expressed an interest in going tarpon fishing. This afternoon at 4 we go off on a half-day charter, with mixed feelings on my part. I can imagine, and will probably thrill to, the experience of being connected (however tenuously) to 160 pounds of leaping, dancing, ferociously terrified fish muscle. The adrenaline rush will also serve to convince me that this is a competition I must not lose. (The spirit of Papa Hemingway still stirs in all boy/men of a certain vintage.)

Still, I have no interest in killing or even hurting a creature that in no way threatens me or mine. I do it, I think, because I hope it will produce a unique, shared memory with my son, a memory we can tap in years to come unfreighted by paternal concerns or authority; just a memory of a few hours when a couple of friends, incidentally father and son, went tarpon fishing.

May 15 / Captiva

Well, not exactly. Even three- to four-foot seas are enough to make me wax nostalgic for seventy miles per hour on a good interstate. It was a four-and-a-half-hour charter, one hour of which was spent getting to and from the mystical seventeen-foot-deep seas in which tarpon love to frolic. One hour was spent drifting and casting a weighted net around the pilings under the causeway for herring—our bait. And two and a half hours were spent lurching from one baited fishing pole to another (the guide did it all—caught the bait, baited the hooks) whenever a bent rod even hinted at a tarpon. But all we saw, all we caught (and released) were black-tipped shark—little ones, two to three feet long. Drew and I have yet to know the thrill of a 160-pound tarpon snatching one of our hooked herring and streaming out toward Galveston. Maybe next time.

May 16 / Captiva

Colin Powell is also adept at Vannatizing America. His widespread popularity is, at least in some measure, a function of only rarely expressing himself on controversial issues. He allows people to project onto him what they would like to believe. My NBC colleague Tim Russert put him on his program, accepting the deal Powell has offered others: Invite him on to talk about "America's Promise" (the social service project to which he has devoted much of these past couple of years), and he'll answer a couple of questions about Kosovo and politics or whatever. Tim kept up his part of the deal: He served up two softballs to Powell about "America's Promise" that elicited lengthy loopers to center field. And then Powell returned the favor, delivering a short right to the nose of the administration on Kosovo: "You're allowing Milošević to determine the timing and nature of his surrender." When asked, "Will you run for president or accept the vice presidency in 2000?" Powell responded with a crisp no. He does, apparently, want to be secretary of state.

Grace Anne and I are closing down the house here until next season. Among the treasures we tuck away in closets are a Hiroshige print that we bought in Japan more than thirty years ago; a complete lion's paw shell that Grace Anne found on the beach one New Year's Day about six or seven years ago; and a phony antique, bronze Buddha that I bought in Thailand thirty-two years ago. I was especially impressed, at the time of purchase, by the statue's heft. I discovered, many years later, that it had been filled with sand. Over time, I've come to love it all the more.

May 17 / Captiva

It is our thirty-sixth wedding anniversary—not the day on which we first married; not even the day on which we married for the second time; but the day on which, thirty years ago, we rededicated our vows at St. Joseph's Church on Garden Road in Hong Kong, with Father Einaudi, OFM (Order of Franciscan Monks), officiating. Because Hong Kong was, in those days, still considered a "missionary diocese," it was not necessary for me to pledge that the children would be brought up as Catholics. I had always found the Church's insistence on my signed pledge to be offensive, despite the fact that I had already agreed with Grace Anne that the children should be raised in their mother's faith.

Anyway, here we were getting married for the third time but for the first time within the Church, meaning that Grace Anne would, once again, be allowed to receive communion. Our daughters Andrea (then five) and Deirdre (then three) were the flower girls. My old friend and cameraman Y. B. Tang stood up for me as best man, and my secretary, Cathy Hope, was Grace Anne's maid of honor.

We celebrated with lunch at the old (since razed and rebuilt as a restaurant-only façade) Repulse Bay Hotel. It was such a lovely occasion, in marked contrast to the bare-bones formality of our civil and Unitarian weddings, that we decided to mark this date, May 17, as our anniversary from that day forward. Hence, our thirty-sixth anniversary is actually the thirtieth anniversary of our wedding in 1969. (Is that all clear?)

May 18 / Washington

It's amazing how the entire Kosovo mess seems to have disappeared from the national radar screen. Once again, President Clinton's political intuition seems right on the money (even though I still believe that this one will rear up and bite him hard, or perhaps he'll be out of office by then). The president appears convinced that as long as Americans are not dying in and around the Kosovo conflict, nothing else matters. British prime minister Tony Blair is pushing hard for ground troops, and some of our own generals are getting ready to blow some sort of public gasket, but America at large is unconcerned and uninterested.

May 19 / Washington

I wonder what it is about our culture that makes us appear to want what everybody else wants. The new Star Wars movie opened at one minute past midnight earlier today, and the lines were long in front of the theaters. There are some movie complexes that have seven theaters, and are, therefore, able to put on forty-nine or fifty showings a day. I don't doubt for a moment the passion of the true Star Wars aficionado, whose every waking moment, these last six months or so, has been filled with a sense of anticipation; but I get the impression that millions of Americans are planning to see this movie only because they believe that everybody else will.

The Pepsico company has reportedly put up $3 billion for the commercial tie-in between this movie, two others (which are scheduled for release over the next five years) and a variety of Pepsico products. It is said of this film that it will make a vast sum of money for George Lucas even if no one goes to see it.

I may be the only one who doesn't.

May 20 / Washington

In a small community outside Atlanta a fifteen-year-old high school sophomore, upset because his girlfriend broke off a two-year-long relationship, brought a gun to school and shot six of his classmates. They will all survive. Meanwhile, we, as a nation, are roused to a fresh frenzy of "How did we all go wrong?" one month to the day since the shootings at Columbine High School. The president was already scheduled to visit with the families of the victims. The vice president rushes back from a campaign tour to cast the deciding vote in a Senate bill that contains new gun control legislation.

You have to make the most of these occasions.

May 21 / Washington

Tonight the last episode of the police drama *Homicide* will be aired. It has always been good, occasionally even great. It's being canceled because of high costs and relatively low ratings. Television is drowning in crap and a wonderful series like *Homicide* can't survive. Unfortunately, quality takes time and costs money. Therefore it takes an even larger audience and higher advertising rates than usual to make a series like *Homicide* profitable. The program was popular, just not popular enough. As the late Baltimore journalist (and cynic) H. L. Mencken noted years ago: "Nobody ever went broke underestimating the good taste of the American public."

May 22 / Potomac

The *New York Times* reports this morning that "White House officials say the President is waging a pragmatic and moral style of warfare that pushes military action as far as it can go in view of the hard limits of American public opinion, congressional dissent and alliance discord. It is the anti-Powell doctrine."

(Of course, the interesting question is what the president will do when his pragmatic and moral styles come into conflict with each other.) General Powell and others before him subscribed to a doctrine of committing troops only when the goals are clearly defined, but then applying overwhelming force to achieve victory.

In the current crisis the White House contends that the Powell doctrine offers the false choice of committing ground troops or doing nothing.

It is the Clinton administration that is offering a false choice. Morality is the cosmetic that governments apply to make necessity more appealing. The moral imperative in Kosovo is saving the lives of innocent civilians. But we do not consider that a *causus belli* anywhere else in the world. In other places where human rights are being violated or where innocent civilians are being killed, we may impose economic and political sanctions, but we do not go to war.

When we go to war, it should only be because a critical national interest is being threatened. If that were so in Kosovo, then one would have to say that we are not doing enough. If it is not so, we are risking too much.

May 23 / Potomac

I saw an apparition from the past today. Grace Anne and I went to a late-afternoon showing of *The Winslow Boy*, a near-perfect film for those, like the two of us, who are thirsting for a simpler age. The film is set in the period immediately preceding World War I and deals with a thirteen-year-old boy who has just been expelled from military (naval) school, accused of stealing another boy's five-shilling money order and then forging the signature. The film actually dwells almost entirely on the impact that fighting to prove the boy's innocence has on the rest of his family. It was an older crowd in the theater, but even so, one man stood out. Well into his eighties, immaculately groomed, the only man in the house wearing a suit (a seersucker at that) and tie, he seemed perfectly at ease. It was Richard Helms, former director of Central Intelligence, who continues to be a little out of step with the times. He is no more inclined to adjust his dress code now than he was willing to trim his sails to accommodate shifting political winds when he was DCI in the mid-seventies.

May 24 / Potomac

There was a somewhat ominous piece on *60 Minutes* last night. The District of Columbia is not prepared for the Y2K bug. The Montgomery County preparations (our home county here in Maryland) are, by contrast, said to be the best in the country. But our county supervisor, Doug Duncan, believes that even Montgomery County residents will have problems.

I feel the first survivalist symptoms stirring in me. I begin making mental lists: water, firewood, extra jerry cans of gasoline. (How the hell long will that last at the sixteen miles per gallon our sports utility vehicle manages?) Maybe I should buy a motorcycle. A gun? Tuna fish and SPAM? How about buying a few cases of MREs (Meals Ready to Eat)? Does the Pentagon have some basement discount store? Chocolate. Coffee. Whiskey and Marlboros. You can always trade for other essentials if you have Marlboros. Screw cancer and emphysema! This is a national emergency.

I don't really believe that the country (actually this is a global thing) is coming to a grinding, apocalyptic halt. But Steve Kroft looked pretty worried last night.

May 25 / Washington

Washington is in a lather over the Chinese theft of military secrets from U.S. nuclear labs, and elsewhere. Actually, that's not quite fair. A congressional committee has issued a bipartisan report that points out that the Chinese government has three thousand business fronts in this country, and that many, if not most, of them are being used for intelligence gathering as well as business. As the current teenage generation might put it: Duh! Has anyone actually been operating under the illusion that a business owned in whole or part by the Chinese government would do anything other than pass on whatever intelligence it can accumulate?

The so-called Cox Report seems, on the face of it, quite fair and evenhanded. It acknowledges that all the administrations beginning with Jimmy Carter's have presided over a leaking ship of state. There does, however, seem to be a mounting partisan storm that will require the casting overboard of a political Jonah. Topping the list, at the moment, Attorney General Janet Reno and National Security Advisor Sandy Berger. Will either or both of them be dumped? Only if the president gets wet.

May 26 / Washington

How are irreconcilable differences handled in this final year of the millennium? On television and in newspaper columns. Rick Kaplan, the president of CNN, got angry the other day at Lou Dobbs, the president of CNNfn (financial network), when Dobbs cut away from a presidential speech to continue with his own program. Rick angrily called the control room and told them to go back to the president. They did, but Dobbs announced on the air that he was doing it because Kaplan had ordered it. Within a couple of days it was all over the papers, in a form that makes it clear that Dobbs or someone friendly to him leaked it. The thrust of the articles made it clear that Dobbs had triumphed in his interoffice fight with Kaplan.

Cindy Adams got dumped from *Good Morning America* by ABC News president David Westin. Under her contract with ABC she wasn't permitted to write anything about *GMA* for a year. After a year and one day she wrote a snippy piece trashing Westin's friend Diane Sawyer. The thrust of the piece was that Diane does not bring in the sort of advertising dollars generated by other ABC News anchors, like Barbara Walters. Take that, David.

Chuck La Bella, a former federal prosecutor who was called in by the Justice Department to investigate campaign finance, determined that there might be wrongdoing by someone inside the White House, and therefore he recommended to the attorney general that an independent counsel be appointed. None was, La Bella was canned and a subordinate of his was appointed U.S. attorney in San Diego, a job for which La Bella was directly in line. La Bella told his version of the story on *Nightline* this evening.

Taking your story to the media is the late-nineties way of dealing with someone whom you can't hurt in any other way.

May 27 / Washington

I feel curiously conflicted about an op-ed piece that Jimmy Carter wrote for this morning's *New York Times*. It is harshly critical of Clinton's Kosovo strategy. I agree with much of what Carter wrote this morning. I think that President Clinton has shown ineffective leadership and is permitting his policy to be shaped by the polls. Having said that, however, I believe that former presidents of the United States ought to have their first amendment rights removed, at least insofar as foreign policy is concerned. It is totally inappropriate for Carter to second-guess the incumbent president. Yes, of course, he's entitled to say anything he pleases. He's entitled to the same freedom of speech that I enjoy. But somehow I feel that former presidents, speaking from the sanctity of their very distinguished but tiny club, should not engage in open criticism of a sitting president who's fighting a war, however limited. It's tacky.

May 29 / Potomac

Rosafina, now an elderly cat entering her eleventh summer, is making it difficult to work. She keeps trying to walk across the keyboard of my computer, clearly for no other reason than that I do not want her to do so. Were I looking for her, she would remain resolutely out of sight. We have lived in the same house together for more than ten years now, and I believe that I know most of her hiding places, but, particularly when we are about to leave on a trip and I need to put her in her carrying bag, she is always able to elude me. She will come to me, as cats are inclined to do, when I seem least interested in her company, and, in her quiet, dignified way, she is able to make me feel guilty by body language alone. Here I am, your friend, her arched back will say as she steps daintily onto the keyboard, and I need you to scratch just above my tail; but you're too busy.

Dogs are easier for men to understand. Less complicated. More like us.

May 30 / Potomac

It does not seem very long ago that our second oldest daughter, Deirdre, and her best friend, Amy, who lived across the street, started up their summer camp for the children of neighbors.

Deirdre and Amy must have been about twelve at the time, old enough to entertain a bunch of four- and five-year-olds for three or four hours (camp was a half-day affair), but not so old as to be intimidated by the challenge. The first session or two, as I recall, took place in our backyard, and then Grace Anne's legal training kicked in and the potential liabilities overwhelmed our sense of hospitality. The kids ended up over at Amy's house.

As I say, that doesn't seem all that long ago, except that we are about to head off to Amy's wedding. She specializes, I believe, in counterterrorism and the Russian Mafia at the State Department's Bureau of Intelligence and Research, and her husband-to-be works over at the CIA. That should be adequate security clearance in the event that they want to start up the summer camp again in our backyard.

May 31 / Potomac

Deirdre and Larry and our grandson, Jake, came down from New York for Amy's wedding. These days any well-prepared couple traveling with an eighteen-month-old baby has—together with the baby aspirin, several changes of clothes, bedtime books, pacifiers and baby bottles—a couple of videocassettes of Barney, the purple, man-sized, cloth dinosaur, whose singing mantra "I love you . . . you love me . . . we're a happy family . . ." begins and ends each of his television programs. Barney is, above all things, "nice." He is so unabashedly, unreservedly, unrequitedly "nice" that, were he not a purple dinosaur, his behavior (particularly since he seems to hang around with young kids all the time) would be suspicious. Even as things are, Barney's influence on these kids (usually about a half dozen or so eight- to twelve-year-olds) is passing strange. These are not normal children. In Barney's world older kids have no problem hanging out with younger kids; boys hang out with girls; black and brown children frolic with white and Asian children in what is clearly the most happily integrated neighborhood in America. These are the Stepford children—alien beings, inhabiting human form. These humanoids might pass as the real thing were it not for the fact that they are always loving and cheerful. They neither quibble nor quarrel. They respond with enthusiasm to the most brainless of Barney's gentle suggestions.

Like the vast majority of children his age, Jake is mesmerized by Barney and his friends. So was I. Reality becomes an unwelcome intrusion while you are adrift in Barney's world. I found myself watching for little snickers or sneers from the young actors perpetrating this fraud on American babyhood, some tiny little flicker of contempt for the sweating goofball inside the purple rug. Nothing. They are clearly hired on the basis of their ability to smile without a breather for hours at a time.

Deirdre and Larry clearly saw through my suggestion that they leave the tapes down here for Jake's next visit as a desperate gambit. As soon as I had the house to myself, Barney and I would have engaged in some serious bonding: "I love you . . . you love me. . . ."

June

June 1 / Cambridge, Massachusetts

Bernie and Marvin Kalb have, at one time or another, been competitors of mine for nearly thirty years. Bernie was Hong Kong bureau chief for CBS when I held the same post for ABC, and then, when I was transferred to Washington in 1971 to take over as ABC's diplomatic correspondent from the late John Scali, Marvin was my CBS counterpart. No man has ever had better competitors.

Marvin went from CBS to NBC and then, in 1986, when it became clear that his clean, no-frills kind of journalism was falling out of favor and giving way to the snappier, less substantive brand of television news, he began looking for a dignified way out. He found it at Harvard, where he was asked to become, simultaneously, the first Edward R. Murrow professor and the director of the new Joan Shorenstein Center on Press, Politics and Public Policy.

Marvin stepped down today after twelve years in that position and Harvard gave him a lovely send-off, made even lovelier by the generosity of a major donor who has funded a chair in Marvin's name at the Kennedy School of Government. When all is said and done, though, one is left with the impression that, even at the greatest of universities, the struggle for ever more donations and endowments dominates the lives of deans and administrators every bit as much as campaign financing dominates the lives of our politicians.

June 2 / Washington

Commercial aircrews in this country are not supposed to work more than a fourteen-hour day. When American Airlines Flight 420 left Dallas/Fort Worth yesterday evening, it had already been subjected to a two-hour delay because of bad weather and an equipment change. Its pilot and copilot had already put in an eleven-hour day. By the time they got to their final destination, Little Rock, Arkansas, they had been working thirteen and a half hours. The weather in Little Rock was worse than the weather had been in Dallas. The plane crashed on landing, killing nine and injuring eighty-three others.

My question is this: When a crew is that close to exceeding the permitted outer limit of a workday, how much pressure is there to get the flight off the ground, no matter what the weather at the point of departure or at the destination, so that the airline won't have to (a) cancel a flight or (b) bring in a fresh crew? I'll never be able to prove it (and neither will the National Transportation Safety Board), but I'll bet economic pressure and the simple desire to bring an interminably long day to a close influenced the pilot's decision not to opt for another airport where conditions would have been safer, but where passenger annoyance, company accountants and endless paperwork would have awaited.

June 3 / Washington

Yesterday, the Russian intermediary, Viktor Chernomyrdin, and the president of Finland, Maarti Ahtisaari, flew to Belgrade to deliver to Slobodan Milošević the terms for an end to NATO bombing.

He accepted and, within hours, so did the Yugoslav parliament, by a vote of 136–74. The document they agreed to is significant on two counts: (1) The Russians agreed to it and (2) it is imprecise. It calls for "verifiable withdrawal from Kosovo of all military, police and paramilitary forces according to a quick timetable."

That may prove to be the easiest part to implement. Top military officers from NATO are expected to travel to Belgrade to hammer out the specifics. (Milošević and several of his top advisors can't, after all, go anywhere else, since they've been indicted as war criminals.)

What is not at all clear is the makeup of the "interim administration" for Kosovo that is to be established. Who will run it? To what body will it report? Will the "international security presence, with an essential NATO participation" called for in the "documents for peace" (as they're being referred to) report to the interim administration, or to the U.N., or to some other body? Who will disarm the Kosovo Liberation Army? Both Secretary of State Albright and Secretary of Defense Cohen today insisted that the Albanians will be held to the terms of the Rambouillet agreement. Good luck.

We are, as I suggested a few weeks ago, beginning the process of defining victory. My concern is that after public attention (never white-hot to begin with) fades again, Milošević will be able to implement his own definition, as he has done so many times in the past in Bosnia.

June 4 / Washington

Lord, how the decades do fly.

Ten years ago today . . . no, if you didn't live through it, you'll never understand how it was unless I back up a little. Mikhail Gorbachev was still president of the Soviet Union, and through his policy of *perestroika* (openness) he had created a new climate, not only in the U.S.S.R., but throughout eastern Europe. The Chinese government was watching closely and nervously; Chinese university students were watching with their hearts in their throats. Gorbachev was about to pay a state visit to China. There were a lot of foreign reporters in Beijing. The death of a relatively moderate Chinese leader inspired students to march in honor of his memory. They marched to Tienanmen Square, read a proclamation on the steps of one of the government buildings and demanded to speak to a leading figure. The government did nothing. The demonstrations continued the next day, and the next, and soon it was like a virus. Thousands of students were joined by union members, workers, Chinese journalists. With Gorbachev about to arrive, the Chinese government was clearly trying to avoid a scene, but they waited too long. Soon Tienanmen Square was jammed with hundreds of thousands of demonstrators. They erected tents and elected leaders. They were in communication by fax with Chinese all over the world. They received support from Hong Kong Chinese, who sent tents and supplies. Gorbachev couldn't even be brought to Tienanmen. It was a public humiliation. Some of the student leaders were brought to meet with Li Peng, the premier. The meeting was carried on live TV. The kids lectured Li. They were actually quite rude.

On June 4, ten years ago today, the government sent in the troops. The army had been assembled all around the area for days. The kids had put flowers in their rifle barrels. They had sung songs to the troops. There was absolute confidence that the People's Liberation Army never would, never could, fire on Chinese youngsters.

That confidence was misplaced. Hundreds of kids were shot, many of them killed. We still don't know the actual numbers. But no one who lived through the euphoria of those wonderful spring days in May 1989 will ever forget it. Nor will we ever forget the violence and repression that followed. For the most part, though, it has become just another anniversary.

Who, after all, remembers when the Berlin Wall was built? In its day, that was a big deal, too.

June 5 / St. Mary's County, Maryland

War should not be an easy thing. We don't know, at this moment, whether everything will go smoothly with the transition from Serb control of Kosovo to the hands of NATO troops, but it appears that this undeclared war, now in its seventy-fourth day of bombing, may be on the brink of achieving several of its stated goals, without a single NATO combat loss. (Two Apache pilots were killed, but that was the result of a training accident.)

I don't regard this as cause for celebration. This entire exercise will leave much of the American public with the impression that war can be waged at little or no cost. Why, if that were true, would it be a bad thing?

We should not, to begin with, be engaged in a war the outcome of which means so little to us. Insofar as the American public believes that this war was fought for any purpose, it was for the entirely altruistic purpose of saving Kosovar Albanians from murder, rape, the loss of their homes and the loss of their country. Many lives and many homes could have been saved if our leaders had been prepared to sacrifice some NATO soldiers. That, however, was a price that none of the governments (save the British) was willing to pay. There's no substitute for good fortune, and this victory owes a lot to that. Washington gambled that it would be able to sustain the cohesion of NATO as long as no lives were lost on our side. Before this conflict is over, though, I am convinced that lives will yet be lost; and I wouldn't be surprised in a few months to find NATO troops safeguarding Serbian civilians against attack from the Kosovo Liberation Army. In all likelihood, though, the Serbs will flee Kosovo altogether. I can't imagine that many of them will want to risk the wrath of the returning refugees without the protection of Serb soldiers or police. Then we in the NATO alliance will have what we sought to avoid: an independent Kosovo, which will doubtless unite to form a Greater Albania with Albania and possibly seek to annex part of Macedonia. NATO troops will have their hands full trying to keep that from coming to pass.

June 6 / St. Mary's County

Two sets down in the finals of the French Open, Andre Agassi is fading fast. His opponent, Andre Medvedev, a Russian, is only twenty-four, but in the hothouse environment of professional tennis, he is considered past his prime and is staging something of a comeback. It is nothing, though, compared to Agassi's comeback. The man who was first in the world slipped, only two years ago, well out of the top one hundred. He has won Wimbledon, the U.S. Open, the Australian Open but never the French Open, and now he's down 6–2, 6–1 and faltering.

His is to be a truly magnificent comeback. He wins the next three sets and becomes one of only six men ever to win all four of the great championships. I revel in his victory. Score one for old age, or at least aging athletes. I feel new energy infusing my own backhand. How old is Agassi anyway? He must be pushing forty. He is, it turns out, all of twenty-nine.

June 7 / Potomac

The Serb military officers who were summoned to a location just on the Macedonian side of the border with Kosovo to receive their marching orders have a few questions, a couple of conditions, some reservations. No, they're not negotiating. They understand that there were to be no negotiations, but how the hell, for example, are they supposed to get out of Kosovo in seven days (two days, actually, for their artillery and armor) when they don't have any gasoline? And anyway, wasn't all of this supposed to be taking place under a U.N. Security Council resolution? Also, the Serbs would like to have the Russians sitting in on all of this. . . .

Two full days of this blather and NATO has resumed bombing, while Milošević reassures the anxious Finnish intermediary that he remains perfectly amenable to the deal he and the parliament signed last week. That, of course, may be the root of the problem, in that the deal they accepted last Thursday is full of destructive ambiguities.

The victors are so eager to be done with this war that they are in danger of being parsed out of their victory.

June 8 / Washington

Mary Ellen Greenfield (whom I never knew as anything but Meg) was given a joyful send-off today at the sort of memorial service that each of us, in his most private moments, hopes his life will engender. Everyone who spoke clearly loved and liked Meg. There were well over five hundred people in the synagogue, among them Defense Secretary William Cohen, Senators Kennedy, Moynihan and Nunn and a ton of media people. Meg was the editor of the op-ed page at the *Washington Post*. As such, she decided the *Post*'s editorial policy and whose opinions would receive space on her hallowed turf. She had clout. Meg also had a wonderful sense of humor and, in some respects, no judgment at all.

She once called me and asked if I would join her and Don Graham, the publisher of the *Post*, for lunch. She and I often had lunch and gossiped like a couple of teenagers, but I couldn't figure this lunch out. It evolved that she thought I might make a good successor to Ben Bradlee as managing editor of the *Post*. It never seems to have occurred to her that I know nothing whatsoever about newspapers. It clearly did occur to Graham, but he was gracious.

I must add, because it is such a rarity in this day and age, that he and his mother, Katherine, were wonderful friends to Meg. They would drive her up to Baltimore for radiation sessions during her three- or four-year struggle with cancer. They took care of her like a member of their own family, which, of course, she was; not blood, but family.

Colbert King, of the *Post*'s editorial board, summed it up beautifully at the service: "People tell me," he said, "that I will find closure with this memorial service. I don't want closure. I want Meg back."

So do I.

June 9 / Washington

I don't have a great deal of time today in that I have to cancel a lot of previously made appointments. Tom and I plan to leave for the Balkans again tomorrow.

Events there are unfolding at an agonizingly slow pace, and with each passing day it seems to me that NATO's determination not to negotiate a cease-fire agreement with the Serbs is eroding. Specific references to NATO being at the core of a peacekeeping force have now been eliminated. The Serbs (in keeping with NATO's agreement that Kosovo remain under Serb sovereignty) are insisting on having observers at their border posts. The Russians are refusing to have their soldiers under NATO command, but are now talking about having as many as ten thousand troops in Kosovo. For a process that is not supposed to be involving any negotiation, there is certainly a lot of spontaneous erosion in NATO's position.

In any event, whether peacekeepers are able to enter in the next couple of days or only early next week, Tom and I are convinced that we need to be there a little sooner, rather than later.

June 10 / Washington

We are in for a hectic week or two of Kosovo coverage, as NATO troops go in and we get a chance to see what the Serbs have left behind, and then I think Kosovo will disappear from the U.S. radar screen. There will be occasional blips, if U.S. troops get wounded or killed by mines or booby traps. The major newspapers will continue to cover the stories of traumatized refugees struggling to come to terms with what they find when they return. Television will cover it, too. But as far as the general public is concerned, this story is over. We won. Nobody on our side got killed by the enemy. Air wars do work. Damn, but reconstruction is going to be expensive. Hey, how about those Knicks!

Speaking of sports: Sandwiched between all the public appearances today by the president, the secretaries of state and defense and the national security advisor to the president was a reception at the White House for the New York Yankees. They are the reigning world champions of baseball, it is true, but they've been that for eight months. Their presence at the White House today gave the First Lady an opportunity to be seen wearing a Yankee cap and a gigantic grin. After all, the best that Rudy Giuliani can do is invite the Yanks to Gracie Mansion.

June 11 / En route to Macedonia

It may just be the dryness in the plane cabin, or a conversation I had yesterday with Sam Donaldson, discussing his bout with cancer, but I'm having a little trouble swallowing, and it's not the "gee I think I'm coming down with a cold" sort of feeling. As Samuel Johnson observed many years ago, it does focus the mind.

The Russians were a little playful today. All of a sudden this morning, 173 Russian peacekeepers assigned to SFOR in Bosnia took a bunch of armored personnel carriers and hightailed it across the border into the Republic of Yugoslavia. Moscow said that Russian soldiers wouldn't cross the border into Kosovo, but the Russians are also making it clear that, while they have no intention of serving under NATO in a peacekeeping force, they do intend to be part of the overall peacekeeping force. What's more, they intend to have a zone of their own—just like the Americans, the French, the Italians, the Germans and the British.

Before leaving Washington, I interviewed Vladimir Lukin, a former Russian ambassador to the United States, now the head of the Duma's foreign affairs committee, who made it clear that most of his colleagues in the Duma believe that the U.N. Security Council resolution passed the other day, the one that authorizes peacekeeping forces to move into Kosovo, does not put those forces under NATO command. When I pointed out that Gen. Mike Jackson believes that he is the commander of those forces on the ground, while Gen. Wesley Clark believes himself to be the overall commander, Ambassador Lukin reminded me that there was a Russian poet who believed himself to be in control of the universe. That, he added, did not make it so.

This will either be fixed quickly or will lead to huge problems.

June 12 / Pristina, Kosovo

I'm sitting at a small desk in the guest bedroom of a large and pleasant home in Pristina, the capital of Kosovo. The Kosovar Albanian family that owns this house is friendly with one of our interpreters, who has brought us here. We are scattered throughout the house, sleeping, for the most part, on bedrolls and sleeping bags that we've carried with us from the Macedonian capital of Skopje. Tom and I flew Washington-Frankfurt-Thessaloniki, Greece, driving three hours from there to Skopje. After an hour in Skopje we jammed into an armored Land Rover and headed off for Pristina. Almost the entire length of the sixty-mile drive from the Macedonian border to Pristina there was bumper-to-bumper NATO traffic, mostly tanks and armored personnel carriers. Alongside the road, there were small units of Gurkha soldiers, protecting the route against snipers.

We arrived here at the house at dusk, and while I was conducting a brief interview with one of the sons (who speaks excellent English) and the mother, there was the crackle of gunfire outside, probably not more than a block or so away. They have heard so much of it that they barely reacted. Just before I came into this room, however, to write this entry, our interpreter stopped me so that we could discuss what we do if armed intruders break into the house tonight. He is mostly concerned about his friends, since it is unlikely we will be harmed. I assured him that I was ready to hand over a wad of dollars immediately since that, after all, is what the thugs who roam these neighborhoods usually want.

The Russians, incidentally, are just about twenty minutes down the road at the airport. NATO is trying to make it seem as though their unexpected presence in Kosovo does not constitute any sort of major obstacle. Nice try.

June 13 / Pristina

Wars and television were made for each other. Whether it is the fighters and their machines, or the victims of war, or the scenes of destruction that punctuate an otherwise tranquil landscape, everything is hopelessly photogenic. We have turned our viewing public into voyeurs of violence, and because there are so many of us (I don't know if this number is correct, but I'm told that there may be as many as two thousand journalists and photographers in and around Kosovo), we are constantly struggling to find new pictures and a new "angle" to keep the viewers from becoming sated. By the end of this day, two photo journalists from the German magazine *Der Stern* had been shot and killed by snipers.

We found ourselves so gorged with material, gathered yesterday and this morning, that we called New York early this morning and suggested that *Nightline* do a prime-time special in the *20/20* time period tonight. Our offer was accepted. It has meant working through the night and depleting any and all material that we might have used on *Nightline* tomorrow. I often joke that certain television news programs should have a "degree of difficulty" label attached to them, just as is done with competitive divers, so that viewers would know how miraculous it is that so much material can be processed and put on their screens in such a brief period of time. One of the lessons I have learned about television, though, is that nobody cares. A program either grips the audience or it doesn't. How hard it was to produce the broadcast is of absolutely no interest.

June 14 / Pristina

We got to bed at 4:30 this morning and were up and out on the road again by 7 a.m. There is no orderly way to cover this kind of story. We get into our armor-plated Land Rover and drive somewhere, anywhere. Sometimes you get lucky and find a story, sometimes you don't. This morning we decided to drive out to the neighborhood of Kosovo Polje. It is among the hardest-core of the hard-core Serbian neighborhoods, named after the monument that commemorates Prince Lazar's losing battle against the Turks in 1389. If a 610-year-old battle (and a disastrous one for the Serbs, at that) seems a little dated and irrelevant to the news of the day—welcome to Serbia! No people has ever celebrated a catastrophe as enthusiastically as the Serbs. It was Milošević's invoking of that battle on its six hundredth anniversary, here in Pristina, that jump-started his rise to the top and reignited Serb-Albanian animosities.

We drive out to the actual monument, which is on a hilltop overlooking the road from Pristina to Belgrade, and spot a small convoy of

Serb farmers pulling out of town. They are leaving just ahead of Serb troops and police, who will be required to get out of the region by tomorrow, under the NATO mandate. One of the farmers tells me that his son is the sixth generation of his family to live in this area. He cannot envision leaving for good and insists that he will be back, but he has to protect his family. As we follow the tractors along the road, there are numerous fires dotting the landscape. These are the homes of Kosovar Albanians, presumably torched by departing Serbs. The farmer tells me that a television crew came to his village three days ago, and their driver set one of the houses on fire so that the crew could film it and the reporter could pin it on the Serbs. Could it be true? I suppose it could, but part of the Serb psychology seems to require that there be a thousand conspiracy theories to explain away the obvious.

Later in the day, we meet a Kosovar Albanian whose house was burned by retreating Serb troops last night. They had requisitioned his house, used it as a mess for the soldiers and then, apparently, kicked over the stove and burned the house down. The Albanian and I were able to talk in German without benefit of an interpreter because he had been a guest worker in Germany for twelve years.

The Russians are still holding the Pristina airport. They can play a pair of deuces better than anyone I've seen. NATO forces have the power and could easily seize the airport from them but, as an English commando captain told me, "That requires political will, doesn't it?"

June 15 / Pristina

We have been on the road all day again, beginning this morning with a visit to Pristina police headquarters. It was hit by three NATO missiles early in the bombing campaign. A number of people were killed inside the building, but there was evidence that the police had gone on using offices there for the last several weeks despite ongoing bombing attacks.

Today, thousands of files were pitched out of the windows and into a courtyard below. Then someone set the files on fire. They were still burning when we got there. We salvaged some of the material and brought it back to the hotel for some of our Serb colleagues to examine. There was one particularly interesting diary entry, apparently that of a senior police officer. The notation is from October 19, 1998, six days after presidential emissary Richard Holbrooke and Slobodan Milošević hammered out an agreement permitting two thousand observers into Kosovo. That's actually when the ethnic cleansing here got under way in a particularly intensive fashion. Our anonymous police official notes receiving orders that "nothing is to be turned over to the Hague War Crimes Tribunal." He appears to be unclear as to what the policy is regarding houses on fire. He writes: "No burning??????"

We leave police headquarters and head off for the neighborhood of Kosovo Polje. We aren't expecting to find much. Indeed, we expect to find it empty, since this is the day police and soldiers must leave the region. For the next four or five hours we videotape literally hundreds of tanks, armored personnel carriers, heavy earth-moving equipment, trucks and cars, all of them loaded with troops and units of the special police (a paramilitary force responsible for some of the war's worst atrocities) beginning their exodus for Belgrade. All the vehicles are flying Serb flags, and the men being transported are cheering and giving the three-fingered Serb salute. The thumb holds down the forefinger, and the remaining three fingers are splayed apart. I believe there may once have been a connection to the Holy Trinity; now it simply identifies the saluter as a Serb loyalist. As we pass one tank, whose crew has "liberated" someone's wine cellar, one of the tankers insists on passing a bottle of Cabernet Sauvignon to Alex Bruckner, our cameraman, who is videotaping from the open roof of our Land Rover. The troops look very tough, and not at all like a defeated army. But they are leaving.

June 16 / Pristina

Today we liberated a village in honor of *Nightline* producer Leroy Sievers's forty-fourth birthday. It was unintentional, actually, and only occurred after we nearly liberated a nearby prison. We'd meant to liberate the prison. The few remaining guards there (who, it turned out were ethnic Albanians, the Serbs having fled) told us we could come in and suggested that we could do whatever we wanted with the prisoners, if only we could provide NATO protection for them. We set off down the road looking for help, and found a willing British sergeant commanding an armored personnel carrier. That was more than enough to impress the prison guards, not to mention the few Serb soldiers who still remained, across the street from the prison. In we walked to find a prison essentially empty. There were just four prisoners remaining, three Albanians and one Bosniac. Everyone else had been set free three days earlier. Not exactly the liberation we'd envisioned, but more than enough. While interviewing the prisoners, though, I asked one of them how long he'd been in. Nine years, he said. *Nine years!* What was he in for? Murder. All of them were in for murder. We'd been on the verge of springing four murderers from prison.

Which is how we came to liberate a village. The prison medic was concerned on two fronts. He needed to keep a NATO presence in front of the prison, so that the Serbs wouldn't come calling to find out what we'd been doing there. He also wanted to demonstrate to us and to the Albanian community that he had always been a pretty good guy. He told us that he could take us to a nearby village where some of the released political prisoners were. They would vouch for him. We drove into the village in our military-looking, red, armor-plated Land Rover, and the residents, believing us to be at least the vanguard of KFOR's liberating army, first trickled, then flowed, then flooded around the vehicle: dozens, then hundreds, then more than a thousand. They cheered, chanted, waved, wept; threw flowers, candy and cigarettes. (I'd always thought the liberation etiquette called for the "liberators" to throw candy and cigarettes at the people.) One old man was so overcome with emotion that he kissed the spare tire of the Land Rover, which is attached to the hood. Nor did the Albanians seem to care when we told them who we were. If we were there, the troops couldn't be far behind. In fact, they weren't. By the time we left the village, Leroy was carrying a giant bouquet of freshly picked flowers, and the French were on the main road setting up security.

It was, Leroy assured us, the most memorable birthday party he'd ever had.

June 17 / Pristina

We have been getting by on two or three hours of sleep a night. The water isn't working in the hotel, which means the toilets don't flush and you can't take a bath. It goes without saying that there's no laundry service, so we're also running out of fresh clothes. But this story is so gripping that none of us is complaining.

Today we visited a mosque near the village of Dyz, about twenty kilometers from Pristina. It's a relatively long ride (about an hour) because the road is so bad to begin with and now it's cluttered on both sides of the road with the burned-out wrecks of cars and tractors and trailers that were left behind during a dreadful weekend in late April. The Serbs essentially herded several tens of thousands of internally displaced persons toward a road near Dyz by firing artillery shells in their direction from three different areas. Once they were on the road, they were stopped by Serb irregulars and special police, who threatened to kill children if parents didn't come up with a thousand deutsch marks. The Serbs randomly reached into cars and into the cabins of tractors, stabbing at the drivers with knives. Sometimes they pulled people out of their vehicles and shot them at close range.

It's hard to know exactly how many people were killed, but a local KLA commander told us he was aware of the graves of sixty-six people in his region. Relative to the number of people fleeing toward Pristina, sixty-six is not many. There was a line of vehicles and people on foot that stretched the entire distance from Dyz to Pristina. I heard estimates of their number today, ranging from twenty thousand to fifty thousand. The apparent intent of the shelling and then the terrorizing was to herd thousands of Albanians first to Pristina and then on to either Albania or Macedonia. It succeeded, as we now know.

June 18 / Thessaloniki, Greece

We arrived here in the middle of the night. It has been an extraordinary week. As I mentioned previously, the water in Pristina has been cut off for most of the week; now we know why. The Serbs cut the dials off the controls at the waterworks before pulling out.

None of us has had a bath or shower in over a week. (Did I mention that before? It's become a preoccupation.) Food has been an interesting mixture of German MREs, fruit, candy and, occasionally, the output of the Grand Hotel Pristina's kitchen. The Grand is surely the most misnamed hotel in Europe. It is the least grand hotel of its kind, which is to say, it aspires to a certain level of grandeur, but achieves only seediness, bad smells and sullen service. For the time being that has no adverse impact on their business, since there are so many journalists, aid workers and others in Pristina that the hotel has all the trade it can handle.

Today we went back to the village of Koliq, about an hour's drive from Pristina, to do some additional shooting on the road (a rutted path, actually) which saw some twenty thousand to fifty thousand refugees make their way to Pristina. Graves of those murdered have been uncovered in Koliq; but for miles before one reaches the village, there is evidence on either side of the road of the panic that must have seized those fleeing. There are the charred wrecks of cars. There are handcarts—some empty, some still carrying a few belongings. Clothes are strewn everywhere. Here lies a cooking pot, there a bowl. A child's doll lies smiling in a ditch.

Serb paramilitaries and special police appear to have killed scores, perhaps hundreds, of people on this road. We were in our armor-plated Land Rover again, yellow adhesive tape stuck to its rear and sides announcing its name as "Jelly 2." (ABC's vehicles were originally white, but they were being confused with one of the U.N.'s humanitarian relief organizations' Land Rovers. ABC News was asked to paint its vehicles another color. Burgundy was selected, but over the white base it came out looking like some strawberry jelly color. Hence the name.) Anyway, Jelly 2 is top-heavy and has lousy tires. At one point today, when we were trying to make our way down a particularly muddy, slippery and fairly steep slope, I put the two right wheels in a ditch. First we tried, unsuccessfully, to winch ourselves out. Then Alex got behind the wheel and managed to drive it out. There were a few times on that road when I thought we were on the verge of tipping over. How the refugees made it up and down those muddy inclines, particularly at a time when they were being harassed, shot, stabbed and terrorized, I will never know.

June 19 / En route from Brussels to Washington

Things are going a lot better than I would have dared believe. The Serbs are pulling out on schedule, and, so far at least, there have been no NATO casualties. Refugees are beginning to pour back into Kosovo at a rate of about four thousand a day. At this rate it would take about six months for all the refugees to return. Obviously, once the mines are removed, the daily return rate will increase dramatically. The Russians have agreed to participate in three of the existing zones, British, French and American, in a fashion that is not altogether clear to me. They will be operating within those zones, but not reporting directly to NATO. We'll see how that works. The KLA is negotiating with NATO generals and appears ready to demilitarize gradually. One KLA unit took over a Serb interrogation facility and promptly tortured one old gypsy to death. He was found chained to a chair, beaten. A number of other gypsies were discovered in the same facility, chained to the radiators, with their arms handcuffed behind their backs. The Albanians are convinced the gypsies collaborated with the Serbs against them. It's too early to tell whether this was just one isolated incident and whether the KLA can keep its own people under control. It doesn't look as though there will be many Serbs left behind in Kosovo. There were two hundred thousand of them when all of this trouble began. After the bombing campaign by NATO that number had been reduced to one hundred thousand. I'm sure it's below fifty thousand now.

It's hard to see where NATO planes caused all of their damage in Kosovo. Most of the bridges are still standing, and those that were destroyed were quickly replaced by substitute feeder-bridges. We saw one fascinating example of a bridge that was camouflaged with branches, while about 150 yards away there was a fake bridge, constructed out of wood, with fake tanks standing at either end. Neither had been hit, although it reminded me of a story that was told about the RAF in World War II. After the Germans painstakingly built a fake wooden factory building, having moved the real factory underground, the RAF reportedly dropped one wooden bomb on the decoy.

June 20 / St. Mary's County

Father's Day. Larry and Deirdre have brought Jake down to spend a week with us. It is literally mind-blowing how jet travel whisks one overnight from a war zone in the Balkans to a diaper pad in southern Maryland. I am not only in a different time zone, I feel emotionally detached from the banner headline in the *Washington Post* announcing that the NRA defeated a gun control bill, from the Sunday-morning talk shows, from the smooth and clear highways and the unravaged neighborhoods. It will take more than an overnight flight, however, to put all of the suffering, danger and uncertainty behind me. We take peace so much for granted in this country that the total lack of interest in Kosovo is off-putting. I will quickly become engaged in the company of our grandson, but I hope I never get over the ache I felt standing in front of those twenty-one fresh gravesites in Koliq.

June 21 / St. Mary's County

Late this afternoon I was swinging Jake on the little swing we set up under the rose trellis that we constructed for his mother's wedding nearly nine years ago. Then I did a variation on the Marlon Brando bit in *The Godfather*, when he's dodging between, and hiding among, the tomato plants. Jake loved it, laughing and giggling. How much we take these sorts of things for granted. Again, I find myself half here and half back in Kosovo, thinking about the horrors some of those little children have experienced. It's not just the children who are marked for life. I'm haunted by the memory of the man we saw as we drove thirty or forty miles outside Pristina to the prison. He was barefooted, walking down the center of the highway. It must have been in the eighties and the tarmac was hot. He was totally oblivious to it and everything else around him, just muttering to himself and occasionally and spasmodically acting out the visions that possessed him. I can't explain how, but we all knew that his madness was something relatively new; it was war-induced. I don't know what it was that happened to him, but it broke his mind. I think of him often. I've mentioned him a couple of times to people here who have asked what it was like in Kosovo. Those listeners nod as though they understand, but I really don't think they do. I don't think they much care either. Man's greatest protection is his ability to block out other people's pain. It is also Man's greatest curse.

June 22 / St. Mary's County

I'm reading *Black Hawk Down*. It's an excellent piece of reporting, the product of its author Mark Bowden's efforts to piece together what happened in October 1993 in Somalia. A year earlier, in late 1992, George

Bush, who had already been defeated by Bill Clinton, mounted a purely humanitarian mission to save the people of Somalia from the horrors of starvation and violence. Over the course of the intervening eleven months there had been growing tension between the Somali warlord, Mohammed Aidid, and the United Nations. A U.N. force of Pakistani soldiers had been attacked by Aidid's paramilitary, and eighteen of the Pakistanis had been killed. Some were subsequently disemboweled and skinned. Aidid had to be brought to justice. A $25,000 bounty was placed on his head at the orders of Adm. Jonathon Howe, a U.S. Navy officer, seconded to the United Nations in Mogadishu. Aidid was so offended by the amount that he had a bounty of a million dollars placed on Howe's head. In any event, one thing led to another, and an operation was mounted to capture some of Aidid's top lieutenants. It involved Delta force troops, SEALs, army Rangers—the best the United States had or has. A couple of Black Hawk helicopters were shot down, and in the effort to recover their crews eighteen U.S. troops were killed and several dozen others were wounded. About five hundred Somalis were killed and more than a thousand were wounded. I don't recall ever hearing anything about that at the time. Indeed, the only thing that captured the American imagination was the image of one dead Ranger being dragged naked through the streets of Mogadishu.

Shortly thereafter, President Clinton ordered U.S. troops withdrawn from Somalia. Things there today are, I believe, not much better than they were before the United States became involved in the first place. I think it explains, at least in part, why President Clinton was so determined not to lose any pilots or troops in Kosovo. We stand for principle until the political cost is too high.

I don't want to rain on the president's parade. He has achieved more than I believed possible in Kosovo. Just as the dead Ranger made future humanitarian operations in Africa unfeasible (that's one major reason why the United States did nothing in Rwanda), Kosovo's ultimate price has yet to reveal itself. I don't think NATO has found its new mission; indeed, I suspect that NATO will never again embark on anything like the Kosovo operation.

It would be a great achievement, though, if Milošević and his ilk were actually driven from office and brought to justice. The Balkans are rocky shoals, though, and no great power has ever navigated them successfully in the long run.

June 23 / St. Mary's County

Jake and I took the Boston Whaler out today. We went out St. Inigoes Creek and across St. Mary's River to Dennis Point Marina, where I gassed up the boat. No one was at dockside, so we went up to the restaurant where, to Jake's delight, we found two parrots. One, the larger and more colorful, does nothing. The other, all green and smaller by half, does a passable imitation of a chicken, apes a hideous laugh and can sing "Hail to the Redskins" (or at least the first verse) and "Jesus Loves Me" (the first two lines). Jake was enchanted. He loves "boids," as he calls them, anyway, and I'm not sure whether he is young enough to be amazed that a bird can talk, or so young that it has never occurred to him that talking is something birds don't routinely do. In either event, it was the high point of his day.

This evening Grace Anne and I went to see *Instinct*, with Anthony Hopkins. He is such a fine actor that we have gone to see anything he does; tonight changed that. I hate to think he needed the money that much.

June 24 / St. Mary's County

Grace Anne and I are taking Jake over to Solomons Island for dinner and then I will continue on to Washington. I have a couple of appointments with doctors in the morning. A lifetime of "enjoying" the sunshine has left me with keratoses, or skin cancers, that have to be "burned" off with liquid nitrogen. They are relatively harmless as long as they are treated early. Since most of them are on my face, it makes good sense to get the work done when I'm on vacation, since it does not leave the treated area looking particularly good for the tube.

Today's big news in the *Washington Post* is that the American Medical Association has voted to unionize doctors. I'm sure my old friend and internist Dr. Edward Gwozdz will have some interesting views on that when he gives me my annual physical tomorrow. Under the current managed-care plan, he makes a big, fat $35 for an hour-long examination. He can't even cover his costs, which is ludicrous. No plumber would come to the house for $35 an hour. Gwozdz is seriously considering early retirement, which would be devastating to his patients.

June 25 / Washington

Late Friday afternoon is no time to be waiting for someone at Washington's Ronald Reagan National Airport. Thousands of people coming and going for the weekend make it a wretched place to drive, and there is no place to wait. You can pull up to the curb, but every five minutes or so a cop asks you to move on. So, you drive the circuit around the airport and try again. All the while you're concerned that the person you're waiting for is coming out of another exit and doesn't see you where you're parked.

I was waiting for our daughter Tara, who is sweet enough to be coming down for the weekend so she can take her nephew, Jake, home on Sunday. A woman approached me and identified herself as the mother of a girl whom Tara has known since third grade, although I think they've drifted apart these last few years. I remember the girl as a talented young singer and dancer (school plays), and the mother as being left with the huge burden of raising three children on her own after she threw out her husband, an abusive cop. Then, briefly, she took him back. That didn't work either, but it did provide her with a fourth child, a son, who's now in his mid-teens. Apparently he's quite a handful and has been running with a bad crowd. So she moved—to Littleton, Colorado.

You can run, but you can't hide.

June 26 / St. Mary's County

Several of our *Nightline* producers have been working with Robert Krulwich, one of television's most creative reporters and thinkers, to put eight one-hour programs on the air for summer prime-time airing. The first is on the subject of time. Robert interviewed some young people on the streets of the Battery in New York, apparently stopping them at random. He used a prop telephone to make the point that, as the devices designed to improve our lives become more efficient, we become less patient. Each of the young people in Robert's "test group" was asked to pick up the phone and listen to it ringing. "How long," each was asked, "how many rings before you would become impatient and hang up?" I tend to become a little antsy after four or five rings, but I would never hang up before six. All of these kids said they would hang up after two rings if they did not get an answering machine or the party they were trying to reach. Two. There is comparable research that shows only about 45 percent of those watching NBC's smash hit *ER* will stick with the program for the entire hour. Consider that for a moment. This is the most popular program on commercial (and, therefore, all) television, but 55 percent of those watching don't stay for the entire program. Viewers, these days, are watching with one finger on the remote control. If, God forbid, we bore them for even ten or twenty seconds, we're gone and they're off to another selection.

The program that Robert and the others have put together is wonderful. It is provocative and entertaining, but I am wondering who will watch it. Hardly anybody watches television anymore to be provoked into thinking. We have undoubtedly brought this upon ourselves. We have been so responsive to what the consultants have told us about the shrinking attention span of the American television viewer that we keep adjusting to meet that diminishing target. We are doing the same thing in terms of E-mail. All messages now demand instant attention, and an instant response. I don't always want to give instant responses; in fact, I believe it to be foolhardy. These days, we do, simply because we can. We rarely ask why.

June 27 / St. Mary's County

Someone on the radio this morning made reference to the top five best-sellers in a particular year in the latter part of the nineteenth century. I was struck by the fact that all the authors are well known to me today. Mark Twain, of course, Louisa May Alcott and Henry James are among them. I'm looking at this morning's list of the top ten fiction best-sellers in the *Washington Post* and wondering how many, if any, of these authors will be known to an audience one hundred years from now: Janet Fitch, Terry Brooks, John Sandford, David Guterson, John Grisham, Jack Higgins, Mary Higgins Clark, Jackie Collins, E. Lynn Harris and Martin Cruz Smith.

Two or three of these are actually wonderful writers, but will they survive the test of time?

I'm tickled to discover that *Tuesdays with Morrie* by Mitch Albom has now been on the best-seller list (nonfiction) for seventy-four weeks. Morrie Schwartz was a gamin elf of a man, a retired sociology professor at Brandeis, and when he was dying of ALS, also known as Lou Gehrig's disease, he decided he wanted to share the process and phenomenon of dying with a larger audience and agreed to a series of interviews with me on *Nightline*, documenting his own demise. Among those watching was Mitch, one of Morrie's former students at Brandeis. He called Morrie and asked if he could visit him. Mitch is a sports reporter in Detroit; Morrie lived and died in Newton, Massachusetts. The first visit turned into a regular weekly event, and those visits and conversations turned into *Tuesdays with Morrie*, which I'm happy to say is one of the most popular American books at the tail end of the twentieth century.

June 28 / St. Mary's County

One of the most persistent tensions, as we come to the end of this century, is between what we in the media always insist is "the public's right to know" and the competing right of individuals to their privacy. In our quiet, rational moments we reporters are inclined to acknowledge that society needs to be broken down into tiers: A politician seeking to attain national office obviously has a lesser claim to maintain his privacy than the family of a youngster killed in a high school shooting. A businessman should expect that his business dealings will be subjected to intense scrutiny; but unless his lifestyle suggests that he's spending far more money than his salary and stock options could support, he ought to be entitled to an assumption of privacy. The same goes for the children of those who are in the limelight. Here, though, celebrities and politicians should understand that once they use their children in political ads or as grist for a daily talk show, they have undermined their right to complain later on if certain segments of the media pursue their children's activities.

The danger lies in our mutual needs. Celebrities and others want publicity, but only at those times and on those occasions when it is useful to them. Having provided them that sustenance, at the beginning of a political campaign, or when they're flogging a book or a movie, we tend to be intolerant when, at a difficult time in their lives, celebrities demand their privacy. To one degree or another, there is nothing new about that level of tension. What is different today is the voracity of the Hydra-headed media beast. There have never been so many mouths to feed. I believe that we are fast approaching a point at which the demands of an overpopulated media industry will be so insistent and uncontrolled that the very values of a free and open press are threatened. As it is, those demands are so great that they have spawned a counterindustry of political, industrial and entertainment world "spinners" far more sophisticated than the simple "p.r." people of years gone by. Much of our national life these days is determined by the choreography involving, on the one hand, those who seek to set the agenda, create the image, shape the argument in behalf of their clients, while on the other hand, legions of us in the media, who are so consumed by our competition with one another that we scarcely have time to weigh and process the material we're putting out.

June 29 / St. Mary's County

I have become a part of the barter economy. Our veterinarian, Peter Eeg, who lives and works in Poolesville, Maryland, heads up a neighborhood coalition that is seeking to prevent the transformation of 220 acres of local land into a golf course. The concern of the citizens is that their aquifer will be overburdened. Each house out there sits on a minimum of twenty-five acres, mandated by the county because of the inadequate water supply. Each house uses about 400 gallons of water a day. The 220 acres in question, therefore, could support nine houses, using a total of 3,600 gallons of water a day. The golf course, by its own estimate, will be using a minimum of 109,000 gallons a day. Peter has been invited to appear on a public television panel program together with the attorney representing the developers. He wanted me to prep him for his television appearance. Since Grace Anne and I are on vacation down here, Peter asked if he could spend a couple of hours with me. We have a particularly ornery and people-shy cat by the name of Phantom (so named because she could never be found during her early days with us). Getting Phantom to the vet is always a problem, so Peter brought the appropriate shots with him today. Phantom got a house call, Peter got his training in spin control and everybody's happy.

June 30 / St. Mary's County

The year is half over. As we begin to slide down the hump of the second half, there will be more and more attention paid to the Y2K phenomenon. From this vantage point, in the middle of 1999, my guess is that it won't be as bad as some people fear, but it'll be worse than most expect.

Simply put, computers (which, after all, have only come into being during this century) were all programmed to recognize which year it is by the last two digits alone. This, then, is 99. Next year, the year 2000, should be 00. The fear is that those computers that have not been programmed to take this into account will assume a reference to the first year of this century, 1900, and that, consequently, systems will shut down, bills will be construed as being one hundred years overdue, and more nonsense than I can possibly imagine will ensue.

This, of course, promises to be a problem with global consequences. It takes only one computer in the global daisy chain to bring an entire system crashing down. There are fears that this will affect the air traffic control systems of many second- and third-world countries. There is growing concern that some countries have made absolutely no preparations. Even normally sober public officials are suggesting the stockpiling of at least some essentials, and the withdrawal from bank accounts of enough money to tide a family over for a couple of weeks. Since we cannot know for sure what will happen, preparing for the worst is prudent. When a vast number of people prepare for the worst, it has a tendency to create its own dynamic, usually bad.

July

July 1 / St. Mary's County

If you want to feel good about how stupid all the experts can be, here's the morning line on the 2000 presidential election. George W. Bush, who has already harvested more than $36 million in contributions, cannot be denied the Republican nomination. Al Gore is still way ahead of any of his Democratic competitors, having collected more than $18 million, but Bill Bradley is doing a lot better than expected. He has pulled in more than $11 million, and during the second quarter of this year he has collected nearly as much as Gore. Still, the nomination is Gore's to lose.

In all the current polls, George W. simply blows Al away. It's not even close. However, who's that glowering on the political horizon? Pat Buchanan is said to be considering pulling up his political roots of a lifetime, bidding adios to the Republican Party and running as an independent. That might sufficiently split the vote of ideological conservatives so as to deny George W. the election and give it to Al.

Note the date. Stay tuned for changes.

July 2 / St. Mary's County

Flashback to 1953, and my penultimate day at boarding school.

At the beginning of each school term we were required to hand over to our housemaster the sum of money from which our weekly allowance would be distributed. Those of us in the third form were not permitted to bring more than thirty shillings, the equivalent of $3.60

today. Each week we would be given one and threepence, the equivalent of about eighteen cents. It doesn't sound like much (nor was it), but you could go to the movies for ninepence; get a newspaper cone full of chips (french fries) with a splash of vinegar and a healthy dose of salt for threepence; and you could get a quart-sized bottle of barley water, with one of those flip tops that allowed you to reseal the bottle after each sip, for another threepence. If you didn't go to the movies, you could afford to buy some sweets (candy).

On the last day of spring term in 1953, our housemaster gave me all that was left of my pocket money. It amounted to a little more than ten shillings. It was more money than I had ever had at one time at Abbotsholme, and I resolved to spend it wisely. I bought half a pound of barley sugar (a very popular hard candy in England; I don't know why it never caught on here) and a five-pack of Woodbines, the workingman's cigarette; they were relatively cheap, but still too expensive for most workers to buy twenty of them at a time.

I took my cigarettes and my barley sugar and, with a classmate, repaired to the top of a haystack. It never occurred to either of us that we could defer the delight of smoking a second or third cigarette to the next day. Nor that we might not eat the entire half pound of barley sugar at one sitting.

I have mixed memories of that day. I still get a pleasant feeling of anticipation at the mere thought of lighting up a Woodbine. I also recall "hurling" (in the current vernacular) over the side of that haystack.

It's a cautionary tale to all young smokers.

July 3 / St. Mary's County

The original house on our property down here was built in 1642, somewhere on this site, and although we have been unable to find any of its remains, there is ample documentary evidence detailing how Thomas Cornwallys was deeded two thousand acres here, after helping to finance the voyage of the *Ark* and the *Dove* from England to the Colonies. Those two boats were, in many respects, the Catholic equivalent of the *Mayflower*, bringing, as they did, the first Catholic settlers to North America in 1629. The house in which we now live, Cross

Manor, dates back at least to 1765. It is our belief that the original house was pillaged and set on fire by a pirate named Ingels.

In any event, this property has seen a lot of American history, including its use during the Civil War as a telegraph office and refueling station for the Potomac fleet of the Union army. The wharf that used to stand just off a point that juts out into St. Inigoes Creek was known as Grayson's Wharf, and we have a photograph that would appear to date back about sixty or seventy years of two white women and a black man standing on the wharf. We thought we knew who the women were, since we know who owned the property at that time, but we never thought to learn who the tall, lean black man standing with them was.

This afternoon we were visited by an African American couple. The husband had been referred to us as an excellent house painter. His wife was with him because they had just come from a funeral. Grace Anne was showing the man what needs to be done, so I showed his wife around the property. When we came to the photograph of the trio on Grayson's Wharf, she put her hand to her mouth and exclaimed: "That's Pop E!" It was her husband's grandfather, who had, in fact, worked here at Cross Manor more than sixty years ago.

I have mixed feelings. The sense of continuity is, at one and the same time, good and discouraging. There are thousands of men here in St. Mary's County, both black and white, doing exactly what their fathers and grandfathers did before them—tilling the same land, living in the same houses. It is said that you could compare the manifests of the *Ark* and *Dove* to the St. Mary's and Calvert County phone books and find all the same names. Still, I doubt if the rate of progress among black residents down here has kept pace with that of whites. This remains a very conservative part of the country.

July 4 / St. Mary's County

Whenever I start to think that my boating skills have reached an acceptable level of competence, small doses of reality intrude.

We have had a twenty-six-foot cabin cruiser for about twelve years. While it is named after Grace Anne, she is not much for boating, and, therefore, we don't use it often or go very far when we do. Last night, in fact, we went about a mile, straight up St. Inigoes Creek, due west. We anchored a couple of hundred yards away from Dennis Point Marina, which puts on a fireworks display from on board an old barge every July 4 weekend. It was terrific. My son, Drew, and his girlfriend, Annie, were along, and we all enjoyed it immensely. All I had to do was turn around and head the boat back one mile, due east. I made it without incident, but being surrounded by dozens of other boats at night is hugely disorienting. The navigation lights create a bobbing miasma of red and green lights that make it all but impossible to distinguish the flashing red and green channel markers even though I've sailed these waters hundreds of times in the *Grace Anne III*, in our little whaler and on my small sailboat.

I was out on the sailboat today. It was hotter than hell—over one hundred degrees—but there was a good wind. I was complimenting myself on my sailing skills because of the progress I was making overtaking a much larger sailboat that had a far greater spread of canvas.

Then I realized that the other boat was coming toward me.

July 5 / St. Mary's County

The July 4 weekend is drawing to a close, and, although this is technically the beginning of the summer season, it is my experience that from this weekend on summer gurgles away like water passing through a wide-necked funnel.

The lead editorial in the *Washington Post* today is titled "The Surplus Illusion." It points out that in 1997, when Congress passed the balanced budget act, the legislators committed themselves to cutting a large category of federal spending in real terms by 20 percent at "some time in the future." The *Post* argues that since everyone at the time knew that this would never happen—that such cuts, in other words, will never be made—all projections made by budget estimators skew the outcome. The rosy assumptions that we will have budget surpluses in the trillions are, then, almost totally wrong. The current wrangling over how to spend the windfall, whether for tax cuts or new social programs, are pipe dreams. And yet no one, not the White House nor anyone in the House or Senate, seems inclined to spell out reality.

As my producer Tom Bettag likes to say, I think I smell a story here.

July 6 / Washington

Why do we revel so in extremes of the weather?

Not content with having the temperature peak at a torrid 105 degrees, we feel obliged to inform future generations that it felt a helluva lot hotter than that. Just as, in the winter, we have something called a "wind-chill factor," so, too, in the summer, we are now encumbered by a "heat index." Each seeks to quantify not how hot or cold it actually is, but how hot or cold it seems. On a cold winter day, the wind makes it seem even colder. On a hot summer day, humidity makes it seem even hotter. Thus, today, incorporating the heat index, we are told that it feels like 115 degrees.

How are our poor parents or grandparents to compete? It may, on some particular day in 1907, have felt even hotter than it feels today, but there is no statistical evidence to buttress their anecdotes. (Of course, there was no air-conditioning, either.)

July 7 / Washington

The first time I met David Halberstam he was a star reporter for the *New York Times* in Vietnam in 1964. I had been with ABC News for only a year. We were doing a radio documentary on what was happening in Indochina. Most attention had been focused on what was invariably referred to as "the land-locked, tripartite kingdom of Laos." Now, attention was shifting to Vietnam. I did an interview with Halberstam, Neil Sheehan of UPI and Malcolm Browne of the AP. I was hopelessly smitten with admiration and jealousy. These three foreign correspondents were everything I wanted to be.

David just called. He wants to come by tomorrow to talk about what's happening to the United States in terms of its world role as we come to the end of the twentieth century. He especially wants to discuss television's role in diminishing the importance of foreign affairs. David told me something that is disturbing but not surprising: ABC is having trouble finding anyone who wants to cover Moscow. Russia has never been more open to television coverage, rarely been more interesting than it is right now, and we can't find anyone to take the assignment.

The problem: The bottom line for a television correspondent is getting on the air. The magazine programs won't touch stories about Russia, *World News Tonight* has lost much of its appetite for foreign stories, and *Nightline* might do a half dozen stories a year on Russia.

If television isn't covering the story and Americans are reading less and less, I suppose it's inevitable that we will become dumber and dumber. And that's very dangerous indeed.

July 8 / Washington

I wish Matt Drudge no ill. He is an agile self-promoter who has made a name for himself by posting a newsletter on the Internet. He has been just accurate enough in just enough stories to earn a great deal of attention, and the attention has been sufficient to distract focus from the many inaccuracies in his overall reporting. The Internet is a relatively new medium, and all of its consumers will have to come to terms with new standards for quality control.

Drudge, however, has apparently been signed up by ABC Radio to do a weekly show. The brass chooses to describe it as a talk show, and insists, therefore, that there is no need to subject Drudge to the same standards that apply to ABC Radio News reports. I disagree.

He presents himself as a reporter, and ABC Radio listeners can be excused for assuming that the standards for one reporter appearing on ABC Radio are the same as for all others. If Drudge's flexible attention to accuracy is to be the new standard, that's not a comparison I cherish.

July 9 / St. Mary's County

I went to see the ear, nose and throat doctor this morning. What had been bothering me is no cause for concern. Great news. In my imagination there is a certain dramatic symmetry in a television anchorman developing throat cancer. I can live without the drama.

The price of gasoline has shot way back up again. It is somewhere in the neighborhood of $1.20 a gallon for Regular.

July 11 / Potomac

Driving home from St. Mary's County I was listening to NPR's Sunday edition of *All Things Considered*. It featured a fairly long interview with Brian Attwood, who has just resigned as the director of the Agency for International Development, AID. Two interesting statistics: Most Americans, said Attwood, seem to believe that the United States distributes about 20 percent of its budget in overseas aid. The actual figure is less than 1 percent. At the turn of the century, the residents of developed countries had about nine dollars in spendable income for every dollar available to people in the rest of the world. Now the ratio is about sixty-five to one. The gap, in other words, between the world's rich and poor countries is seven times greater as we come to the end of the century than it was at the beginning of it.

What particularly frustrates Attwood is that we now have a significant number of congresspeople who take pride in the fact that they have never applied for and do not intend to apply for a U.S. passport. These legislators who never travel do not believe there is any reason that they should travel; they are confident that everything they need to know about the world is available to them here at home. Unfortunately, this coincides with a growing tendency among the television networks to reduce, if not eliminate altogether, coverage of foreign news.

We're in trouble.

July 13 / Lansdowne, Virginia

We're at the Lansdowne Conference Center, not too far from Dulles Airport. When I write "we," I'm referring to all of *Nightline*'s editorial and production staff—correspondents, producers, director and many of the other support people. We're having our annual retreat. This is either the third or the fourth one, and it's an opportunity for people to air their gripes and their fears and to talk about where we all think the program is going or ought to be going.

Tom Bettag is a great believer in the efficacy of these sessions. They're a little New Age for my taste. Since Tom is a far more effective administrator and manager than I, however, I defer to his instincts.

There is a great deal of concern this year about what will happen to *Nightline* (and therefore to the members of its staff) when Tom and I move on to whatever the next phase of our careers will be. We have, in any event, decided that nine years of sixteen-hour days is more than enough for him, and twenty years of what began as sixteen-hour days and is now down to about seven- or eight-hour days is also enough for me.

We gave notice of our intentions to ABC management about eighteen months ago, and we've been talking to our own staff about it for at least three months; but no one seems quite sure that we really mean what we say. There seems to be a sense that when the time finally comes, we will reconsider.

Whatever happens, it is best that it be spelled out soon, with precision and definitiveness. The uncertainty is making people very nervous. They all seem to wonder, as my old friend, *Nightline*'s first senior producer Stuart Schwartz, once did: Are these the good old days?

In fact, they were, and they are.

July 14 / Lansdowne

Our sessions here have been run by three very nice people who are part (or, for all I know, they may be the entirety) of an organization that helps senior executives or, in our case, an entire staff, come to terms with their inner selves, their interpersonal relations, their fears, their concerns, their ambitions. It is all, as far as I'm concerned, a lot of blather and psychobabble. Last night, for example, several of us volunteered, in much the same manner as members of an audience agree to be hypnotized for the amusement of the rest of the audience. We then sat in a file of chairs, one behind the other, representing various aspects of our inner selves: "fear, pain, the golden child, aggression, defensiveness." I like to think myself fairly open-minded to new techniques and ideas, but this was pure drivel.

Still, our session this morning, which was devoted to suggesting new approaches and ideas for developing and expanding *Nightline* in the next few years as Tom and I move into other areas of programming, was terrific. Our "facilitators" took the position that yesterday's exchanges of "angst" were the necessary prelude to today's productive exchanges of ideas. I think it's a load of crap. But whether by luck or design, today's was a very good session, and I said as much before the group. I believe that our staff now has a better handle on what lies ahead and how they will deal with it. That was what Tom and I hoped to accomplish, and he deserves credit for taking the risk and making it happen.

July 15 / New York

Tout le monde a son nature,
L'un le merde et l'autre le confiture.

There is no accounting for taste.

Grace Anne and I were invited to see the musical *Titanic* at the Kennedy Center last night. It wasn't exactly dreadful, but it's not very good either. The actors do what they can with the material, which is to say, they have wonderful voices. But the music is mediocre and the lyrics are banal. On top of that the story is so well known that, absent any internal plot development, there isn't even any element of drama or surprise.

This, however, is one of the most honored musicals of the last few years. I know that taste is a very personal thing, but there have to be some objective standards by which something like this can be measured. *Titanic* is not original, certainly not groundbreaking, nor is it charmingly old-fashioned. It's well staged, although even in that regard it felt claustrophobic to me. I have gone into other productions (*Cats, Evita, Phantom of the Opera*) wondering how it was possible to make a great musical out of such material. In each of those cases I left the theater thrilled to discover how wrong I could be. I have gone to revivals, like *Chicago*, and wondered whether I would be satisfied with a remake of something old. Grace Anne and I loved it so much, we went to see it again.

Titanic is a bust.

July 16 / Washington

I feel a little better after reading this morning's review of *Titanic* in the *Washington Post*. It turns out that the Washington production of the show was far less ambitious (and also far less impressive) than that staged on Broadway. Scenes in New York literally occurred on three levels, sometimes simultaneously, and when the ship "sinks" she does so far more dramatically than at the Kennedy Center. The *Washington Post* reviewer described the local production here as being no better than a black-and-white Xerox copy of the original.

As I say, that answers some of my questions about how and why Grace Anne and I saw the show so differently from those who awarded it Tonys for Best Musical, and for Best Music and Best Lyrics.

I'm still left wondering, however, how the staging and set could have done so much for the music and the lyrics, which, I'm afraid, I still think are banal.

You can look at this morning's radically different reviews of the new Stanley Kubrick movie, *Eyes Wide Shut*, and marvel at the question of taste. The *New York Times* gave it a rave; the *Washington Post* panned it in all its aspects.

July 17 / Washington

John F. Kennedy Jr., the young man who put a lump in the nation's throat thirty-six years ago when he stood saluting the army caisson carrying his father's coffin, is missing. He was piloting a single-engine plane from New Jersey to Hyannisport, Massachusetts. On board were his wife and sister-in-law. They left last night around 8:30 and haven't been seen since. Some debris from their plane has been found, and it's hard to believe that anyone from the plane will be found alive. If, as they once said about John's uncle, Ted Kennedy, his name were Ted Smith and his accomplishments were no more nor less than they are, it would be a very minor story indeed. Young John Kennedy is/was by all accounts a very nice young man, clearly a very attractive person, but his accomplishments have been modest.

Put his apparent death, however, at the end of the list of tragic events that began with his uncle Joe Jr. early in World War II. That list is so overwhelming that it has riveted the attention and the sympathy of the entire nation.

July 18 / Potomac

John Kennedy Jr., his wife and sister-in-law are still missing and are now presumed dead. It continues to be a huge story, almost to the exclusion of any other news. Why? Well, JFK Jr. is, of course, the only direct male descendant of President Kennedy, and perhaps there lurked in the hearts of many Kennedy loyalists the notion that he might someday reclaim the throne. But that's what so mystifies me. I don't think there are that many Kennedy loyalists left. I believe it's fair to say that most Americans alive today have absolutely no memory, were probably not even alive, when Kennedy was shot. And even among those of us who were alive and politically aware at that time, some of the luster has been tarnished by all the revelations about the Kennedys in general and JFK in particular.

Perhaps it has something to do with the fact that we are all lovers of legend. We treasure our Paul Bunyans, our John Henrys, even our Billy the Kids. This is a family that has painted on a larger canvas, used brighter colors, dared more outrageous themes than most of us do. If they had all died in bed in their eighties and nineties, if they had been allowed to achieve all of their goals, we would probably have tired of them. The Kennedys symbolize unfulfilled goals, unrealized promise, and the fact that these have been curtailed by acts of mad violence or reckless bravery or even poor judgment only serves to make us ache a little more for what might have been.

July 19 / Washington

Two young Americans were killed in Kosovo yesterday, three others were injured, when their armored personnel carrier overturned.

I cannot imagine how difficult it will be for their families to absorb such news at this time. It wouldn't have made it any better for the families if the accident had occurred three or four weeks ago, except then they would have been joined in their mourning by an entire nation. At that time, everyone's attention was riveted on what was happening in Kosovo.

Today Kosovo is already a fading memory in the minds of most Americans, and the attention of the nation is riveted on the loss of JFK Jr.

July 20 / Washington

Today marked the thirtieth anniversary of Man's first landing on the moon—the "One small step for a man, one giant step for mankind" landing. Neil Armstrong, the man who spoke those words, was the first one down the ladder, Edwin "Buzz" Aldrin the second.

What none of us knew at the time was that a NASA official had placed a call to the White House—specifically to William Safire, now a columnist for the *New York Times*, then a speechwriter for Richard Nixon—to ensure that President Nixon had something appropriate to say in the event that the lunar module didn't make it off the surface of the moon. Armstrong and Aldrin would have been left to die because there was no way of launching a rescue mission.

Aldrin was my guest on *Nightline* tonight. I wanted to follow up on that point but couldn't get through the "Well, that was the mission and we didn't think all that much about not succeeding" line. I'm sure that, to a degree, that was even true. They had to focus on the expectation of success, rather than the likelihood of disaster. Still, you'd think that thirty years later it might be all right to concede at least a touch of apprehension. But I suppose that wouldn't qualify as the "right stuff."

Whatever it is, it still works. I'm in awe of all those original astronauts. We were out to beat the Russians whatever it took, and if getting to the moon first would have meant leaving Armstrong and Aldrin behind, well . . . Safire had written an eloquent eulogy: "These brave men, Neil Armstrong and Edwin Aldrin, know that there is no hope for their recovery. But they also know there is hope for mankind in their sacrifice. . . . For every human being who looks up at the moon in the nights to come will know that there is some corner of another world that is forever mankind."

Safire is probably pleased that his memo has finally seen the light of day.

July 21 / Washington

The bodies of JFK Jr., his wife and sister-in-law have been recovered. It will, at least, foreclose the stories that would inevitably have arisen that the accident was an elaborately planned scheme to afford them a new life of privacy. It will not, I'm afraid, end the spate of stories questioning Kennedy's experience as a pilot and, therefore, his judgment in leaving New Jersey so late that he could not possibly reach Hyannisport during daylight.

The young man struggled mightily during his life to establish some small measure of independence from the Kennedy myth. In death, it will be unavoidable and inescapable.

July 22 / New York

I flew here early this morning in order to get my picture taken—many times over. ABC News is launching a promotion campaign that, at its core, will be an artsy collection of its "stars" at work. The fact that I rarely, if ever, work in New York is irrelevant. We borrow the office of a news executive and I am posed leaning on the edge of her desk looking pensive.

Understand, these things are not performed by a photographer alone. He has two assistants; then there's someone or other from the ad agency; then there's some minor honcho I never heard of from the network; and then, for good measure, they've imported a familiar face, one of *Nightline*'s producers, Ted Gerstein, whose unenviable task it is to "engage" me. The charade moves down to the ABC News assignment desk area, which I rarely visited even when I worked in New York. Then, on to a control room, where some shots are taken of me walking through the corridors. Finally, there are some exterior photos on Sixty-seventh Street, shot to make it look as much like Washington as possible. I hate it. It's nonsense. But I'm always among the first to engage in the Kremlinology of studying how the photographs are arranged and presented in the lobbies and conference rooms of ABC News buildings. When you see how these photographs are laid out and whose pictures dominate, you'll know who's in and who's out at ABC News.

July 23 / St. Mary's County

It has been a year since we first met Peter, who is one of the country's more prominent architects. We would like him to build a house for us on a piece of property we bought some years ago. Grace Anne and I hope this will be our last home. We are planning it with an eye to making it compatible with old age. Corridors and doorways should be wide enough to accommodate a wheelchair. We would like everything to be on one floor. It is meant to be a home for two people, but it will be designed with the knowledge that other family members will be coming to stay for a few days at a time. This is an intricate mating dance. We have to get to know the architect. He has to get to know us.

We like him very much. He seems to like us. Once you embark on a project like this, however, you are stuck with one another for at least a couple of years. I feel a little like my graduation from buying suits off the rack to ordering my first custom-made suit. Over the course of our thirty-six years of marriage, Grace Anne and I have spent the past twenty-eight in a house that another couple had built for themselves. A very few years after the house was complete, the wife died of cancer, and the husband, understandably, didn't want to live there anymore. That couple must have been roughly as old as we are now. It's one of life's little ironies that, by the time your family is fully grown and you have enough money to build a house for yourself, you probably don't have that many more years left. This will be the one and only time we build a house specifically for ourselves. I wonder who'll be living in it a few years from now.

July 24 / St. Mary's County

The front page of this morning's *Washington Post* unintentionally captures much of what has been wrong about the media's obsessive coverage of JFK Jr.'s death. It has been exactly a week since he disappeared, three days since his body and those of his wife and sister-in-law were found. Yesterday his family held a memorial mass, and Ted Kennedy delivered a moving eulogy. Clearly, there has been a great deal of public interest in every aspect of this story, so it is not surprising that the *Post* would cover it with a color photograph on its front page and a good-sized story to match. But down in the bottom left-hand corner of the front page, within a box labeled "INSIDE," is a tiny color picture of King Hassan II of Morocco. The accompanying copy reads ". . . the Arab world's longest-ruling monarch and a key figure in the Middle East peace process died at 70. . . . WORLD, Page A13."

For seven straight days now we have been examining and reexamining the life of a young man whose greatest accomplishment was the accident of his birth into one of America's most storied families. Because he was a Kennedy, his untimely death was of huge interest. But when the seventh day of covering the death of a man whose real achievements fall into the category of unfulfilled promise exceeds the first word accorded to the death of a world leader, whose accomplishments were genuine, courageous and protracted, then we have lost our sense of proportion.

July 25 / En route to New York

Maryland, particularly southern Maryland, has been in the grip of a severe drought. Temperatures have been in the nineties for a good deal of the summer and the corn, while stunted and no higher than a man's shoulder, is tassling out prematurely. This is the second year in a row we've had unremitting heat and little rain. Some of the local farmers aren't going to make it through another bad harvest. It's a brutally hard way to make a living.

I'm on my way to New York where, tomorrow morning, I'll be meeting up with Bob Barnett, the lawyer who is serving as my literary agent. This is the first time we have worked together; he also represents a number of my broadcast colleagues, and Bill and Hillary Clinton, for the books they undoubtedly hope will reduce, if not eliminate, their multimillion-dollar legal bills. Bob and I are meeting with senior editors from Random House, Farrar Straus, Knopf and a couple of other major publishing houses in search of a good home for this work in progress.

I long ago lost any sense of perspective as to what a book like this will be worth. Ironically, I think its real value will come for readers many years from now, who can use it to get some sense of our times and values. Whether it will be a popular read in the immediate future, I can't tell.

Tomorrow, when we meet with the various editors, however, will not be the time to give any hint of those doubts. Writing this book, in any event, has been easier than planting corn or soybeans.

July 26 / New York

I'm in a sweltering dressing room waiting to appear on the David Letterman show. The producers asked that I be at the theater by 4:30 p.m. The show doesn't start taping until 5:30 and the first guest is never introduced before 6:30, but television producers are a nervous lot, whose future does not depend on the goodwill or comfort of their occasional guests. I'm appearing tonight in the expectation that I can say a few nice words about the eight one-hour *Nightline in Prime Time* specials that feature Robert Krulwich. Letterman, who has no interest whatsoever in that subject, will grant me a few seconds to plug the programs, and, in return, we'll banter for a few scintillating minutes, providing what passes for entertainment these days.

Minimal as the talent may be, the ability to be an acceptable guest on a variety of television programs is much in demand among the producers of those programs. It is also a valuable commodity from the vantage point of author and publisher. In each of the conversations my lawyer and I had today with representatives of five major publishers, the conversation, sooner or later, got around to publicity. Was I willing to go "on tour"? What that actually entails (along with autograph signing sessions at a variety of large book chains) is a sequence of often mind-numbing interviews on television programs with names like "Good Morning, Cleveland," where the questions run along the lines of—So, what made you decide to write a book?

July 27 / En route to Washington

Tom Bettag and I have spent the day sailing with one of the top ABC/Disney (or as Disney might prefer, Disney/ABC) corporate executives. It was a particularly pleasant way of discussing what Tom and I may do once we begin to withdraw a little from the daily responsibilities of turning out *Nightline*. Will it make a difference in the long run? In the final analysis corporations have to base decisions that will cost them a lot of money on something other than personal relationships and pleasant days spent sailing off the coast of Long Island, but it is still helpful. So many creative notions go unfulfilled simply because those who have them are unable to convince those who can facilitate their development. In that sense, today was a good day.

July 28 / Washington

Flashback to November 1953. My parents and I had just arrived in New York as new immigrants. It was certainly a more pleasant arrival and occurred under better circumstances than prevailed for most immigrants. But there I was sitting on a bed in the Alden Hotel, somewhere in the lower Eighties on Central Park West, crying my eyes out. It was my first or second day in America, I was thirteen and felt that we had just made one of the biggest mistakes of my young life. I had been listening to the radio (televisions had not yet made it into most hotel rooms) and one commercial in particular had hit home, if not precisely in the fashion that the advertiser intended. It was an antacid commercial:

> *Eat too much?*
> *Drink too much?*
> *Try Brioski's, try Brioski's . . .*

It was a silly little jingle but certainly no more offensive than hundreds of others I would hear over subsequent years. What hit me so hard at the time, though, was that we had just come from postwar England and Germany. World War II had been over for eight years, but many foods were still scarce in Germany, and there had been rationing for some items in England until 1951 or 1952. The notion that we had come to a country where people needed to take a product to deal with the consequences of "eating too much" or "drinking too much" bewildered me. Wouldn't it just be simpler, I wondered, if these overconsumers simply didn't? (It didn't take me long to join their ranks.)

The moment came rushing back the other day in New York when one of the editors at a major publishing house wondered whether I would be writing anything about immigration.

July 29 / Washington

We are in the middle, yet again, of an evolving story of madness and violence. Today, Mark Barton, forty-four years old and apparently someone who engaged in a fair amount of day trading in the stock market, went to the Atlanta offices of the All-Tech Investment Group, which had handled his trades, and opened fire. There are already five people reported dead in one location and four in another, and he appears to have killed three members of his own family in still another location. Those killings seem to have been committed several days ago. Just to further complicate this story, two other members of Barton's family were murdered five or six years back, and he was a primary suspect. Charges, however, were never filed. It is in the immediate welter of confusion that inevitably surrounds a story like this that we, in this business, sometimes stumble into a series of inferences that turn out later to have nothing to do with actual events.

The first live television reports have all emphasized that Barton appeared to have been a disgruntled day trader. The implication has been that he held some of the folk at All-Tech responsible for his losses. That may, indeed, ultimately turn out to be true, but All-Tech's CEO is already being quoted as saying that Barton hasn't been trading recently. It's relevant because day trading itself has come in for a great deal of criticism, in that people tend to make and lose huge amounts of money very quickly, acting on impulse rather than considered information.

This may yet become the first mass murder blamed on Internet trading methods.

July 30 / Washington

The Barton story overwhelmed everything else yesterday and continues to unfold in bizarre ways. He ended up, yesterday evening, being cornered by police at a gas station. He shot and killed himself. His second wife and his two children by an earlier marriage were found at her apartment (she had moved out on him earlier this month) bludgeoned and drowned. Barton left notes on each of the bodies and a letter addressed "To Whom It May Concern," giving some insight into his own torment and warning that he would be going after "many of the people that greedily sought my destruction." It now turns out that he couldn't meet his margin at one trading company, where he shot and killed five people, and lost as much as $90,000 the day before yesterday trading at another company, where he shot four others. Both of these are places that have become fashionable in recent years, where a day trader can, in effect, rent a computer position where trades can be made instantaneously.

There is still some mystery surrounding the deaths of his first wife and mother-in-law, both of whom were murdered just across the Georgia border in Alabama. Barton insisted to the end, in the letter he left behind, that he hadn't killed them. "There's no reason for me to lie now," he wrote. Investigators from Georgia who have been tracking this homicide case remain convinced that Barton simply got away with it. It does make you wonder what would have happened if Alabama's authorities had pursued the case a little more intensively.

Fourteen murders and one suicide. Unlike the shootings at the school in Littleton, Colorado, I don't think the debate over this one will linger. What's to blame? Day trading? Barton appears to have been a killer before day trading was fashionable. Guns? He bludgeoned and drowned his second wife and two children. An unsuccessful investigation six years ago? Maybe. But then, maybe someone else was responsible for those murders, as his lawyer continues to insist.

Barton was indisputably a deeply troubled man who will now have a card file along with dozens of other troubled American killers who dominate our interest for a few days or weeks and then become the answers to obscure trivia questions.

July 31 / St. Mary's County

The heat is oppressive and enduring. The East Coast, in particular, has been sweltering under temperatures in the high nineties together with high humidity for most of the month now. Baltimore has announced that it has only enough water to last the city for another fifty-six days. We must assume that it will rain heavily sometime between now and the end of September, but still, it's an indication of how severe the drought has been. Well over a hundred people have died from heat-related causes.

Cities have set up cooling centers, where people who have no air-conditioning in their residences, or who have no residences, can get some relief. Many transit systems are offering free bus rides as a means of convincing people to leave their cars at home.

Air-conditioning, which has become a familiar part of the American scene only during the second half of this century, has probably changed the way we live and where we live as much as any modern invention. It is, unfortunately, another line of separation between the rich and the poor. Those of us with money can afford to keep our living and travel spaces as cool as an early-spring morning, while those without means are as helpless to deal with the heat as our grandparents were in 1899.

Almost lost this week, with the attention lavished on the Atlanta killings, were two aftershocks from the president's dalliance with Monica Lewinsky. Federal judge Susan Webber Wright fined Clinton more than $90,000 for his various perjuries during legal depositions in the Paula Jones case. That money is to help Jones pay for some of the legal expenses that were incurred. Judge Wright also referred the matter to the Arkansas Bar Association, so that it can consider disbarring Clinton. But we have become so accustomed to the president's indiscretions and lies that this news caused barely a ripple.

Meanwhile, Linda Tripp, who has emerged from these seedy proceedings as tarred and scarred as the president seems untouched, was indicted yesterday on two counts of wiretapping. That is to say, she recorded her telephone conversations with Lewinsky without informing her of it. This is against the law but is rarely, if ever, prosecuted. If convicted, Tripp will face a maximum penalty of five years in prison on each count. I can't imagine that will happen, but there is a message here for anyone seeking to play hardball with a popular president.

August

August 1 / Potomac

It seems the president was abused as a child, though it is not altogether clear who did this. So says Hillary in an interview she gave to a writer for a new magazine called *Talk*. *Talk* is the brainchild of Tina Brown, the Englishwoman who has enjoyed previous success editing *Vanity Fair* and, more recently, *The New Yorker*. Tina, who comes across in person as a demure English rose, has the instincts of a pirate. More on that in a moment.

Hillary told the interviewer from *Talk* that young Bill was abused at the age of four. It is not quite clear whether this abuse took sexual or psychological form, although the suggestion seems to be that it was the latter. He was trapped between two strong-willed women, his mother and his grandmother. That is the thrust of the revelation. Washington is all aflutter. I think this story will last about a week. If anything, I think this will only endear the president even more to those who admire him and identify with the troubled times of his life.

But back to Tina Brown. She asked Tom Bettag and me to have lunch with her a few months back so she could pick our brains on the prospect of starting up a television show (or at least a series of television specials) that might create synergy with the new magazine. That lunch led to an amusing meeting in New York involving Tom, Tina, Harvey Weinstein (one of the heads of Miramax Films) and me. Harvey suggested the "Ted and Tina" show, although I have this strange feeling that I wouldn't have had top billing for too long. It all went by kind of quickly, but I think Harvey was also suggesting that Tom and I would get 50 percent of the profits. I told him I already had a job, and anyway, I rather like the solo gig. Harvey feigned embarrassment. Tina actually did seem embarrassed. Anyway, the magazine seems to have landed with a splash.

August 2 / New York

Our son, Drew, and I left Potomac this morning shortly after 7, fortified by two large cups of Starbucks' finest, piloting (actually he was piloting; I was riding shotgun) a twenty-four-foot-long Ryder rent-a-truck loaded with many but not, I believe, most of his belongings. Drew has found an apartment in Brooklyn that he can have for a modest—for New York—$850 a month. At that price there has to be a catch, and there is. The apartment is being rented by someone else, who wants to share what in any other part of the country would be considered fairly cramped quarters. Such is the shortage of good, cheap apartments in the New York metropolitan area these days that this is considered a "good deal."

Anyway, we made it to lower Manhattan shortly after noon and were just congratulating ourselves on how well we had done, when Drew misjudged the length of the truck while navigating a turn and took the right front fender off a parked vehicle. Fortunately, it was an old Datsun. Unfortunately it was parked right in front of a police (transit police, but still . . .) precinct and belonged to one of the young ladies who worked there. Fortunately, she and most of her colleagues who joined her on the sidewalk appeared to be *Nightline* fans. The offended party wanted (and who was I, under the circumstances, to deny her) a photograph with me in front of her damaged Datsun. She was very sweet, agreed that the whole damn car isn't worth more than $900, and she and Drew exchanged phone numbers. She will let him know what it costs to fix her fender and he will pay for it.

By the time we got to Brooklyn it was about 2 p.m., and the parking space closest to his apartment was next to a fire hydrant about fifty yards from the front door. It took us three hours to unload the truck. It will take Drew three months to unload all of the boxes. I hope he loves his new apartment.

August 4 / Washington

I had a visit this afternoon from a man who was executive producer of *World News Tonight* about twenty years ago. He and I have been friends for even longer than that, going back to the early seventies, when I had just returned from Southeast Asia and he was a senior producer on ABC's evening news program. Howard K. Smith and Harry Reasoner were coanchoring in those days. When Roone Arledge came into our collective lives, we regarded him as the barbarian at the gate. Now he is generally acknowledged to have ushered in ABC News's golden age. I don't think Roone changed all that much. It's just that industry standards as a whole have shifted so much in the direction of the prime-time magazine shows that what we regarded as crass commercialism in the mid-seventies looks now, on reflection, as having been one of the high-water marks of our profession.

August 5 / Washington

The news out of Kosovo is discouraging. The Kosovo Liberation Army has taken over the administration of the province. NATO troops were never intended to fill that role and the U.N. administration is neither in place nor likely to be soon.

Predictably, Kosovar Albanians are extracting revenge. Serbs and gypsies who are believed to have collaborated with the Serbs are being beaten, terrorized and killed. The exodus of Serbs has already been such that only a fraction of the two hundred thousand who once lived in Kosovo remains. They will most likely leave soon, too. What is emerging is a de facto Albanian state. Whether it will merge into part of a greater Albania remains to be seen, but prospects for a multiethnic Kosovo are dimming, day by day. When all the Serbs are gone, what will NATO's role be?

August 6 / Potomac

I remember a quotation from a book flap promoting the virtues of the humorist and writer S. J. Perelman, something to the effect that

"*Before* they made S. J. Perelman, they broke the mold." Much the same can be said of Robert Krulwich. His quirky sense of humor, harnessed to his lively inquisitiveness, makes Robert one of the genuinely few "originals" in television. He, as I indicated earlier, has been working with some of our staff on an eight-part *Nightline in Prime Time* series, to fill a few of the gaping voids in summertime television. The subjects to be dealt with in the series of shows range from cloning and the nature of a family to musings on man and machine, time and even string theory. My role in these programs has been peripheral, but I think they are truly marvelous. They begin to show us what television can be. The first two, however, have been ratings disappointments.

All of us in commercial television are confronted by a difficult choice that commercialism imposes. Do we deliberately aim for the lowest common denominator, thereby assuring ourselves of the largest possible audience but producing nothing but cotton candy for the mind, or do we tackle difficult subjects as creatively as we can, knowing that we may lose much of the mass audience? The good news is that even those who are aiming low these days are failing, more often than not, to get good ratings. In those cases, then, the failure is twofold. At least Robert and my colleagues have tried something fresh and daring, and though they may have failed to attract the audiences they hoped for, they have succeeded in doing something memorable. On television that doesn't happen very often.

August 7 / New York

What a remarkable experience "live" theater is. Grace Anne and I took our children (minus Andrea, who's in Colorado for a friend's wedding) to see the current revival of *Cabaret*. I've seen the movie, know the show from its original production and was not expecting to be surprised or particularly moved. I was wrong. The staging of this production in the old Studio 54 works amazingly well. The set designer had the brilliant idea of turning the audience quite literally into a cabaret audience, by the simple expedient of removing theater seats and replacing them with tables, café chairs and small lamps on each table. The set design is remarkably simple but creative, and the final scene, in which the master of ceremonies reappears one last time, following the Nazi takeover of Germany, is brilliantly staged. The orchestra is arrayed, throughout the production, on a stage above the main stage, framed by a rectangle of lights, slightly askew. At times that second stage is obscured by a garish curtain, as it is in the penultimate scene. You hear the music of the orchestra, loud and jarring, but when the curtain opens the places are all empty. The compère appears on the ground-level stage, wearing the same black leather coat he has worn on previous occasions, but as he appears, the brick, rear wall of the theater itself is revealed, bathed in a harsh, white light. The members of the orchestra, several of whom are also dancers, are seen standing, like so many broken dolls, in a spare, concentration camp–like setting. The compère drops his black coat and is, himself, wearing the striped pajamas of the concentration camp inmate, emblazoned with a yellow star of David and the pink triangle, used to label homosexuals. The impact is shattering.

Still, I find myself walking away from the production wondering whether the extremes of total permissiveness, represented at one end by the Berlin cabaret culture of the 1920s and early thirties, and at the other by the brutal, totalitarian, fascist state, are, at least by implication, meant to be the only alternatives available to us.

It's a great production, but that's a false choice.

August 8 / En route from New York to Washington

We are at LaGuardia Airport early, which is to say, we're booked on a 2:30 p.m. shuttle but are at the terminal in plenty of time to make the 2 o'clock flight. The clerk is decent enough to tell us that that plane is having mechanical problems and that it will be faster for us to make our way over to the Marine Terminal to catch Delta's 2:30. We drag the bags out to the curb to wait for the transit bus that will take us from one terminal to another, and while Grace Anne is good about it, I know she hates flying so much that this will simply increase the tension for her.

I'm not sure it can be taught (or learned), but I'm coming to believe that there is a peculiar mind-set that can be helpful in coming to terms with the process of being flung around the globe in this day and age. Call it the Zen of traveling. It requires an ability to put one's mind in neutral, to flow from ticket counter to boarding gate in a state of detachment. I certainly don't always follow my own advice in this regard (see my earlier musings on United Express overbooking its flights to Florida), but the fact is that most airline personnel have either become inured to irate passengers or they have learned not to react in kind. In any event, it's my experience that unemotional hovering ("I know, you told me it might be another two to three hours before you'd have any further word, but I just wanted to be sure you could find me. . . .") usually accomplishes more than thunder and lightning. If you can cultivate the frame of mind that you will, eventually, get where you're going, and that this is, in any event, a wasted day, it will cut the stress. The point is this: You are in the hands of others who control your fate. Ticket clerks can be helpful or they can find any number of reasons not to put you on the flight you want. Remember: Flight crews have your life in their hands, and (a) nothing you suggest to them is likely to make a difficult flight easier, and (b) if you go down, they go down. Read a book. Take a nap.

August 10 / Washington

I've decided to go for laser eye surgery. I now need glasses for both distance and close up and find myself squinting just to read the Tele-PrompTer, on which the print is very large. The ophthalmologist holds out a vision (a little ophthalmologist pun, there) of no glasses needed for driving or even for working on this computer. I will still need reading glasses, but at half the strength I now use. There is, I guess, in most of us a certain cringe factor involved in having anybody slicing and dicing on our eyes, but I'm persuaded that it's about as safe as any such procedure can be. If the nine-page legal release form doesn't cause me to change my mind, Friday's the day.

August 11 / Washington

We were here late again last night to cover the rampage of another maniac. This time it is a thirty-seven-year-old with connections to a white supremacist group. He walked into a Jewish community center on the outskirts of Los Angeles and opened fire with a 9mm. Five people were injured, four of them children—a sixteen-year-old, two six-year-olds and a five-year-old. The shooter sprayed the inside of the lobby with thirty bullets. Obviously, it could have been much worse than it was, but that's scant consolation to the families of those young-sters, or to the sixty-five-year-old receptionist, who was also hit.

We struggle again to find meaning in chaos. What's the angle? Hate crime? Gun control? Mental illness? (The shooter has apparently spent time in a mental institution.) Today, there are a thousand barn doors slamming shut across the country. Jewish schools and commu-nity centers are under special watch by police. Questions are being raised about why this particular man was released from a mental insti-tution. Since his name was carried on a number of "watch" lists main-tained by groups that track hate crimes, why was he able to obtain the weapons and ammunition he used and those found in two vehicles he abandoned yesterday?

In reality, these are questions asked and answered for virtually no other reason than that the asking and answering seem to sooth us. Unfortunately, each of these cases carries the seeds of constitutional and civil rights issues that are far more difficult to resolve than any of these individual cases may suggest. Should the actions of some racist maniac determine whether millions of hunters should be allowed to carry rifles? Shall we, in our zeal to avoid violence at the hands of a few seriously disturbed people, inhibit the freedom of millions of disturbed but harmless people? In the wake of each such incident, however, the various lobbying groups spring into action, fearful they may lose an opportunity to make converts.

August 12 / Potomac

It's 11 p.m. I have to get up around 5:30 in the morning in order to be at the laser center before 7. If all goes well, I'll be out again by 8 and a skillful doctor will have turned the clock back ten or even fifteen years, at least in terms of my vision.

This is discretionary surgery. It would be entirely possible simply to go on strengthening the lenses in my glasses. This is not, I can hon-estly say, a matter of vanity, either. It is, quite simply, a matter of conve-nience and quality of life. I strain now to read the TelePrompTer. I have to wear glasses in order to drive and glasses in order to read. I played tennis the other day and found that I was having a hard time focusing on the ball as it was coming across the net. None of this is a great hardship, but I believe that the relatively tiny risk factor involved (anytime someone is playing around your eyes with a laser there's always the possibility that something could go wrong) is worth the benefits of a successful procedure.

August 13 / Potomac

What is, to me, most significant about this entry is the manner in which it is being made; that is, without glasses. My vision is far from perfect. Dr. Melanie Buttros (the surgery seems to have gone well, so she's entitled to full credit) warned me that for the first few days after the procedure I would be seeing the world through a thin haze of Vaseline. The amazing reality, though, is that I can read this computer screen without benefit of any enhancement. The procedure was essentially painless and very quick—less than half an hour for both eyes. The preoperative paperwork, however, is not for the faint of heart: eight or nine pages of closely printed paragraphs enumerating the many disastrous things that probably won't but definitely *could* go wrong. The fact that the Food and Drug Administration has not yet given its blessing to the procedure must also be acknowledged. Each separate paragraph, in fact, must be initialed; *and* (on the off chance you're contemplating a lawsuit anyway) at the end of the document you are required to copy a few thoughtful sentences, in your own handwriting, which are craftily designed to seal your doom in any courtroom:

Ladies and gentlemen of the jury. I direct your attention to exhibit 23c. Here, in the plaintiff's own hand, is his acknowledgment that he knew full well the risks that he was taking. You will have to ask him what it is that causes him to engage in such blatant risk-taking behavior.

The procedure is not cheap and we'll see how long the benefits last, but in these first postoperative hours, I'm thrilled.

August 14 / Potomac

The news from overseas is not good. The Russian military is fighting Islamic militants in Dagestan who, in turn, are being supported by

Chechen commandos. The new Russian prime minister, Vladimir Putin, is threatening air strikes against Chechnya. The Russian military did not fare well in its first war with Chechnya; indeed, for all intents and purposes, Chechnya is an independent republic. I'm not sure what makes Putin think conditions have improved for his army.

Jiang Zemin, the president of China, is threatening military action against Taiwan, where President Lee Tung-hui's recent suggestion that Taiwan and China engage in "state to state" talks has shattered the happy fiction that there is only "one China." What's happening on that front could actually involve the U.S. 7th fleet. If China does launch any sort of attack against Taiwan, the United States has long been committed to come to Taiwan's defense.

Meanwhile, in Kosovo, the KFOR troops from the United States, England, France, Germany, Italy and Russia seem already to be wearing out their welcome among Kosovar Albanians. That's not surprising in the case of the Russian troops; they were always perceived as sympathetic to the Serbs. But now isolated cases of violence against the French, the Americans and the British are increasing. They, too, in their efforts to protect the few Serbs who remain in Kosovo, are now seen as pro-Serbian. The United Nations, meanwhile, has been excruciatingly slow about getting its own police force on the ground. So, naturally enough, elements of the KLA and Albanian thugs who are interested only in seizing power and making money have stepped into the vacuum. It is likely to get much worse.

August 15 / Potomac

My family probably started going to the Montgomery County Fair in Gaithersburg, Maryland, about twenty-five years ago. We used to make an afternoon and evening of it, eating dinner at one of the events sponsored by a local church. It's only about a fifteen-minute drive from where we live, but it is truly another world from the cluster mansions that have sprung up all over Potomac. These looming monuments to wretched excess repeatedly demonstrate that money and good taste do not necessarily go hand in hand. In order to build the huge mansions that sprawl across Potomac's mostly two-acre zoning, their owners have had to eliminate most of the trees and shrubbery that marked

Potomac as a largely rural area when we first moved out here nearly thirty years ago. What were once rolling meadows have been bulldozed to produce what I refer to as "helicopter pads," on which the houses themselves are erected to attract as much attention as possible. It makes it easy to forget that Montgomery County is still predominantly agricultural.

We stopped going to the county fair when the kids went off to college and moved away from home, but today Andrea, our oldest, and her boyfriend and I decided to spend the afternoon there. The fair has not changed at all. The livestock exhibits, the various harness competitions, the pig races are all as I remember them. There was a wonderful moment when the fellow running the pig races asked for a moment of silence to pay tribute to a friend of his who had died two weeks ago. This, it turned out, was the man who had brought pig racing to the Montgomery County Fair. My first reaction was a bit of a snicker, but on reflection, he did a helluva lot more for the aesthetics of the county than the contractors and architects who dumped all those monster houses on the landscape.

August 16 / Potomac

In Kansas the other day there was a court ruling that, in effect, precludes the teaching of evolutionary theory in high school. The ruling does not technically do so; it merely prohibits the inclusion of any questions on evolution in any statewide tests. The impact, however, will be the same as if the court had ordered an outright prohibition. I suspect few, if any, teachers will want to devote precious time to teaching something that is rejected by many of the families of their students and by many of the churches which these families attend, when that will not help students on their exams.

In an outlying community of Boston today a number of camp counselors were dismissed because they had invoked God's blessing on their day's session. The camp's name includes the words *Bible Study*. The locus of the camp is on the grounds of a church. The counselors, however, are paid, in part, with federal funds; therefore, God is persona non grata there.

These are two examples of the idiocy that informs our national dialogue on the subjects of religion and science.

August 17 / Washington

I always believed that television would move the world in the direction of greater understanding and compassion, if only because it has the capacity to bring distant places, people and their problems into our homes. How could we not be moved by scenes of distant suffering when they are unfolding right before our eyes? In fact, there are some among us who redeem the apathy of most by responding with care and charity. Most among us, though, react simply by switching channels to less troubling images. And the networks have learned that.

Today, for example, there was an earthquake in Izmit, Turkey. The shock waves were felt 160 miles away in Ankara. There was significant damage in the huge and ancient city of Istanbul, with its population of ten million people. As of this writing, Turkish officials already say that more than two thousand people have died in the quake. There is every reason to believe that the number will spiral much higher. Hundreds of thousands, if not more, are homeless. It is a human tragedy of enormous proportions. Our evening news program, of course, led with the story. We will be going live tonight on *Nightline*. But there will be no specials, the magazine programs will not scramble to redo their broadcasts. Neither Princess Di nor JFK Jr. was among the dead or injured, so I suppose the two thousand or more dead Turks are of insufficient interest to warrant any kind of live coverage during the normal broadcast day.

Once upon a time, when we in television believed there might be even scant interest in a story of consequence, we felt an obligation to make a statement, to say, "This is important and you should care." Most of the time, in fact, when we did our jobs well, we were able to stimulate public interest. The twenty-four-hour cable news networks have made it easier for us to duck our responsibility. Since we know they will cover these stories, we feel less pressure to do so ourselves. It's a mistake, even from a business point of view. There is little enough to distinguish the three commercial television networks from the cacophony of new media voices. The traditional news divisions, however, with their familiar teams of anchors and correspondents, are among the few remaining "brands" that cannot easily be duplicated. Instead of accentuating the difference between ourselves and the media newcomers, too much network news programming emulates them.

August 18 / Washington

Maintaining privacy these days is not easy. If my home telephone number were available through the phone book or the information operator, we would be inundated by calls from people who have story ideas or other less benign suggestions for me. For years, therefore, we've had an unlisted number. We pay a monthly fee for this privilege. It surprised me the other day, though, when I called my old friend and college roommate Ray Foster, to hear him answer his phone with "Yo, Teddy, nice to hear from you." "How'd you know it was me?" I asked. "We have Caller ID," he said. So this morning I embarked on a search for a sentient human being at my telephone company, AT&T, to learn about Caller ID.

It is 9:40 a.m. "We apologize for the continued delay; however, all of our representatives are still busy. Please stay on the line and the next available representative will be with you as soon as possible." It sounds like the second or third in a sequence of recorded messages. It is the first and I hear it often enough that I have time to check my spelling. There is some bland, mind-numbing piano music in the background.

After ten minutes, I break through the first gate and into the world of options: "If you are looking for . . . press 1. If you are looking for . . . press 2." Apparently no one has ever called to inquire about revealing unlisted numbers on Caller ID. I press one of the other keys and am rewarded by a pleasant living lady who tells me that this is a matter for my local telephone company. I live in Maryland, I tell her. That would be Bell Atlantic South, she tells me, giving me the number, and kindly offering to connect me.

Of course I then hear another recording: "Welcome to Bell Atlantic. . . ." The thrust of this message is that I shouldn't bother. They're totally overloaded. "We may [note that there are no promises here] be able to help you better if you call later in the day." Not to be deterred, I try the number the nice lady at AT&T gave me. "Due to the heavy volume of calls," this message begins, "the expected delay is three minutes." Not a problem, I'm a mere fourteen minutes into this exercise. Indeed, within the promised three minutes there is another living human; unfortunately, she informs me that I have reached Bell Atlantic Boston. She gives me another number in my region and also offers to "pass me over." She does so.

"Thank you for calling Bell Atlantic," I now hear. "Due to the unusually heavy volume of calls . . . call back later."

No, dammit, I am going to call now!

I am rewarded with a recording that once again thanks me for calling Bell Atlantic, and once again I am advised that anybody who could help me is busy helping somebody else. I am asked to stay on the line.

A mere twenty-three minutes after beginning my quest, I am in the care of a male operator who has an immediate answer. All we have to do is punch in *67 before each and every call and even those with Caller ID will not become privy to our telephone number.

I begin to complain about the idiocy of a system that charges me for maintaining my privacy in the first place, and then requires of me, my family and anyone who may place a telephone call from my home, that we all remember to preface our calls with *67 in order to guarantee that privacy. And then I realize that this nice man has no more power over the system than I do. I thank him for his time and wonder whether there is a fee for the *67 service.

August 19 / Washington

George W. Bush is going through one of the initial phases of the hazing process that attends all presidential campaigns that seem to have some life in them. As the early odds-on favorite to win the Republican nomination, Bush was sailing serenely through the summer, carrying a campaign bankroll that must now be in excess of $40 million. It is enough money so that he can afford to turn down matching federal funds, and, as long as he does not accept those funds, there are no limits as to the amount or timing of what he can spend in promoting his own candidacy.

Bush and his advisors knew that he would be hit, at one time or another, by questions having to do with his reputation as a young man. He was known as something of a rake, a party animal. He defanged most questions relating to that behavior by acknowledging that he used to drink too much, but, he insisted, from his fortieth birthday on, alcohol has not been an issue in his life. As to the question of womanizing, Bush has responded by saying that he has been faithful to his wife.

For some reason, though, he will not directly address questions having to do with the use of cocaine. He has drawn a line around that particular subcategory of misbehavior, labeling it a rumor (which is all it is at the moment) and part of the "Washington game of playing 'gotcha.'" By refusing to deny the use of cocaine, he has ensured that he will be asked about it almost every day, sometimes more than once. The noose keeps getting a little tighter on the issue. Over the course of the past two or three days he has been asked about the questionnaire that would-be White House staffers are expected to fill out. At first he was asked whether he would be able to affirm (as potential staffers are expected to) that he has not used illegal drugs at any time during the past seven years. He said that he would. What about while his father was president? he was asked. (That means before 1988.) Again, he said he would have been able to make the affirmation. Today, some diligent researcher has uncovered the fact that the White House questionnaire actually inquires about illegal drug use as far back as the applicant's eighteenth birthday. Bush refuses to answer.

Should he?

On one level I have great sympathy for candidates who believe they should be judged on their positions, their careers and their present moral state. Let him who is without sin cast the first stone. . . . On the other hand, Governor Bush's tough stand on drugs and crime in his own state of Texas has certainly contributed to the fact that untold thousands of young men and women are in prison because they were found to be in possession of very small amounts of hard drugs. George W. doesn't owe me an answer on this question; but those inmates, who were imprisoned when they were in their twenties, do deserve an answer. They won't get a chance to question Bush. I may.

August 20 / Washington

I went for my one-week, postoperative eye exam today and my distance and intermediate vision is just about 20/20; the close-up reading vision has slipped to 20/40. I'll probably have to get slightly stronger drugstore magnifying glasses. All of this is as advertised. I was given a choice: Was I more concerned about being able to read without glasses or was I more concerned about being able to do everything else without glasses? I opted for everything else. I relish the freedom of being able to drive again without glasses; look forward to being able to play tennis this weekend and to see the ball coming at me from the other side of the net. My nonreading life requires no further magnification and I am grateful.

August 21 / St. Mary's County

The *Enterprise* is the newspaper of record down here, and I've been leafing through the obituaries. I read them not because I expect to find a familiar name or face but because I have always found it a humbling experience to realize how little our lives amount to in the eyes of disinterested others. The writers of obituaries are, almost by definition, disinterested. The job is not held in particularly high regard at most newspapers (although obit writers at the *New York Times* have a certain cachet, I suppose) and is usually reserved for very young and inexperienced reporters or those who are, effectively, washed up.

The obits in the *Enterprise* seem to follow a pattern: name, age, nickname (if any), place of death, place of birth, blood and marital relationships. Most of the rest of the obit is reserved for the social details surrounding the disposal of the dear departed: "Friends may call at the Mattingly-Gardiner Funeral Home. . . . Pallbearers will be . . . Memorial contributions may be made to . . ."

What is mysteriously absent from each and every obituary in the edition I'm reading is anything that gives even a clue as to how the dearly beloved left this vale of tears. One of the men who passed on, for example, was only thirty-nine. Not a clue as to how or why he died.

Saddest of all, though, is the absence of anything about who these people were. References to their lives are sparse in the extreme: ". . . a lifelong resident of St. Mary's County. He served in the U.S. Navy during World War II. From 1945 to 1986 he was a carpenter for the Public Works Department at Patuxent River Naval Air Station." And that's one of the more descriptive biographies. The women who died are disposed of in a single biographical line: "Mrs. N. was a lifelong county resident." "Mrs. E. was a homemaker." Now, in the blood relationship segment we learn that Mrs. E. had five children of her own, thirteen grandchildren and thirteen great-grandchildren. Something must have happened. One of those survivors must have a memory or two about poor old Mrs. E.

I can see it now: "Edward James Koppel: He was away from home a lot."

August 22 / St. Mary's County

We may prove to be altogether too successful in our current enthusiasm for blaming the media for everything from discouraging promising political candidates to the spread of toe fungus. It's a tempting sport and, to the best of my knowledge, mostly victimless, but we had best be careful. There is no denying that we reporters frequently present ourselves as irresistible targets, but the press continues to be an essential court of last resort, and those who undermine the public's tolerance and support for that function do so at their own peril.

Several newspapers have run lengthy articles these last few days reporting the claims of workers at the Paducah Gaseous Diffusion Plant in Kentucky and its sister plant at Oak Ridge, Tennessee. The workers say they were required to work under conditions that exposed them to dangerous levels of radiation. This, apparently, has been the case for many years and is only now coming to light because the bones of a long-dead uranium worker have been exhumed and examined. It appears that workers may have been exposed to levels of radiation dozens of times above federal limits. The fact that these plants are owned and operated by the U.S. government and that they were, and continue to be, engaged in matters of high security and of critical importance to the national interest simply underscores how essential it can be to have an institution such as the press that is more or less free of government intervention.

When the press raises questions about issues that bring national security into conflict with the fundamental rights of an individual to be safe in his workplace, the press may be criticized for jeopardizing the national interest. When the press raises questions that bring a business operation's free enterprise rights to make a profit into similar conflict with a worker's rights, the press may be criticized for failing to appreciate the requirements of capitalism. The miraculous paradox of the American systems of government and free enterprise is that each continues to require a vigilant and free press to act as watchdog in order to ensure the necessary survival of both. And while I worry sometimes that denunciations of the press and the media are so widespread and vigorous that they could undermine the process, I recognize that the paradox extends to us. To keep any part of the democratic system healthy, it must be subject to inspection and criticism. The media are oftentimes the mechanisms for that. We must, however, accept the fact that they will, on occasion, be its targets.

August 23 / Potomac

It's a preseason game, so the outcome is essentially meaningless, but it's Denver (albeit without John Elway) and Green Bay (with Brett Favre) and it's Monday Night Football. The inescapable conclusion is that summer is almost over and serious matters are about to be undertaken again.

No sooner were those words written than Brett Favre fell backward on the AstroTurf and caught himself on his right hand. He left the field in obvious pain, but it's too early to know whether the injury is serious.

Coaches like the momentum that a series of preseason games gives their team. They might prefer to shield their stars and veterans from preseason injuries but even those players need the playing time that these games afford. It does sometimes have the aura of being less than completely serious, but even in the slightly artificial atmosphere of preseason games, the injuries are for real.

August 24 / Washington

The surprise movie hit of the summer is a film called *The Blair Witch Project*. The premise is charmingly simple. Three college students embark on making a film documentary. Their focus is a rural Maryland community in which, legend has it, a witch has caused the deaths of several people. The making of the documentary itself is chronicled by one of the trio using a hi-8 video camera. The film that we are watching is actually made up of intercut segments of the "documentary" and the video. Both, we are led to believe, were found after the disappearance of the three young people.

The Blair Witch Project was made for about $30,000. It has now grossed in excess of $100 million. It's well done, and my hat's off to the young filmmakers who produced it. The nature of the film, however, in which long segments of jerky camera movement are included to cover the panicked flight of the college students, or segments in which they are disoriented but still shooting, can easily induce a form of motion sickness.

I rejoice, with the filmmakers, in their success, but it is another example of the "when pigs fly" phenomenon: It is such a marvel that a group of young filmmakers with neither studio nor big-business backing beat the odds that it would be uncharitable to critique the technique.

One interesting footnote: The filmmakers did a brilliant job of building prerelease interest in their work by creating a *Blair Witch Project* website on the Internet. Where major studios would have spent tens of millions of dollars promoting a big movie, these young people accomplished the same end at almost no expense.

August 25 / Washington

Perhaps our children are now of an age at which the question of birthdays should become a private matter. In any event, today is our youngest daughter's birthday and I'm filled (as I usually am on these occasions) with nostalgia.

There is apparently nothing that we can do, as we grow older, that prevents us from becoming the clichés we found so amusing in our elders. I remember the day of Tara's birth "as though it were yesterday." I still have a difficult time thinking of her and the friends she grew up with as adults. My problem, not theirs.

The other day we were having a little farewell party for one of our interns, a young man who had done particularly well. He spoke warmly of how he had come to look upon the *Nightline* staff as "family," and I (thinking to make a joke of the reputation of *Nightline*'s staff at ABC News of being almost cultlike in our devotion to one another) offered him a paper cup full of what I said was Kool-Aid.

He looked at me blankly and then I realized that, of course, the "Jim Jones mass suicide in Guyana" story had happened long before he was born. He had no way of knowing that several hundred members of that particular cult had committed suicide by drinking Kool-Aid laced with cyanide.

He came up to me later and told me that he was the first *Nightline* intern to be born after the program began in March 1980. He probably meant that to be reassuring.

August 26 / Washington

"Wrestling" has become one of the great growth industries of the 1990s. I put the word in quotation marks to distinguish "wrestling" from the Greco-Roman style of wrestling that is still practiced in colleges around the country, throughout the world and in the Olympic Games. "Wrestling" has had its place in the American culture since the early days of television. It's cheap to put on the air and has always attracted some of the least likely fans, including, some forty years ago, my mother. That Alice Koppel, trained in classical music, cultural worlds away from the phony theatrics and violence of professional "wrestling," so enjoyed watching it on TV never failed to amaze me. I remember once taking her to St. Nicholas Arena, then on Sixty-sixth Street in Manhattan, so that she could see her particular favorite, "Killer" Kowalski, at work. I think she was more astonished by the antics of the audience (an unruly lot) than by those of the wrestlers themselves.

But those were relatively simple days. "Wrestling" today is huge. The WWF, the World Wrestling Federation, may not quite rival the National Football League or Major League Baseball, but it's getting close.

Tomorrow night we will focus, however, on a variation, perhaps more accurately described as a mutant, of professional "wrestling." It calls itself "extreme wrestling," and puts great emphasis on producing generous amounts of blood for its fans. What is particularly unsettling about this offshoot, however, is that, despite ratcheting up the level of violence, it purports to be for family consumption; and, indeed, parents are bringing their five-, six- and seven-year-olds in droves to watch the combatants hit each other with everything from rolling pins to baseball bats wrapped in barbed wire. It's all incredibly hokey and, within the parameters of trying to produce the requisite amounts of blood, the participants are clearly trying not to hurt each other more than necessary. Still, the question is to what degree the children are capable of drawing that subtle distinction.

Punch and Judy were violent, but at least they were puppets and there was no blood.

August 27 / Washington

Some of the "brass" came down from New York today to meet with the staff and talk about the impact of the new technologies. There are a lot of interesting ideas floating around and, before too many more years have passed, we will no doubt be "interacting" like crazy with our audiences. Certainly the technical capabilities exist, and there is lots of eager talk about giving our viewers "toolbars" and "options" and "access"; some of that may even appeal to our audience. Still, the transition is likely to take many years and the development of secondary or tertiary ideas before new technologies take off.

The "horseless carriage" needed gas stations all over the landscape before automobile travel could be viable. And even then it was not until the mid-1950s, when President Eisenhower ordered the development of the interstate highway system, that cars began to become the indispensable tools they are today.

In such matters I tend to be conservative. Network news organizations are unique enough that they are worth conserving. My hunch is that before too long CBS News will exist only as a shell organization housing its magazine programs, *60 Minutes* and *48 Hours*. NBC News long ago went down-market and in the direction of tabloid. ABC News still has the capacity to be a world-class news organization with a global reach, but I'm not sure the corporate will or money is there to make that happen. It's a shame because it's the one thing we can still do best. CNN may try it, but I think we could actually achieve it.

August 28 / St. Mary's County

We are hosting some of my French cousins. Until a few years ago, I was unaware of their existence. One of them heard about me through another cousin who had read about *Nightline* and me in the German magazine *Der Spiegel*. He wrote to me care of ABC News in Washington. I actually get quite a few letters from people who believe we may be related, but that hardly ever is the case. This letter, though, written in broken English, referenced a number of names from earlier generations, names that seemed familiar. Our grandfathers, it turns out, were brothers. This particular branch of our German/Jewish family (that is to say, my cousins' father) fled Germany in 1939 and settled briefly in Denmark. When the Germans headed in that direction, he fled to France. He was a farmer, and he took refuge with a French farm family, the head of which was also a Lutheran minister. This minister had a daughter. The daughter and my cousins' father fell in love and married. And so it is that I now have cousins by the names of Christophe and Jean-Baptiste. They are not Jewish, but they have gone to great lengths to track down all of their Jewish relatives, myself included.

Very little of my family is left, and I rejoice in these unexpected additions.

August 29 / Potomac

Sometimes when I am driving home to Potomac from southern Maryland on a Sunday evening, I tune in to listen to one of Washington's legendary radio broadcasters, Ed Walker, who hosts a collection of old radio broadcasts from the thirties, forties and fifties. It's a wonderful way to kill a couple of hours of driving. But the truth of the matter is that most of those old broadcasts were pretty mediocre. Some of them, like the Abbott and Costello program, were just dreadful.

That's not a bad thing to recall. Abbott and Costello have gone down in entertainment history for a couple of classic numbers and for the slapstick humor they brought to films, but their radio show was so bad that nothing like it could possibly survive on the air today.

What is worth remembering, before we drown in nostalgia, is that broadcasting, in particular, has expanded so much (in terms of overall hours of available material) that we often lose sight of how much quality material is being produced these days. By the time you include the many new cable channels, public broadcasting and what is available on direct satellite television, there is (in addition to all the trash) also much more excellent material available to the viewer than ever before. It is true that one has to search for it. But along with what is best on ABC, NBC and CBS, there are treasures to be found on PBS, HBO, A&E, Discovery, ESPN, Nickelodeon, the Disney Channel, the History Channel and so many more outlets that did not exist thirty years ago.

August 30 / Potomac

Do the great corporations that control our destinies have any idea how infuriating and idiotic some of their systems are? Tim, the technician from Bell Atlantic, is here installing our new Caller ID system. Grace Anne and I have had nightmares wondering how wires would be snaked from the control panel, which is downstairs in the basement, up to her office. Not a problem. Tim finds enough prefed wires in the office to service an entire communications network. He speaks the words that gladden every homeowner's heart: "This'll only take a few minutes."

Then I ask him about the actual Caller ID unit, the little box that will permit us to know who is trying to reach us. "Oh," he said. "I don't carry those. They're supposed to send you those when you order the service." I ask Tim if he can get through to the sales department of Bell Atlantic more quickly than I can, and, indeed, he gets through in a couple of minutes. The nice saleslady there tells me that until August 13 they would have provided such a unit for free, but that since I ordered our Caller ID unit on August 20, we'll be charged. I am perfectly content to be charged. I never harbored any illusions that I would get anything from Bell Atlantic for free. But wouldn't it have made sense for someone to tell me, at the time that I was ordering Caller ID, that the unit doesn't come with the service? After all, the service without the unit is roughly the equivalent of a new car without tires. The sales lady is apologetic, acknowledges that I should have been advised that the service comes without the unit. She asks if I can wait for a moment. When she returns, she says that she can send me a unit but only a single-number unit (we have ordered the service for both of our telephone numbers); otherwise I will have to call "TeleProducts of Bell Atlantic." This process began at 10:30 a.m. By 12:30 I am, on paper at least, the proud owner of a "two-number Caller ID unit."

August 31 / Washington

There can be an important nexus between commercial television as we know it today and the Internet. I was reminded of that once again today when we aired a program on one of the biggest credit card companies in the country and complaints that it has been imposing late fees on customers who paid their bills on time, and changing the interest rates on customers who signed up for what they believed to be "fixed" rates.

The company representative who appeared on the program did not much help her cause when she tried to define "fixed" for me. The legalistic gobbledygook simply made the point that outraged consumers had made in our setup piece. No ordinary human being is going to be able to figure out all that nonsense in the fine print. The late fees, the company representative insisted, were imposed by an independent contractor in Phoenix who worked on behalf of the credit card company. That did not help explain all the late fees charged to people on our program, whose bills came from Louisville, Kentucky. In any event, we are now encouraging consumers who have experienced similar problems to post them on a bulletin board on *Nightline*'s website.

A consumer specialist who appeared on the program insisted that the banking and credit card industries make so many and such large campaign contributions that there is no reason to expect remedial legislation out of Congress. But the reach of the Internet, married to the impact of network television, may still be able to achieve something. We will see.

A postscript to the sentiment I expressed on the occasion of Tara's birthday a few days back: She is smart, lovely and charming. And she has been working several years now for a company started and nursed into significant profitability by our terrific son-in-law, Larry. Our two oldest children went into my field of television journalism; our son has followed in his mother's footsteps as a lawyer and gives us great pride with his work for Legal Aid. It never occurred to either of us, I think, that Tara would be such a dynamic businesswoman. We tend to expect our children to be reflections of ourselves. When they (as we once did) assert their independence and separateness from who and what we are it always comes as a surprise. It shouldn't, but it does. Grandfather Erwin Koppel, a business dynamo in his day, is smiling somewhere.

September

A piece in the *New York Times* this past weekend and one on National Public Radio this morning on the subject of sports and our diminishing standards of ethical behavior were both very interesting. The broader piece was by Frank Deford, who frequently writes for *Sports Illustrated* and is a contributor to "Morning Edition." He began by citing pivotal moments in two enormously important games: The first was during the women's World Cup final. It had come down to a shootout between the U.S. team and the Chinese team. They had played to a 0–0 tie in regulation time and in overtime. On one of the Chinese penalty shots, the U.S. goalie, Briana Scurry, moved forward beyond the goal line and toward the shooter. That is against the rules, but it enabled her to block the shot. The referee did not call a violation and Scurry's "save" gave the U.S. team its margin of victory.

The other game occurred last December. The New York Jets were near the Buffalo goal line in a key National Football League game. On one play the quarterback of the Jets, Vinny Testaverde, was stopped just short of a first down, but, after the whistle was blown, ending the play, he jerked the ball forward for a first down and got away with it. "Bye-bye, Buffalo," Deford said. "Jets proceed to conference championship."

The story in the *Times* focused on President Clinton's propensity for awarding himself "mulligans" whenever he plays golf. A mulligan entails taking a second, third, or fourth shot, when the ball you've hit before has gone awry. It usually involves the permission of the other players, but the president, by all accounts, simply does it. What annoys golf purists about this practice is that Clinton records his score according to the best shot that he's made, appearing, thereby, to be a better player than he is. He is, in fact, an excellent golfer, but his behavior on the golf course is consistent with his lifestyle.

Deford's conclusion: "Where once we valued sportsmanship, now we prize what we have come to call gamesmanship."

And, indeed, you have only to spend an hour or so along the sidelines observing parents watching their children play soccer or football, and you cannot help but despair a little. The need to win (for most parents) is, at times, so overwhelming that the children must draw the conclusion that winning is their first obligation. That is also the only lesson they can draw from watching most professional athletes these days. The "trash-talking," the "preening" following any good play, the constant effort to gain an edge, whatever the cost, all these are examples that will leave their mark on our children.

September 2 / Washington

When fundamentally honorable people are caught in a lie, it tends to undermine their credibility as a whole. When ranting lunatics stumble across a truth, we tend to examine the remainder of their ravings with fresh and probably unwarranted respect.

For years now, the conspiracy theorists have insisted the FBI started the fires that destroyed the Branch Davidian compound in Waco, Texas. Some eighty people, including about twenty-five children, died in those fires. One of the charges has been that the FBI used what are called pyrotechnic tear gas grenades. These grenades not only emit tear gas, they can set fire to anything flammable in the immediate area. The FBI has denied that charge since 1993, as has the attorney general.

Those denials now turn out to be wrong. An infrared tape, shot from an FBI helicopter on the morning of the Waco inferno, picked up the sound of a conversation between two FBI agents, one requesting permission to use a pyrotechnic grenade, the other granting it. An internal memorandum, found in FBI files, makes reference in 1995 to the use of pyrotechnic tear gas grenades. The fact is that those grenades (two of them) were fired at a concrete bunker hours before the actual fire began to blaze at Waco. No one is suggesting that the grenades started the fire. But the credibility of the FBI and the Justice

Department is, relatively speaking, in shards today while the conspiracy theorists are rejoicing in their enhanced stature. When are Washington bureaucrats going to learn how much damage they do with their foolish cover-ups?

September 3 / Washington

I flew to New York for a couple of hours today to attend the memorial service for an old friend and colleague, Walter Porges. He was one of the quiet pillars of the network news establishment, unknown outside the industry but widely loved and respected within.

Occasions such as these bring together those who retired (or were forced out) years ago and those who have gone on to work at other networks or in other fields. It was, as someone said this morning, a gathering of the old guard. Many of these people held the fate and future of ABC News in their hands twenty or thirty years ago. As with any former colleagues, it is quickly apparent whether you had a genuine relationship with them, or merely a relationship dictated by the work environment. With those in the latter category, the conversation is forced and stilted. With the men and women who were and still are friends, these encounters at funerals reinforce the knowledge that we treat these friendships too cavalierly. Careers that seemed so vital and important in their prime have a much more trivial quality to them in retrospect. The friendships, which we tend to take for granted, loom much larger.

The massive turnout today (there must have been at least five hundred mourners) was a tribute not to a man's title or status, but to his quality.

September 4 / St. Mary's County

It is probably fair to say that almost every culture values age more than America does. Our fixation on the appearance of youth, though, is really getting creepy.

Character lines (can you believe that we once regarded the outward imprint of life's ups and downs in a positive light?) and the bags under people's eyes are being erased at an alarming rate. Breasts are being enhanced or diminished to whatever the fashionable ideal is supposed to be. Hair is being implanted and transplanted with reckless abandon.

Diets are pandemic, but for those who fail even the "infallible" weight reduction programs, there is liposuction. The older among us (which is to say those over fifty) are having so many hair grafts and face-lifts that I find myself casting quick glances at people's hands and necks to establish some sort of age reality check.

A well-known comedienne appearing on *The Larry King Show* the other evening had made it into her late forties or fifties without feeling any apparent need to resort to a face-lift. It used to be one of the more charming things about her. That is no longer the case. She now has had such radical plastic surgery that it looks as though she has trouble closing her eyes.

We have convinced ourselves that almost any outward appearance of age is either an insuperable hurdle in the daily competition of life or, even worse, an acknowledgment of impending death. There is no denying the existence of "ageism," that awkward term that is supposed to convey the prejudice of employers, in particular, toward anyone who seems older than forty. What troubles me is the embarrassing spectacle of millions of mature Americans cringing behind dye jobs and tummy tucks. We should be mining the wisdom of our older citizens and celebrating their accumulated experience rather than driving them into cosmetic plastic surgery.

And if it's the acknowledgment of impending death that they're trying to avoid, I don't think Death will be impressed.

September 6 / Potomac

Summer is over—not strictly, not literally, but it's over nevertheless. Even if the weather remains hot after Labor Day, it's still fall. The kids are back in school, the power brokers who took most of August off are back at work and the television commercials are beginning to focus on cold weather clothing again.

Mercifully, no one has started up yet with much millennium nonsense. I think it's being saved for November and December. Then you won't be able to turn around without someone reminding you that you're about to get your "last haircut of the millennium," and the like.

I am still somewhat amazed at how little public attention has been given to the Y2K problem. Again, I suppose, it's not the sort of thing that puts its clammy hands around our throats until the days are short and gloomy and cold. Then it will be appropriate to start worrying about brownouts and blackouts and temporary bank closings and whether or not it's safe to fly. For the moment, though, it's only Labor Day and the nation is largely preoccupied with getting back home from the beaches and mountains and making the practical adjustments autumn requires.

September 7 / Potomac

I am in the third stage of my new relationship with Bell Atlantic. During our last episode, Tim, the helpful Bell Atlantic technician, came to the house to install the wiring that would make it possible for us to have our own Caller ID. I had thought that he would also bring with him the boxes on which the caller identification is actually made, but that was just foolish optimism on my part. Those had to be ordered from TeleProducts of Bell Atlantic. My excitement when the boxes arrived a mere three days later soon gave way to disappointment, however. It turns out that the cords by which you connect the phone to the Caller ID box and the Caller ID box to the outlet in the wall are not compatible with AT&T's Merlin phone system. I probably should have brought that to Tim's attention, but it's not the sort of knowledge the average consumer brings to the table. Maybe Tim knows such things; if he does, he didn't mention it.

I have spent the better part of three hours today trying to find a human being at Bell Atlantic who can deal with this problem. However, the only people I reach advise me that this is a problem only TeleProducts of Bell Atlantic can handle. TeleProducts has a phone tree (". . . If you know the name of the party you're trying to reach, press 1. If you're trying to reach sales, press 2. . . ."). This particular phone tree does not offer a number for incompatible cord connections. I did reach one human being at TeleProducts (by pleading my case with another human being whom I reached at the other Bell Atlantic; he personally connected me), but she believed I wanted my money back. She offered to return it if I would return the Caller ID boxes. When I explained that, having paid for the wiring in my home,

I really wanted functioning Caller ID boxes, she was stumped. She did offer to connect me to someone at "customer services," which sounded promising. After listening to twenty minutes of Muzak, though, I gave up.

I know, I lack persistence. I did have other things to do today, but if I really cared about my Caller ID, I would have canceled everything else on my schedule. As Scarlett O'Hara said: "Tomorrow is another day."

September 8 / Washington

If I needed further evidence that today is merely yesterday's tomorrow, I needed only to pick up where I left off on my quest to get a functioning Caller ID system.

I am wise now to the self-sealing nature of TeleProducts of Bell Atlantic's phone tree. You can listen to its various prerecorded options; but, failing to find one that suits your need, there appears to be no way out (short of hanging up) and no indicated path to a living human being.

Suffice it to say that I eventually connected with someone at TeleProducts (but only through another friendly intermediary at Bell Atlantic), who confirmed for me that there is no way their product can be used with AT&T's Merlin system. He acknowledged that someone at Bell Atlantic sales, or Tim, the technician, should have advised me of this before they bored holes into the walls of my house and pulled wires through them. He admitted that one hand does not know what the other is doing. Finally, one young man at TeleProducts confided to me that I could reach him again by dialing into their phone tree and hitting oo. At that point I can connect to his extension, which he also gave me. I put the question to him this way: At which point up the Bell Atlantic pyramid would I be likely to find someone who can resolve my problem for me? Who, in other words, can either authorize a complete refund or make the technological adjustment that makes Merlin compatible with a Bell Atlantic product? He professed not to know. I asked him for the number of the president of Bell Atlantic. He gave it to me readily, willingly. A little too readily, as it turned out. It was simply another phone tree, in Philadelphia.

My wife finally suggested that I call the folks at Merlin Lucent

Technology. They recognized the problem immediately. There is, they told me, a general-purpose adapter, 267a, which can make the two pieces of equipment compatible. One little problem, though. It can only be installed on the main equipment box, which, in our house, is in the basement.

The good news is that we can have Caller ID. The bad news is that were we to avail ourselves of this option, we would have to run down to the basement every time we want to look at a caller's name and/or number.

September 9 / Washington

East Timor is, I fear, destined to become another of those places like Somalia, Haiti, Bosnia and Kosovo that features prominently on our national agenda for a few months, weeks or only days, and is then relegated to the "former crises" file. The United States has scrupulously (or, some might argue, unscrupulously) avoided putting too much pressure on the Indonesians to clean up their act in East Timor. Indonesia is far too important to U.S. national interests because of its position astride critical sea lanes, its importance as an oil producer, its being the world's largest Muslim country and its staunch anti-Communist position. (Let us not forget that in the 1960s President Sukarno ordered the slaughter of about a half million of his own people because of their Communist or left-wing sympathies.)

Eventually the United Nations will, I suppose, intervene in some fashion in East Timor. But the great powers, including Russia and the People's Republic of China, are far too concerned about international intervention against the suppression of independence movements (think only of Tibet and Chechnya) for there to be a lasting U.N. role in East Timor.

Let us at least hope that an end can be put to the systematic killings.

September 10 / Potomac

All Jewish holidays begin at sundown. This evening marks the beginning of the year 5760. I must confess that the older I become the more

I treasure the contemplative nature of the Jewish New Year celebration, which is marked by religious services in the evening and then again during the following day. Since I attend a Reform synagogue, only the first day of Rosh Hashanah is observed. Most Conservative, and all Orthodox, synagogues also observe a second day.

In any event, I've never felt particularly comfortable with the forced hilarity of our secular New Year's Eve celebrations, although I can remember how important they were to me when I was in my teens and early twenties. Having permission to stay up and out all night, finding a place where we could acquire and imbibe alcohol, all of that seems quaintly silly. These days, kids tend to stay out until all hours from their early- and mid-teens on. There is now a tragic relief among many parents when they discover that their teens are "only" consuming alcohol. I am anything but an observant Jew, in that I neither follow dietary restrictions nor keep the Sabbath, but these High Holy Days link me to my heritage. They are, in a sense, the only tangible cord that binds me to my past. I try to apply the ethical strictures of Judaism to my daily life, but many of those have been adopted or adapted by various branches of Christianity. My wife is Catholic, my closest colleague, Tom Bettag, is Catholic. Our ethical perceptions are largely interchangeable. It is only by holding or attending a seder at Passover or attending the High Holy Day services that I deliberately and visibly reassert my place in the Jewish community. They have always been important to me, but I treasure them more now than ever before.

September 11 / Potomac

I stopped at the Giant supermarket on the way back from services to pick up a couple of items. One of the men at the checkout counter is someone I've known for several years. I asked him how he was doing and he said he guessed he could hold out until 1 p.m. tomorrow. That momentarily confused me. I thought he might be talking about some marathon overtime that he was working. Instead, it was a reference to the opening of the National Football League season. In particular, he was referring to the opening game of the Redskins' season in nearby Washington against the Dallas Cowboys.

The new owner of the Redskins, who is, I believe, only about thirty-four, has let it be known that he expects the team to win. That is a thinly veiled way of saying that heads will roll if the team loses. I wonder if there is any owner who hasn't let it be known that victory is expected?

The point, though, is that there are tens of thousands of Washingtonians whose reason for living seems largely dependent on the fortunes of the Redskins.

Grace Anne and I used to be invited on a fairly regular basis to attend the Skins' home games. Jack Kent Cooke, the owner then, got so depressed when the team lost and expected all of his guests to be so jubilant when the team won that Grace Anne and I felt uncomfortable. So we stopped going to the games. I imagine that my checkout friend at the Giant would have a hard time fathoming that.

September 12 / Potomac

Pat Buchanan is, apparently, on the verge of announcing his defection from the Republican Party and his intention to go after the nomination of Ross Perot's creation, the Reform Party. That will come as bitter news to George W. Bush. I suspect that Buchanan will siphon off some considerable support from the GOP's right wing, and that might be just enough to win the day for Al Gore or Bill Bradley.

Buchanan and I have had our problems. Four years ago he launched an angry public assault on me for being anti-Catholic. He cited as evidence of that a *Nightline* show about him in which I made reference to instances of anti-Semitism cropping up in the parochial school that Pat and his brothers attended. I also quoted an item from the *Washington Post* suggesting that Pat's father had been a fan of the late Father Coughlin, a virulent anti-Semite whose radio broadcasts in the late thirties and early forties were among the most popular of their time. Buchanan denounced me for slurring the good name of the nuns who had taught at his school, and denied categorically that his father had ever listened to Father Coughlin. It would have been extraordinary indeed if the elder Buchanan had not listened to Father Coughlin. There was no television in those days, so the most popular radio broadcasts of that time were even more ubiquitous than Laura

Schlessinger or Rush Limbaugh are today. Even so, my only source was the *Post*, so I apologized on the air the next night, conceding that the Buchanan family was better equipped than I to know what transpired in the Buchanan home. The public attacks on my "anti-Catholicism" continued for a few weeks, but got no traction. I am, after all, married to a Catholic, have four Catholic children and will happily put my record for religious and racial tolerance up against Buchanan's.

September 13 / Potomac

There is another hurricane building and headed toward the east coast of Florida. The worst hurricanes are given the designation of Category 5. This one, Floyd, almost falls into that classification. Its winds are blowing at 150 miles an hour and it's gusting at over 200 miles an hour. The hurricane is 250 miles across, surrounded by another huge band of tropical-force winds that makes the overall package more than 600 miles wide, which is to say that if it hits Florida (and that is its current course) it could blanket the entire state with killer winds and rains dropping two to three inches an hour. We've called a local contractor, who has done work for us before, and he has promised to put up the hurricane shutters for us. If this kind of a storm were to hit Captiva head-on, it would probably cut right through the island. The beach-front homes are a joy most of the time, but you can lose them in the blink of an eye.

On a totally different front there is another storm brewing. Indonesia's President B. J. Habibie has now given his permission for a U.N. peacekeeping force to move into East Timor. He is conceding, in effect, that he cannot control his own military there. He is truly between a rock and a hard place. If he doesn't let the United Nations in, he loses the loans he desperately needs from the International Monetary Fund. U.S. arms sales to Indonesia have already been suspended because of the atrocities committed by militia members, supported by the Indonesian military. On the other hand, bringing in foreign troops to subdue violence by members of his own armed forces may cost Habibie his presidency, and may lead to another military coup in Indonesia.

September 14 / Washington

Floyd is wending its way up the coast of Florida and drawing a bead on South Carolina. Somehow, naming a hurricane makes it seem less violent, but the dimensions of this storm almost immediately eliminate any sense of whimsy. Literally millions of people are evacuating low-lying areas along the coasts of Florida, Georgia and the Carolinas.

It is indeed an ill wind that blows no good. We are compiling a five-part series on bioterrorism, to be shown sometime in October. The premise of the series is a conclusion, reached at the highest levels of the federal government, that it's no longer a question of whether such an attack will be launched against the United States, simply a question of when. We are hypothesizing an anthrax attack, in which jars of the virus are broken on the rails of a major urban subway system. The trains would act much like plungers in a hypodermic, distributing the virus throughout the system of tunnels.

We have been searching for video of the kinds of mass exodus that would take place once the public found out about the anthrax. Today we found it.

This journal was purchased today by the publishing house of Alfred A. Knopf. I'm happy it has found a good home.

September 15 / Washington

Trying to predict the news rarely makes sense. Our assumption for most of this day and into this evening was that no story could possibly push Hurricane Floyd aside. It remains, after all, one of the biggest and most powerful storms in recent history; it is scheduled to make landfall along the North/South Carolina border at just about the time we go on the air, and it has already driven more than three million people out of their homes and in search of shelter.

And then, around nine o'clock this evening, the first bulletins start moving out of Fort Worth, Texas. Some maniac has entered a South Fort Worth Baptist church where a youth rally was in progress. He opened fire, killing at least seven people, among them three children; then, he took a seat in the back of the church and blew his brains out. A number of other people were also shot and a pipe bomb exploded. All in all, there are at least another eight people wounded, some of them critically.

It's not altogether clear whether this part of the story is true, but there seems to have been some connection between the youth rally—which was designed to focus students going back to school on appropriate values—and the shootings earlier this year in Littleton, Colorado.

What a tragic irony it would be.

September 16 / South Bend, Indiana

It's almost midnight. I've just come back to the "Inn" here at Notre Dame, after having a drink with Father Ted Hesburgh in his apartment at the top of the Hesburgh Library. It was good to see this eighty-two-year-old priest, more than twelve years retired from his post as president of Notre Dame, blind in one eye, but still as smart and vigorous as ever.

It has been a good day. I accepted an invitation to deliver the annual Red Smith memorial lecture here for two reasons: Red was a legendary sportswriter and columnist for the *New York Times* whose prose I greatly admired. Coming here also gave me the opportunity to bring my father-in-law, Eugene Patrick Dorney, to the college he loves best. He never attended university himself. He stuttered badly as a boy and his father determined that there was little point in wasting scarce money on a son who couldn't speak well. So Gene's younger brother, Dan, went to college. Gene (Pop, as we now call him) became a passionate Notre Dame "subway" alumnus, someone who adopted Notre Dame (as so many Irish Catholics did) as though they had gone there.

The undisputed high point of the day was attending the football team's practice session in their huge stadium. Pop got to talk to the head coach, Bob Davie, for about fifteen minutes. He met and talked to a young player from the Maryland area he had heard about. He watched practice and discussed last week's loss to Purdue with Davie, whom he now adores. Tomorrow we will attend the evening pep rally and on Saturday we'll watch Notre Dame demolish Michigan State. If there was any doubt in anyone's mind about the outcome of that game before today's practice session, there is none now.

My speech went well—a standing O. Here's what I said in summing up:

> What I do believe is that the community of professional journalists has a greater obligation than ever before to lead by example. Information on all the media is now so voluminous that it tends toward the chaotic. We can still serve a critical function bringing order to information.
>
> The new technologies are all geared toward speed. Speed has always been an important part of journalism, but it's not mandatory. Traditional journalism requires a sorting out of good information from bad, of the important from the trivial. That sort of commitment and expertise may be out of fashion, but the need for it is greater than ever before.
>
> There are at least two kinds of extreme ignorance. The first exists in a vacuum, where no information is available. The second exists in a world of informational anarchy, where so much information abounds that the mind doesn't know what to believe. That pretty much describes our world as we move into the third millennium. In such a world there is more of a need for good journalists than ever before.
>
> Should some of you choose to make your careers in journalism, I'd like to leave you with a few random thoughts to help you on your way. The technologies of delivering information have changed, but the fundamentals of honest reporting haven't. There's nothing new about deadlines; even quarterly journals have them. Although we now live in a world in which immediacy is valued so highly, never publish or broadcast a story before you're comfortable with its accuracy. Remember that some things seem important and other things are. It's easy to write about the first batch; try to reserve some of your energy for the second lot, too. Establish a set of guiding principles for yourselves—reasonable ones, this is not the priesthood—but stick to them. Emphasize honesty, fairness, decency. Don't

be afraid of questioning authority. Skepticism is all right, but try not to lapse into cynicism. Provide a voice to the powerless. Never lose your curiosity. You have this incredible license to talk to anyone, to go anywhere. Make it interesting.

Don't be afraid of losing your job. You'll find another one.

September 17 / South Bend

Pop is definitely surrounded here by kindred spirits. I confess that I have never been able to muster the sort of "school spirit" that is so much in abundance among some college loyalists, but here at Notre Dame it approaches unique (and to me, baffling) heights. It is, no doubt, generated by more than simply an appreciation for the long tradition of winning football teams. This is a great university and those who went to school here clearly value the entire experience. Still, the excessive attention to football becomes, at times, a caricature of itself. The handsome tile mosaic of Jesus, arms outstretched, that adorns one side of the Hesburgh Library and overlooks the football stadium is referred to as "touchdown Jesus." The huge and brooding statue of Moses, clutching the Ten Commandments and holding up one finger, to denote the singularity of the Almighty, is known on campus as "We're #1, Moses." The life-sized bronze of Father Gorman, onetime chaplain to the Irish Brigade of the Union army, holding up his right hand in benediction as he offers absolution before the Battle of Gettysburg, is known for all time among Notre Dame football fans as "fair catch Gorman." There is, in other words, here among the faithful, two very distinct cultures in operation: a real and devout Catholicism and a distinct subculture that acknowledges a near-religious devotion to the Fighting Irish football team. As Pop put it, when he was explaining his own attraction to Notre Dame football from earliest childhood on, "There was, in those days, very little for Irish Catholics to yell about."

As we come now to the eve of tomorrow's game with Michigan State, the campus is bursting with portly, silver-haired fans sporting their hats and caps adorned with shamrocks, wearing their infinite variety of sweatshirts of blue and gold. In some respects, it is much the same on most college campuses around the country, and yet the devotion here seems just a shade more fervent.

This evening we were invited to the home of the athletic director, Michael Wadsworth. He is a former Canadian ambassador to Ireland and I am sure he is very proud of that, but his association with the Fighting Irish and the fact that he once played for them seems just a shade more important to him. Among the invited guests this evening are Rocky Bleier, once captain of the football team here and later a legendary player for the Pittsburgh Steelers, and Ara Parseghian, one of the team's most successful coaches. On this campus, the truly great coaches, like Knute Rockne and Frank Leahey, are rewarded with life-sized bronzes.

Pop seemed equally awed by the living presence of Parseghian and the statuary presence of the departed. It's been a great weekend for him, and the game is yet to come.

September 18 / South Bend

The game is over. Michigan State triumphed, and Pop's new friend, Coach Davie, is going to be feeling the heat. These football games permit, indeed encourage, a certain degree of "ersatz" emotion; jubilation in victory, mournfulness in defeat. But a surprising number of the fans take it very seriously.

There is no question that a place like Notre Dame, though an excellent academic institution, depends for much of its alumni support on the achievements of its football team. That puts a huge amount of pressure on the coaches and players. There is, even now, a new scandal brewing here on campus. One of the tutors assigned to help a member of the team is believed to have written a paper that the player turned in as his own. That means the university itself is directly involved, which could lead to serious sanctions from the National Collegiate Athletic Association.

The highest level of college football in this country is not really played by a great many "scholar" athletes. The football team is predominantly African American. The percentage of African Americans among the student body in general is a mere 3.5 percent. There can be no question that the football players are being recruited, almost exclusively, to win games. They are treated like heroes and given every possible opportunity to achieve academic success, but without their football prowess not many would be admitted to Notre Dame in the first place.

This is a profound ethical dilemma on university campuses around the country. There's a direct relationship between victorious football and basketball teams on the one hand and alumni donations on the other. Postseason play and seasonal network contracts (all Notre Dame games, for example, are carried by NBC Sports) are hugely lucrative, and they do not come very often to universities that crack down hard on academically unqualified sports stars. Given the financial pressures on all but a few of the most generously endowed universities, it is not a problem that will go away soon.

September 19 / En route to Pittsburgh

A postscript to yesterday: Hearing that Muhammad Ali was watching the game from one of the boxes near our seats, I rounded up my son, Drew, Tom Bettag and his son Andy and wandered down the hall to pay a courtesy call. I thought that perhaps there would be a coterie of people around Ali but found him standing at the rear of the enclosed luxury box, alone and appearing somewhat bored. ("Are you a big Notre Dame fan?" I asked him a little later, and he held his forefinger and thumb about a centimeter apart to indicate just how big a fan he is.) He seemed genuinely pleased to see us, which I attribute at least in part to the boredom. The late, great sportscaster Howard Cosell first introduced us about fifteen years ago, and I remember being struck by how huge Ali's hands are, truly formidable weapons. Even now, somewhat stooped and much diminished, Ali is an impressive-looking man. His eyebrows are thatched with white, but the astonishing thing about Ali is still his eyes. It seems like a trivial word, but his eyes are "merry." Ali is amused by all the nonsense that surrounds him, which is, when you consider it, an extraordinarily useful defense against the corruption of self-importance.

I mentioned to Ali that I had seen him and his wife on *Good Morning America* the other day. She is frequently his "voice" these days. When Charlie Gibson asked how difficult it is for Ali (whose advanced Parkinson's disease causes severe trembling and makes it difficult for him to speak) to deal with his affliction, she spoke movingly of his faith. He believes, she said, that everything that happens in life is a test, that perhaps God had found him too talkative in his youth and that this is an opportunity for him to become more "pensive." I don't know whether Ali ever said that to his wife or whether he even thinks it. Others speak a lot in his behalf these days. I heard a sportscaster on NBC enthusing about how much of a Notre Dame fan the champ is. He certainly seemed to be suggesting a greater enthusiasm than the centimeter's worth Ali indicated to me. Anyway, I told Ali how moved I was by his wife's remarks, and what a great symbol of moral strength I thought he had become to his fellow countrymen. His voice tends to be just a whisper now, and I wasn't sure I heard him correctly the first or second time that he responded. I asked him to repeat it. The eyes were still twinkling, but I am sure I heard the same phrase three times: "Still just a nigger," he said.

The phrase is open to everyone's own interpretation. Unfortunately Ali has a hard time speaking for himself. My own interpretation of what he said, though, is as simple as it is sad. For all the awards and celebrations, for all the fawning and admiration, the truth is that even for Ali, who will probably be crowned "athlete of the century" before this year is out, his race has still been his defining reality in the context of living as a black man in America in our time.

September 20 / En route to London

Grace Anne and I are off to Ireland for a week and looking forward to a relaxing time. The trip has been organized by Disney chief Michael Eisner and his friend Barry Diller. It's to be a biking vacation. We've done one of these before and it is anything but "roughing it." You stay in fine hotels or inns and eat extremely well. During the day you bike anywhere from twenty-five to fifty miles, but there's always a van available to pick up laggards.

I'm looking forward to the opportunity of a longer, relaxed conversation with the man who owns, among the many other parts of the Disney empire, our news division. I say "our" news division, even though it's technically his, because after thirty-six years with ABC News I feel both possessive and protective. Eisner has his theme parks, his feature-length cartoons, the rest of the ABC network, ESPN and a couple of Hollywood studios. I truly believe that a network news division falls into a unique and very special category; we're not just another "budget" or "cost" center. But I'm increasingly nervous about the prevailing attitude at the network.

There seems to be no particular distinction drawn between the entertainment division and the news division when it comes to responding to the corporation's demand for budget cuts. To a certain extent we are reaping the whirlwind for years of profligate spending, but lately the corporation has been cutting into muscle. It makes no sense to me that thirty-five years ago ABC News was getting by on $5 million a year and had news bureaus all over the world. We were not expected to make money. In those days we did almost as much foreign news coverage as domestic. Now the world is infinitely more interdependent, news divisions have annual budgets of $700 million and deliver a profit of about $100 million a year, but news bureaus are being reduced and closed for "budgetary reasons." Paradoxically, perhaps, because I hold no executive position at ABC News, I am more free to speak bluntly about these matters than the people who run the news division. In any event, I am old enough and sufficiently well off that I have little to lose. When I was much younger and still had four children to put through college, I might have been a touch less blunt, but, in fact, when I was in my mid-thirties and the children had both high school and college ahead of them, I did quit when I found it impossible to get through to my then-boss, Roone Arledge. He and I eventually worked out our differences, but not before I stayed home for a couple of weeks, thereby making it clear that I was serious about resigning.

September 21 / Galway Bay, Ireland

We are staying at Gregans Castle Hotel in the Burren. It overlooks Galway Bay about four or five miles off, and it's quite lovely. Our driver, Tony, talked informatively and entertainingly for most of the way here from Shannon Airport. Some of the lower roads are flooded because of heavy rains and so the ride took nearly two hours. Normally, it takes one. Ireland, or at least this part of it, has a sleek and prosperous look about it these days. Seventy percent of the Irish, according to Tony, now own their own homes. He puts the average salary (I find this a little hard to believe) at about thirty thousand

pounds per annum, about $47,000. I have been able to find no inde-
pendent verification for this extraordinary claim. But new schools are
sprouting up everywhere and Irish children are growing into a well-
educated workforce. Ireland's entry into the European Union (E.U.)
and the subsidies it receives from the E.U. have made a huge difference. That, together with the fact that wages and operating costs here
in Ireland are still cheaper than in most of the rest of Europe, has
drawn large segments of the information industry here. Ireland is
becoming a modern and prosperous country. Still, modernity has its
limits. On the drive here, we passed a section of new highway under
construction. It had mysteriously stopped at an open field. Tony
explained that a lone tree standing in the middle of the field was the
cause of the holdup, and that, in fact, the road was being diverted. The
tree, it turns out, is a "fairie" tree. Cutting it down would bring bad
luck to the "woodsman" and his family, and no one has been found to
do the job.

It's good to know that old legends die hard, even in the information age.

September 22 / Galway Bay

Hiking through and biking around the rocky slopes that rise up from
the ocean, we have been guided through the burren (as barren as the
name suggests) by Michael Gibbons, a charming local archaeologist
and environmentalist. He put the passion of local farmers for their
land into stark relief by taking us to a rocky plateau overlooking the
Atlantic—giant slabs of limestone with deep crevices between them.
Then he pointed up into the burren where, occasionally, you can see a
green field.

"Do you know how those fields were made?" he asked rhetorically.
None of us, of course, did. "They carried the seaweed up there and put
it in the fissures between the rocks."

Eventually, as the seaweed decayed, it would form a kind of mulchy
soil in which crops could be planted. It must have taken years.

He also put the fairies and the superstitions surrounding them into
a broader context, claiming that many of the legends surrounding
them and their habitat were spun to prevent the eradication of forests,
an early Irish environmental movement. Whether or not that's entirely

so, it's a lovely thought. A little later in the day as we were standing outside a local pub having a Guinness, Gibbons pointed out to the Atlantic and quoted a local poet on the subject of its frigidity: "The scrotum-shrinking Atlantic." Indeed.

September 23 / Galway Bay

Last night we went to the town of Lisdoonvarna, drawn by the whimsical report that this is the town of matchmakers. Sixtyish farmers, who have been too busy to get married, come to town to meet women. A certain degree of order is allegedly imposed by the aforementioned matchmakers. I'm not quite sure what we expected to see (perhaps some sort of public presentation: "Here's a fine sixty-two-year-old farmer, with holdings of forty-two acres. . . ."), but what we found was a pleasant enough pub with someone playing country western music, which is said to have its roots in Irish country music. Sitting around an empty dance floor were a bunch of grim-faced elders. They did not speak to one another, nor show any pleasure whatsoever in one another's company. Two rooms away, connected by a sort of open air lock with chairs, was a game room, in which there were three pool tables and a couple of arcade machines. Young people gathered there with not much more enthusiasm than their elders. Nobody appeared to be having a good time and certainly no one was making any matches.

The locals, when they communicate at all, seem most proud of the films that have been made around here. *The Matchmaker* is one; *The Field*, in which Richard Harris plays the part of a farmer who has lugged years' worth of seaweed up into the limestone flatland next to his cottage in order to create some arable farmland, is another. (I had seen the film but didn't connect to the reality of it until Gibbons's minilecture on the subject.) These are rugged, taciturn people and, after biking through the unforgiving landscape for a couple of days, I can understand why.

September 24 / Connemara, County Galway

A bus took us within striking distance of our goal today (a restaurant in a town about twenty-five miles away), and then we biked through the bogs. The landscape is starkly beautiful, but put the emphasis on stark. In the bad old days criminals were exiled to the bogs and they repaid the kindness by robbing anyone else foolish enough to pass through by carriage or otherwise. It is (and I am relying here once again on the wisdom of archaeologist/environmentalist Gibbons) an ecological treasure trove. The Irish, who are themselves environmentally inclined (in part because many tourists come to visit and admire the wild beauty), are much encouraged in doing so by their European Union partners, the Dutch. They ravaged their own bogs in earlier times and have lived to regret it.

There is something bizarre about this whole biking party. A couple of the wealthiest and most powerful communications barons in the world, Eisner and Diller, have invited an eclectic bunch of lawyers, investment bankers, a couple of reporters, a newly married pair of former ballet dancers, the head of Disney's animation department and Fran Lebowitz. I imagine that Dorothy Parker, in her day, must have inspired the same timid admiration that Fran produces. She feigns a fearlessness that I doubt she feels, but it is sufficient to cow anyone in this group. She has what can easily become a scathing wit. Her primary gift, however, is that she is faster at being witty than anyone else around. She is a passionate liberal who seems to despise New York mayor Rudolph Giuliani and all things German. As she says: "I don't even have a decent knife or coffeemaker around the house." It comes out as a hoarse burst. She does not linger over words. The hoarseness is a product of smoking. Fran is a passionate, or perhaps better, an unapologetic smoker. She smokes in the bathrooms of airliners. There!

What's bizarre about this group, though, is that most of its members are wealthy enough to do more or less whatever they like, and they have chosen to bike through the rain, up and down uncomfortably hilly terrain. The hotels in which we're staying are among the best in Ireland but can't compare to the best in Europe or the United States. Still, it's an invigorating mind rinse for all of us and has enabled me to have a couple of relaxed and uninterrupted conversations with Eisner.

September 25 / Ballynahinch

She appeared to be the night manager, and she was genuinely shocked. There, frolicking around before a roaring fire in one of the public sitting rooms of this restored old castle, was a Jack Russell terrier. He, the day manager, not the dog, had been briefed: "She's emigrating to America in the morning, Bridgette. This is to be her last night in Ireland, and she wanted to spend it at Ballynahinch." Curiously, that seemed to satisfy Bridgette and it was certainly true as far as it went, but it's only part of the story.

When our group stopped for lunch yesterday, about thirty miles from here, a little Jack Russell terrier was hanging around outside the restaurant. It didn't have a collar and no one seemed to know to whom it belonged, but it immediately caught the fancy of everyone, most particularly Barry Diller. Yesterday afternoon and evening Barry unsuccessfully pestered our guides to find out who owned the dog. By this morning Diller was getting a little morose. This afternoon, as we arrived for lunch at another restaurant following this morning's bike ride, there was the dog—newly acquired by Barry. One of the guides had tracked her down. The general belief is that she was homeless. Anyway, a family was holding her in their garden. The homelessness part was yesterday. Now she belongs to one of the richer men in America, who has already arranged a house call from a local vet, who pronounced the dog healthy, about nine months old and has now given her all the shots she needs for her big trip tomorrow—to America.

Shannon, as she is now known, will travel aboard a private helicopter, tomorrow afternoon, to the airport at Shannon, where Diller's private jet will transport her to New York. Shannon's future address (should anyone wish to communicate with her) is the Diller apartment at the Carlyle Hotel in New York. If it is possible for a dog to experience culture shock, this one has a massive dose coming.

September 26 / Cong

There is a silly old joke about two grandmothers who meet while one is pushing a carriage with her grandchild in it. The other grandmother oohs and aahs appreciatively over the baby, to which the first responds: "Yes, but you ought to see his picture." We are in the middle of one of the most picturesque areas in Ireland. The loveliness of the setting and the generous charm of its people continue to draw tourists from around the world. The residents, though, seem fixated on a forty-five-year-old Hollywood image of themselves that, in many respects, defines them in their own minds more than reality does.

The film *The Quiet Man* was shot in the shadow of our bizarre hotel, Ashford Castle. It's almost impossible anymore to identify what belongs to which era in this patchwork of a building that overlooks the huge and spectacular Lake Corrib. There are pieces of an ancient castle interwoven with an old country home. In one wing, the parapet of an ancient castle was razed to make room for three floors' worth of hotel rooms. Most of the work was done by various generations of the Guinness family, the beer barons. The entire structure looks much older than it really is, but it's more or less what the original owners might have done if they'd had the money for it. The view of the lake is wonderful, seventy square miles of breathtaking salmon and brown trout fishing water, dotted by 365 small islands. There is an ancient abbey in the village of Cong, dating back to the twelfth century. It is set in the sparkling, verdant countryside that everyone who has never been to Ireland imagines. But none of that seems to evoke the level of local pride felt in "the film."

John Ford shot *The Quiet Man* with John Wayne, Victor McLaglen, Maureen O'Hara and Barry Fitzgerald in the 1950s. One of the sequences was set in a nearby inn, and "the fight" took place in a meadow close by. Stephen, the old gilley, or fishing guide, who took Grace Anne and me motoring on the lake in the fine larch, elm and oak boat he and his son built with their own hands, provided the information on the boat only after I inquired, but he proudly volunteered the fact that he had been an extra in the movie. He was "holding the tub of water in the fight scene," he explained, as though every precious frame were as indelibly engraved in our minds as they are in his.

Half the buildings in the village reference one relationship or another to the film. Meanwhile, at the "castle," there is a sign in the lobby that informs guests they can watch *The Quiet Man* on channel zero every afternoon at five.

There is also a photograph of Robin Leach, proclaiming that he once featured Ashford Castle on his series "Lifestyles of the Rich and Famous," demonstrating once again that people who run expensive hotels can be impressed by the most extraordinary things.

Today, incidentally, would have been my father's 104th birthday.

September 27 / En route from London to Washington

Judging by this morning's edition of the *Herald Tribune*, not a great deal has changed since we left a week ago. East Timor is still spinning out of control, despite the presence of an Australian and Ghurka peacekeeping force. There have been demonstrations in Djakarta protesting new legislation that gives the military in Indonesia greater powers. Several students have been killed, and it seems more likely than ever that civilian rule in Indonesia will eventually fall victim to events in East and West Timor.

The market seems to have had a bad week, apparently linked in part to the strengthening Japanese yen, but I'm inclined to think that we're due for a "bearish" year, or maybe several.

As I think back on this week, I'm more and more taken by the importance to many Irish of American films shot in their country. It is almost as though the fact that their struggles and hard times have been acknowledged by Hollywood takes away some of the pain. I can remember hearing similar importance attached to the shooting of *Exodus* by Israelis when Grace Anne and I first visited there in 1967.

In part, of course, it's also a way of referencing a common or shared perception. You couldn't possibly know our country as we know it, but did you happen to see *The Quiet Man*? Or, We know you don't know much about this castle/hotel's history, but here it is as featured on *Lifestyles of the Rich and Famous*. You are familiar with that, aren't you?

We all recognize the same Disney icons, we all recognize the same Coke cans; we have, most of us, at one time or another, perceived different parts of the world through Christiane Amanpour's eyes. The world has definitely shrunk during this century, but I'm not convinced that we actually know much more about one another than we did a hundred years ago. We cannot help but be more aware of the diverse cultures that exist in expanding rings around us, but our principal focus remains inner-directed. We are bombarded by images of other places, needs and conflicts, but unless we can see a direct impact on our own lives, it remains largely background noise.

September 28 / Washington

This was our bioterrorism day. Leroy Sievers, one of our most experienced producers, has spent weeks pulling together the five-day scenario I referred to earlier in which unknown terrorists break several glass containers containing anthrax bacteria on the rails of a major city's subway system. In the scenario, which was designed by one of the country's leading experts on the subject, approximately fifty thousand people eventually die. Anthrax, we learned, does not immediately present itself for what it is. For the first two or three days, those who have inhaled the spores either exhibit no symptoms at all, or they appear to be suffering from some kind of flu. By the time the anthrax has been identified, it's usually too late to treat those who have inhaled it. And the terrorists are, of course, long gone.

We brought in a number of city and state officials from around the country to act as our "city officials," that is, the people who would have to deal with such a crisis. Our panel includes John Timoney, the police commissioner of Philadelphia, and Bill Campbell, the mayor of Atlanta. What was frightening to observe (and it clearly scared the hell out of the two of them) is how unfamiliar they were with the peculiar dangers of bioterrorism: the long delay between the act of terrorism and the manifestation; the counterintuitive nature of the medical treatment, which is to say, not wasting antibiotics on those with symptoms because it's already too late for them.

Campbell told me later that he was so shaken by what he learned that he's going to set up a special emergency task force in Atlanta to deal with the potential dangers. If other city officials react in a similar fashion, it may prove to be one of the most useful programs we've ever done.

September 29 / Washington

We have become embroiled again in one of these artificial debates over freedom of speech and expression that, in truth, has little or nothing to do with either. Mayor Giuliani has ordered that city funding be withheld from the Brooklyn Museum, because it is currently exhibiting some British works with "offensive themes." The prime example is a painting of a black Madonna on which flying vaginas and jewel-encrusted elephant dung have been superimposed. The ultimate cynicism here is that these works of art belong to the advertising magnate Charles Saatchi, who will probably follow his customary pattern of putting the works up for auction when the show is over. All this publicity, then, is simply going to drive up the price. Does this really have anything to do with censorship, though? Actually, it has much more to do with politics.

This is a great issue for Giuliani, who is appealing to Catholic voters in particular. His order to withhold city funds from the museum will, in all probability, be overturned by the courts. But the larger issue is this: The First Amendment ensures our right to freedom of expression. And painting is a form of expression, whether we like a particular work or not. Still, the First Amendment does not require government to use public funds to underwrite what each of us wants to say or paint. There will be a few days of public venting and, when it's all over, works of art that would otherwise have gone largely ignored will have become famous; the Brooklyn Museum will have received more attention than it has had in years; and Giuliani will have placed another marker in his undeclared race with Hillary Clinton for the U.S. Senate.

September 30 / Washington

The lawyers and standards and practices people at ABC are doing what they should be doing—worrying. After all, our bio-war scenario is pieced together with pieces of real news video, showing real people, and no matter how many times I stress the fact that this is a fictional scenario, depicting the act of an imaginary bunch of terrorists, there will be some viewer who tunes in ten minutes into the broadcast only to see his uncle Francis being described by me as dying of anthrax. There's some wonderful lawsuit potential there.

Still, I don't know of any other way to present the danger in a sufficiently graphic way so that people will truly come to understand that this is something they need to start thinking about. My hope is that, when all is said and done, it will heighten the consciousness of city mothers and fathers around the country. They need to be aware of the terrible prospect that, one of these days, real terrorists will launch a real biological-warfare attack against a real American city. If these next few nights can heighten that awareness and, ultimately, save some lives, it will have served its purpose.

October

October 1 / Washington

One of the horrors of life in these United States at this particular time is that the pornographers have access to a greater number of vulnerable targets than ever before. They are using cable television, they are using the Internet, they are using the telephone system.

The twelve-year-old daughter of a friend of mine has accumulated more than $1,500 worth of phone bills, at home and in the homes of relatives, calling a telephone number with a 900 prefix that puts her in touch with men or women (basically, verbal prostitutes) who will, literally, "talk dirty" for 95 cents a minute. I'm not altogether sure how these phone hookers would know, or why they would care, that the caller is underage, but it is clearly unacceptable that children should be able to pick up a telephone and dial their way into these costly, pornographic swamps. The fact that our friend is from an Asian country and has a difficult time understanding what her daughter is talking about when she's speaking English on the phone only complicates the problem. I cannot believe, though, that these companies can be permitted to traffic to children without suffering any consequence. I sure as hell do not believe that they should be able to collect on their bills.

Our beloved First Amendment guarantees each of us the right to freedom of expression, but I still think there has to be some level of control over the distribution where children are involved.

October 2 / St. Mary's County

A few random observations: In Potomac, which must rank now as one of the wealthier neighborhoods in the Western world, the price of High-test gasoline is now hovering at $1.70 a gallon. That is still cheap compared to Japan or Western Europe, but it's a good 30 cents a gallon more expensive than almost any other gas station in the region. Remember, too, that only a few months ago, the price of Regular gas was less than a dollar a gallon. Still, the price of gasoline is a relatively unimportant matter in this neighborhood; but then, money is never important unless you don't have any.

Grace Anne and I went to a movie in Lexington Park this evening. One of the young women behind the candy counter looked familiar. It turned out that she was one of the nurses at St. Mary's Hospital who attended Grace Anne after she was stung by a "horse" hornet last summer. The young woman works at the hospital, the movie theater on weekends and at a local college. She's cheerful about it, but she doesn't do it because she wants to—she has to in order to make ends meet.

October 3 / Potomac

In the 1920s my father purchased a small bronze of a lithe, young woman frozen in the act of running. She is naked and her hair is streaming out behind her. The bronze was titled *Fleeting Time*.

It has occurred to me several times over the years, as Grace Anne, the children and I age, that the bronze was aptly named, but that she symbolizes a truth that is sometimes difficult to accept. She has not changed since the time my father purchased her seventy-five years ago. But my father grew old and died; I am approaching sixty; our youngest children are nearing thirty and the older ones are in their mid-thirties. We, in other words, are changing constantly. Time remains immutable. We are the ones in motion. Time stands still.

October 4 / En route to Chowchilla, California

Nearly ten times as many women are imprisoned in the United States than in all of Western Europe. You can, in other words, compare two population bodies of roughly the same size, driven by similar democratic engines, and in ours we incarcerate ten times as many women. Why?

Essentially, there are two reasons: race and drugs. The number of black and Hispanic women in our prisons is vastly greater than their proportion in the general population. Of the women in prison, about 40 percent are there for having used illegal drugs. The number of drug users in prison is much higher, close to 70 percent. Those women who receive drug treatment while in prison have a recidivism rate of only 20 percent. Those who do not, return to prison at a rate more than three times that number.

Eighty-seven percent of the women in prison have children. Hardly any of them have husbands or male partners who accept the responsibility of raising those children when their mates go behind bars. The children, therefore, end up being raised by their grandmothers or aunts, if they're lucky, or being distributed to foster homes, if they're not.

All of these statistics are merely indicators of the deep malaise that continues to afflict American society. There can be no question but that drug trafficking and addiction have to be brought under control. The importance of stable family life to the successful future of children is indisputable. But merely cataloguing these problems on statistical charts and putting the products of these failures behind bars or into foster homes is not addressing the problems. We need to devote at least as much time, energy and money to treatment as we do to punishment.

I'm on my way to the Central California Women's Facility and the Valley State Prison for Women. They are, essentially, just across the street from each other and share facilities, but our producers tell me they are as different as night and day. We're about to devote another week to our ongoing prison series. Insofar as women's prisons get attention at all, it's mostly related to the sexual harassment by male correctional officers. We'll focus on that, too, but there's a great deal more to be covered.

We are creating, in this country, a huge disposable population of well over a million people whose welfare is largely regarded as irrelevant, in that they have either used or dealt drugs. The punishment of these people, which the law intends to be limited to incarceration, is frequently intensified by sexual molestation and, increasingly, by long periods of isolation, such that prisoners are driven mad.

October 5 / Chowchilla

Prison stories—and we have done a lot of them over the years—always present the same paradox. Convicted criminals are charging the men and women who control their lives behind bars with improper acts; that is to say, the wrongdoers are accusing those whom society has empowered to keep them incarcerated with mistreating them. The prison staff deny the charges. Whom do you believe?

It is incredibly easy—it has been made easy for those of us outside the loop of law enforcement—to ignore what goes on behind prison walls. For much of the past twenty years here in California, under the administrations of George Deukmejian and Pete Wilson, the media have been largely kept out of the state prisons. Both governors were basically law-and-order types, and they encouraged their prison administrators to conduct their business without the intrusion of media scrutiny. The new governor, Gray Davis, appears to believe otherwise. In any event, his office has made it possible for *Nightline* to spend this week inside the two largest state prisons for women.

The man who is the chief doctor at the Valley State Prison was reluctant to sit for an interview. We made the point, all the way up the line to the director of prisons, that it is the medical care at Valley State that keeps cropping up as one of the biggest problem areas. The inmates charge that they have a hard time getting to see the doctors, that they are frequently medicated for illnesses they don't have and not treated for illnesses they have had for years. The prisoners also charge that they are frequently abused verbally and sometimes abused physically. Specifically, they charge that some of the doctors give them unnecessary pelvic examinations. In short, they're charging a form of sexual abuse.

Whom to believe? The doctors, who have neither been charged with nor convicted of any crimes, or the inmates, who have been convicted or encouraged to plead guilty to a host of crimes?

The chief doctor was encouraged by his superiors to talk with us and does so. He would have been wise to resist. I am not sure he will be forced to resign after what he said, but my hunch is that he will.

In essence, he accused the women inmates of "asking for it." He suggested that because they are in prison they are unable to find the kind of sexual gratification they need and that, therefore, they come to the doctors looking for unnecessary Pap smears and pelvic examinations. As for those who are not motivated by their sexual drive, he suggested that they make such charges because of "storefront" lawyers who are drawn by the "deep pockets" of the state treasury. I asked him how many such cases had been brought in his experience. "None," he conceded. Didn't that shoot his theory down? "No," the chief medical officer insisted, it merely made his point. If there were anything to these charges, there would have been some lawsuits, and since there are no lawsuits, that must mean that the charges are untrue.

The allegations made by the inmates are difficult, if not impossible, to prove. With most situations cited in charges of sexual impropriety, there are only two people present. In these cases, one of them is a convicted felon. Whom are you going to believe?

I suggested that it was difficult for these women to file charges because of the danger of reprisals. Everyone against whom such a charge can be made is in a position of power vis-à-vis any inmate who levels one. The doctor wasn't buying that either.

The warden was sitting in on our interview. I did not have the impression that he thought his medical colleague had done himself or the system much good.

October 6 / Chowchilla

Thirteen women inmates, now sitting on risers in the middle of the exercise yard, asked to be interviewed. They have a lot to say, and they are an eclectic bunch. The only thing they appear to have in common is their criminality. They are old and young, white and black and Hispanic. There is even one Native American. Then again, they actually do have something else in common: They all have stories of abuse as children, as teenagers, as young women. One striking young woman explains, matter-of-factly, how her common-law husband terrified her into coconspiracy in a murder. He tied her to a chair in their kitchen, she tells me, and then he skinned a live cat in front of her, explaining that this was what he would do to her family if she betrayed him.

Eleven out of thirteen are mothers. They have children on the outside and bemoan the fact that they can do nothing to prevent their youngsters from following in their paths. They don't minimize the things they did that brought them into prison: "There is nothing that anyone can say to me," one of them tells me, "that I haven't said a thousand times to myself."

They explain their affection for one another and the unusual bonding that takes place among women of different races and economic backgrounds when they speak of their low self-esteem. It comes as a revelation to them that so many other women feel as they do. It is one reason why they are so resentful of being called "whores and bitches" by some of the correctional officers.

There is, it must be said, a reason for the common root of the words convict and "conning." It can be difficult to know what is genuine and what is said for effect. But it is impressive to see the level of mutual support these women give one another. Although it would not be healthy for society to leave these women on the outside, unpunished and untreated, I find it difficult to believe that the consequences would be any worse than they are now. Ironically, those who emphasize family values as the most basic building blocks of any functioning society have it exactly right. But the mindless determination to imprison drug addicts without simultaneously treating their addictions is simply incompatible with any hope of reestablishing functioning families capable of any reasonable values whatsoever.

October 7 / Chowchilla

Five correctional officers joined me for a farewell chat. There had been some question about whether the officers would be allowed to talk to me on camera in a group. We couldn't figure out why. Then it turned out that the union took the position that we couldn't take five officers off the job at the same time unless all were put on overtime at the end of the day. The state said no to that, but somehow it all got worked out.

Not too surprisingly, all the officers feel that the inmates are pulling a colossal con much of the time. What's all this concern about mothers being separated from their newborn babies? These women have been mothers several times over already, and they leave their babies with their mothers and their aunts while they go out and shoot up dope. The newborns are better off being put into foster homes.

And I think of Mary. Mary is twenty-three and the mother of five children. The youngest of her children was born just four days ago and, for some reason, the system closed one eye and allowed the mother of the baby's father (they are not married) to pick the baby up and take him home. The father, who is thirty-two, is also in prison on a drug-related charge.

This afternoon, Mary and I are sitting in her room, which she shares with seven other inmates at Valley State Prison for Women, and the tears are pouring down her cheeks. She knows that her life has been a disaster. She has no particular expectation that it will get any better. She has held a variety of jobs in the past but quit all of them because she was bored. I don't have to say anything. She is wondering out loud, recalling what a careless mother she's been. Where will the money for her children's needs come from? She doesn't know. What kind of work will she do? She doesn't know that either. Perhaps the children will have to get state assistance. She knows only that she doesn't want to come back to prison again. She couldn't stand the thought of coming back to prison. She's going home tomorrow. Well, not really home; it's her "mother-in-law's" home.

Mary has no idea how she will ever bring her five children together (they are being cared for by various relatives in different locations), and it will be another two years before the father of her latest child is out of prison. It is simply more than she is equipped to handle. The tears roll down her cheeks and little droplets hang from her chin.

October 8 / En route to Los Angeles

The chief medical officer at Valley State Prison for Women has been relieved of his duties and "reassigned." Just as we were leaving the facilities this morning on our way to the airport, the warden asked if he could have a private moment with me. He had just received a call from the governor's office asking him to give me a statement on camera to the effect that the medical officer's comments in his interview with me were unacceptable and that he had been removed from his position. By the time we got to the warden's office, there was a call from the director of prisons, who wanted to talk to me. The essence of his comments was the same.

My old friend Mark Nelson, who is one of *Nightline*'s senior producers, has been directing traffic on this story all the time we've been out here. He and I talked about the doctor's removal on the drive from the prison to the Fresno airport. We both regret that the doctor was removed from his job, but he was neither tricked nor trapped into saying the things he did. He could have defended his staff against the inmates' charges without suggesting that the women were looking for some kind of sexual gratification. It shows a complete lack of sensitivity to the role and responsibilities he had. If we had chosen not to use his interview (and I don't think that option was open to us), it would have meant that the inappropriate behavior toward the inmates would have continued.

I have regrets, but no second thoughts.

October 9 / Potomac

Donald Trump appears to be giving consideration to running for president of the United States. I know of Trump only through his various self-promotional activities, which seem to consist largely of accumulating as much money as he can through real estate transactions and the operation of some gambling casinos. "The Donald," as the New York press likes to call him, has variously gone bankrupt and made hundreds of millions of dollars. He is currently said to be on the upswing, with an estimated worth of $1.5 billion. I believe it's his estimate. He is also well known for unsuccessful marriages and squiring women young enough to be his daughters to sporting events and other public festivities.

Since we have just had one president with a taste for very young women, I'm not sure that the country is ready for another. Come to think of it, Clinton was also involved in a real estate transaction that was supposed to make a lot of money, though Whitewater did not pan out. Trump's real estate holdings, on the other hand, are big and garish.

I'm not sure I understand what it is that makes him think he is qualified to be president, but then again, perhaps all Trump cares about is the simple act of running. "Donald Trump, the former presidential candidate . . ." Yes, I think he'd like that. It could certainly be useful from a promotional point of view, just as long as he doesn't expect anyone to take him seriously.

October 10 / Potomac

Neither Mark McGwire nor Sammy Sosa broke any records this year, though they both hit more home runs in a season than anyone had before 1998. They both got their share of coverage in the sports press, but what only a year ago had the entire country riveted seemed largely irrelevant this year.

We are a nation that thrives on obsessions. Donna Rice and Gary Hart are replaced by Jim and Tammy Faye Bakker. The hostages in Iran are replaced by the Contras in Nicaragua. Ollie North is replaced by O. J. Simpson, who is replaced by Monica Lewinsky.

I wonder how many of the following names will even be familiar to the public at large ten years from now: Gary Bauer, Steve Forbes, Pat Buchanan, Al Gore, Bill Bradley, John McCain, George W. Bush. One of them will be, obviously. The others? Who cares about unsuccessful presidential candidates?

American Express had a successful advertising campaign a number of years ago in which it had people of note (whose faces, however, might not be known to the public) hold up an American Express credit card and then ask, Do you know me? The point being that with an American Express card it didn't matter whether you were known or not. One of the first people featured in the campaign was a man by the name of Bill Miller. He had been Barry Goldwater's running mate during the 1964 presidential race. It took only a couple of years to make him totally anonymous again.

October 11 / Potomac

I'm not quite sure how such things are calculated, but sometime tomorrow the population of the world will hit six billion. At the turn of the last century we were at one billion six hundred thousand. It is an interesting comment on the bipolar nature of the twentieth century. On the one hand, we have slaughtered more of one another than in any previous century in history. Stalin is said to have killed between twenty and thirty million of his people. Mao may have done even better. We have endured two world wars, in the second of which the Nazis alone killed six million Jews. The Khmer Rouge killed a couple of million of their people, which, on a per capita basis, may have been the bloodiest slaughter of them all; there were only seven million or so Cambodians to begin with. More recently, in Rwanda, the Hutu killed about half a million Tutsi. There have been similar horrors in other parts of Africa, and more modest slaughters in Latin and Central America. On the other hand, the human condition has improved in terms of health care, nutrition and overall living conditions as never before in the history of Man. The improvements have been so extraordinary that, despite our best efforts to eradicate one another, despite the existence of the most efficient killing devices ever, we continue to thrive and multiply.

God help us if universal peace ever descends.

October 12 / Washington

The Pakistani military has overthrown the civilian government in that country. The Pakistani prime minister apparently incurred the wrath of the army chief of staff when he acted as though he had been less than complicit in decisions to take military action in Kashmir. The Clinton administration encouraged the prime minister to take that position during his recent visit to Washington. I have no idea where this will ultimately leave U.S. policy in south Asia, but the foreign policy of this administration is not much to brag about. Haiti is in shambles, as is Somalia. Colombia is a quagmire just waiting to suck U.S. forces in. Russia is a fiasco and U.S. influence there is going up in smoke. Kosovo is turning into a quasi-Albanian state, which is something I thought we were trying to avoid. The U.S. Senate is not only refusing to pass the Nuclear Test Ban Treaty, but the Republican majority is warning President Clinton that he must promise in writing not to push for its passage during the remaining fifteen months of his term, or they will reject it out of hand.

Whether or not this will ever have any direct impact on Clinton's legacy is hard to say, but for some perverse reason, the failures of the Clinton-Gore administration seem to be sticking to Gore as though he had been running the whole show all along, while Clinton conveys the impression that he was simply an innocent bystander.

October 13 / Washington

News and history, history and news. The grand jury has returned its finding in the case of JonBenet Ramsey. She's the little girl who, during her very brief lifetime, appeared in beauty pageants and was brutally murdered in her parents' home some three years ago. The conventional wisdom has been that some member of her family, either one of her parents or her older brother, was connected with her death. The grand jury has been unable to reach any kind of conclusion, however.

That's the story that will capture the public's imagination. It is a story that lends itself to simplistic analysis, on which every reader or viewer can easily express an opinion. But it is not news that is going to make any kind of history.

Meanwhile, the U.S. Senate has rejected the Nuclear Test Ban Treaty. I'm still not sure I understand its reasons for doing so, except, perhaps, the belief that verification of the treaty would not be possible and that, therefore, the United States must retain its option to test. I've been told by experts that we can do all the testing we need by computer simulation, but I don't know enough about the subject personally to have an informed opinion. In any event, I have the sense that in years to come this decision may cost us in terms of nuclear proliferation. This is an historically important event, but, in large measure because it is so complex, the public will tend to ignore it and the commensurate news coverage will be relatively small.

Finally, the world's largest producer of cigarettes, Philip Morris, has acknowledged publicly that cigarettes are addictive; they believe the public should rely on the opinion of public health experts that smoking causes cancer, emphysema and heart disease.

It sounds like a major breakthrough—but it isn't. First and most important, industry lawyers will never make such a concession in court, where it counts; second, tobacco companies are now obliged, under the terms of the tobacco agreement reached with sundry states, not to tell untruths publicly about smoking. Curiously, that agreement has no effect on what the tobacco companies can claim in court. The event is neither historic, nor does it deserve to be treated as though it were big news.

October 14 / Washington

Our culture seems infected by a desperate need to celebrate. A significant percentage of the population is probably depressed because those people are operating under the illusion that everybody else must be having a good time.

I just got off the phone with an old friend who operates a restaurant in Captiva. We have invited our entire family and a number of friends to join us down there over this millennial New Year's celebration. It seemed like a wonderful idea: Let's not be part of the big-city madness; let's just surround ourselves with people we love and usher in the next thousand years with a certain aplomb.

Easier said than done. Where is everyone going to stay? Well, I managed to get some rooms at a nearby hotel, and we'll have people in sleeping bags on the living room floor or (if the weather is good) out on the beach. But where (assuming that Grace Anne and I don't want to spend every day cooking for fifteen to twenty people) do we eat? Hence the call to my restaurant-owner friend. I now have reservations for a small army for a couple of nights. I'm also trying to arrange for a beach barbecue on New Year's Eve. The problem with all of this merrymaking is that it takes a ton of preparation. A few dinners out will be nice, but somehow we're still going to have to feed twenty people three times a day for five days.

When these holidays are first conceived, the sound you hear is the murmur of good conversation and the laughter of people having fun on the beach. You forget the sounds of the dishwasher, the washing machine and the dryer going more or less round the clock.

October 15 / Washington

There was a farewell party here at the bureau this evening for a number of engineers and cameramen who are taking an early buyout from

Disney. The party nearly didn't come off because so many people throughout the news division are being urged to move on that the company is trying to discourage lavish good-byes. Well, I don't know about lavish, but it was a really nice party. I've known a lot of these men (no women this time) for thirty years or more. A couple of them are good friends, and I have no doubt that our relationships will continue. But we have lived in and through our work for so long that conversations in the future will probably focus on the stories we covered together in the past.

I will especially miss Vinny Gaito, a bearded, burly cameraman who bitterly resented me when we first worked together. He and the late ABC correspondent Lou Cioffi had been covering the Hubert Humphrey presidential campaign. I was covering the Nixon campaign. Lou and I were ordered to change places for a couple of weeks so that we wouldn't get too close to our candidates (there was less danger of that happening on the Nixon campaign than on Humphrey's). I was twenty-eight and looked about eighteen. Lou was already a veteran in those days, and Vinny idolized him. He wasn't prepared to like me for even two weeks. Over the past thirty-one years, though, we have come to love each other. I can barely believe how long it has been.

October 16 / En route to Istanbul

Somebody mentioned that Joe Paterno is now in his fiftieth year of coaching football at Penn State University. I realized that I was watching teams coached by Paterno when I was a student at Syracuse from 1956 to 1960. In other words, the first time I saw Penn State play, Paterno had been coaching for only seven years.

I wonder why many of us have such a difficult time realizing that we are getting old. I have no trouble at all appreciating the fact that Paterno is aging (although he still does a credible job of running off the field at halftime). But I continue to be resentful of glimpses caught unexpectedly in a shop window or a lurking mirror. Am I the only person I know who has a "mirror" face? Perhaps you know what I mean. It is a way of composing one's features so that the reflected image comports to the memory of how one looked many years ago. I squirm at the cliché, but I really don't feel that old. My right knee has an awkward way of buckling when I step into an unseen depression, and it is nearly impossible for me to touch my toes without bending my knees, and my lower back hurts most of the time. But, old?

The other day, at Valley State Prison for Women, I was talking to an inmate who conceded that she had little or no hope of ever getting off drugs. She would, she admitted, be back on them again as soon as she got out. She was, she said sadly, too old to change. I thought she might be in her fifties, but she was thirty-eight.

Age is truly a matter of perspective.

October 17 / Istanbul

On the flight in from Frankfurt, Captain Schmidt, our Lufthansa pilot, thoughtfully brought his cabin full of American tourists up to date on the outcome of the Malaysian Grand Prix. Judging from the blank stares, I don't think there was anyone among us who even knew there is such a thing. This crowd would have liked to hear the outcome of the Yankees–Red Sox game, but that clearly did not occur to Captain Schmidt. It is amazing how one man's sports fanaticism leaves another totally cold.

We were stopped at immigration in Istanbul because neither Grace Anne nor I had a Turkish visa. Not to worry. There was a perfectly genial official, not even wearing a mask, who, for $45 each, stamped a visa into our passports without requiring us even to fill out an application. It took less than a minute.

We piled our suitcases into a tiny Turkish taxi. I could see the young driver eyeing me in the rearview mirror. He spoke some English because, it turned out, he is a merchant seaman who is on a month's home leave; he's hustling a few extra bucks terrifying tourists with his kamikaze style of driving. I had a feeling he recognized me. Much of our *Nightline* coverage of the recent Turkish earthquake had been shown on Turkish TV, and only a few weeks ago a Turkish crew came by our studios to do an interview with me. I was preparing to demur modestly when the taxi driver blurted out: "You look like . . . Prince Charles."

It is true that *Mad* magazine once ran a contest to see whether its readers thought that David Letterman, Prince Charles or I looked most like their cartoon icon, Alfred E. Newman. I believe Charles won.

October 18 / Istanbul

Topkapi Palace is breathtaking, wonderful, magnificent—but a couple of hours touring it were more than enough. After seeing golden thrones and forty-eight-kilogram golden vases and a golden dagger, the hilt of which holds three emeralds the size of eggs (not your lousy little pigeon eggs, either: full-size chicken eggs!), you yearn for a nice, simple piece of plastic. The limestone was dragged in from one part of Turkey, the marble from another. The tilework is truly fantastic, as are some of the stained-glass windows. We are, after all, talking about a palace that was constructed in the fifteenth century. Nevertheless, to return to an earlier observation on the Medicis of Florence, any middle-class American living today has an infinitely more comfortable and healthy existence than did Sultan Süleyman the Magnificent.

There is, of course, the matter of the harem: one thousand young lovelies, ranging in age from fourteen to about twenty-five. The first couple of years for these women were given over to training in concubinage, and then they were expected to put in a seven-year term. Only four out of each thousand were ever bound to the sultan in marriage, and, periodically, he would divorce those ladies, in order to find another four who could provide him with more sons. Still, I'd never heard that the concubines were only temporarily employed. When the sultan was through with the ladies, they were given a generous dowry, a lady's maid and married off. Apparently, it was tradition that one or more Jewish matchmakers (who also brought jewelry and fine clothes to the harem, since the concubines couldn't exactly spend an afternoon at the Grand Bazaar) found husbands for the sultan's castoffs. Then, as now, you demonstrated your real wealth not by what you accumulated, but by what you discarded.

October 19 / Istanbul

Menay, our guide, appears to be in her late twenties. Her husband is a travel agent. We were on our way to visit the onetime church of Saint Sophia, built by the Emperor Constantine, and she had asked whether we had been in Istanbul before. Yes, we said, back in 1985 and then again about five years ago. She then talked about how many additional millions of Turks had come here during the intervening years. Istanbul is now a city of ten million.

I mentioned that I noticed a lot more Turkish women wearing the chador, the traditional Muslim head scarf. That set her off. Did we know about the woman member of parliament who had so scandalized everyone by insisting on wearing her head covering inside parliament itself? Yes, we said, that had made the news even back in the United States. But it didn't seem as outrageous to us, perhaps, as it was here. Menay herself seemed quite upset by the gesture. What was that woman up to? How would our members of Congress have reacted if something like that had happened? I suggested that it probably wouldn't have had much impact at all, although I can understand a different set of sensitivities here. Iran and Iraq are right next door. The one has been dominated for years now by its clerics; the other is a military dictatorship. In this part of the world such gestures can have enormous consequences. Still, it surprised me that Menay was so emphatic in her disapproval, especially when later, inside the Blue Mosque, she told us that she is Muslim herself. Clearly, most modern, educated young women here have no desire to see Turkey turn into a theocracy, so it must have been particularly unnerving to see a modern, educated young woman who had been elected to parliament make such a forceful stand, so offensive to conventional sensibilities.

October 20 / Cruising the Aegean

Grace Anne's birthday is in a few days and sailing the Aegean and the Mediterranean seemed like a wonderful way to spend a rare ten days alone together. Her life as a lawyer and mine as a journalist make time alone our most precious commodity.

It strikes me that, while tourism existed long before this century began, the twentieth century has seen an unprecedented explosion in travel. Millions of people are constantly in motion. Some, like us, are doing it for the debatable pleasure of the exercise. Travel by ship remains a wonderfully relaxing experience, although it does strike me that the organizers of these cruises are under the impression that leaving us without some sort of activity or meal at any hour of the day and night could lead to revolution. They also seem unwholesomely devoted to the proposition that whenever the ship is in port, buses should transport us as far away as possible, for as long as possible.

Be that as it may, we are not obliged to be active. Churchill may have had it right when, expressing himself on the subject of exercise, he said, "Whenever I feel the urge to exercise, I lie down until it goes away."

Certainly the media have had a great deal to do with encouraging movement for the sake of movement. Those of us who have the freedom and the money to travel do so in some large measure because we have seen those distant places in films or on television and yearn to see them for ourselves.

Those who move not for recreation or pleasure but to better their lives, whether from rural areas to the cities or from poor countries to wealthy ones or from war zones to peaceful regions, are also clearly encouraged by what they have seen on television and heard on the radio. There are, of course, still places in the world where people are born, live and die in the same village. There are places where veneration of ancestors roots families to a single place, generation after generation. In all, though, the intersection of mass communication, the combustible engine and air travel with a virus of a belief in the inherent right to move, has set the world in motion.

In such a world, nationalism has become an archaic notion, more suitable for attracting tourists than true believers. One day, the trappings of nationalism itself will become little more than folkloric curiosities, as they already are in the remnants of expired empires like those of the Greeks, Romans, Ottomans and Persians. We wander through their ruins and wonder, simultaneously, how they achieved all they did and what it was that ever made them believe their glory would last when nobody else's ever has.

October 21 / Velos, Greece

This has been a disappointing week for Elizabeth Dole. She is an attractive and impressive woman who, most recently, served as president of the American Red Cross. She previously served in two cabinet positions, as secretary of transportation and secretary of labor, but she has never been elected to any public office.

Victorious generals have, at previous points in American history, been able to overcome that void in their careers, but voters normally expect presidential candidates to have some sort of experience in public life. That doesn't seem to faze Pat Buchanan, Alan Keyes, Gary Bauer or Steve Forbes, but in the first three cases the men running for the presidency seem focused less on the expectation of victory than on enhancing their real careers. Buchanan and Keyes can return to preaching their political gospel as television and radio commentators; Bauer will have enhanced his standing as a social conservative and a prominent figure on the right wing of the Republican Party. Only Forbes and Senator John McCain (who has, of course, been elected to the U.S. Senate) have any real expectation of challenging GOP frontrunner George W. Bush. In Forbes's case that has less to do with the power of his message than with his personal fortune, which can keep his campaign going even when his ideas and personality falter.

What is extraordinary is how bereft the world seems these days of the kinds of gigantic figures (great and evil) who strode the political stage sixty or seventy years ago: Hitler, Stalin, Mao, Mussolini, de Gaulle, Churchill, Roosevelt, Franco, Gandhi. You would think that the explosion of mass-media coverage in recent years would have contributed to the rise of more such figures. Perhaps, instead, the harsh, intrusive cameras and microphones have too quickly revealed the feet of clay.

October 22 / Mykonos, Greece

This island clearly belongs to the "if you build it they will come" category of business operation. I'm sure there's a fair amount of fishing that has always been carried on here, but the industry of Mykonos is tourism. This place exists expressly so that people can visit. The whitewashed houses clustered on the hillsides, the narrow alleys snaking haphazardly between and among the houses, the bougainvillea cascading over the sides of walls, all are incredibly lovely, but without the jewelry shops and the quayside cafés there would be nothing to sustain the population; and the shops and restaurants are primarily for the tourists who arrive aboard the cruise ships, ferries from the mainland and private yachts.

It's a little like the Hamptons, only instead of displacing potato farmers, the seekers of sunshine, glorious views of the Aegean and the company of other well-off people seem to have displaced fishermen.

October 23 / Navplion, Greece

The ruins of the ancient city that overshadows its modern counterpart loom at the top of a craggy and near inaccessible mountain just a few hundred yards from the pier where we are moored. Mycenae was founded in 1300 B.C., just about the time Moses led the former Jewish slaves out of Egypt. Homer immortalized the Myceneans (albeit as Achaeans) in *The Iliad* and *The Odyssey*. This was the home of Agamemnon, of the ill-fated House of Atreus, who led his troops in battle at Troy.

I am trying, over breakfast, to absorb an article in the *Herald Tribune* by Howard Kurtz. It is about the Internet culture and how dominant it has become. Indeed, that is one of the opaque realities of our era, as we end one century and move into the next. Theoretically, we have all been thrust deep into the bottomless well of knowledge. We can at least "access" with alleged ease almost all that is known. If I only knew how to get on the damned Internet I could pull up all kinds of fascinating background on Agamemnon, Homer and Mycenean culture, but I am teetering on the very brink of computer illiteracy, saved from myself only because of my marriage to a computer-literate woman and because of my association with computer-literate colleagues.

Even as I give vent, then, to this slightly curdled observation, I caution you to consider the source. I believe that we have crossed over some invisible line and that we are now floundering in a world of too much knowledge. Homer's epic poetry has survived all these years because its subject was stirring and its language magnificent—but also because it was clearly visible in a relatively uncluttered world of literature. These days, it is hard to separate the good from the bad, the trivial from the important, simply because there is so much of it. We are already in danger of leaving the poor, the illiterate and the technically challenged further behind than ever before. I believe that we are also on the verge of creating a gigantic population made up of the confused, those for whom information is available as never before, but who are bewildered both by its volume and by a lack of clarity over which information is credible and which is not. Neither *The Odyssey* nor *The Iliad* was published in Homer's time, of course. I believe that both were initially passed down through oral tradition. And yet they have survived for thousands of years. Homer wouldn't have to worry about finding a publisher these days; he could simply put *The Iliad* on the Net. But would it flourish there or drown? I have my suspicions.

October 24 / Athens

A postscript to yesterday's entry in Navplion. Not a hundred yards from where we disembarked was an Internet Café. Over a couple of cappuccinos we struggled (unsuccessfully) to download our E-mail from home, but succeeded in sending several messages to New York and Washington.

Much as I marvel at our technical ability to maintain this sort of quasi-instantaneous contact with the United States, and as much as I would appreciate the ability to do so in an emergency, I am struck, yet again, by the inanity of the perceived obligation to do so when none really exists. We wasted part of a perfectly good afternoon of vacation time communicating, only because we could. I think there is actually an inverse ratio between the capacity to communicate and the importance of what is being communicated. You have only to think back to the days when the arrival of a telegram struck the recipient with a sense of foreboding, since no one would engage in such an expensive form of communication for anything less than a significant tragedy. Now, insomniac executives, flying at thirty thousand feet or cruising through the South China Sea, wake their subordinates at all hours of whoever's day or night it may be to communicate the most trivial insight, because technology has given them the ability and their corporate status gives them the right.

Who would have believed, twenty or thirty years ago, that one of our rarest and, therefore, most precious privileges at the end of the millennium would be the ability to claim, truthfully, that we are out of touch?

October 25 / Ephesus, Turkey

Today is Grace Anne's birthday, and a lovelier day we could not have expected. We began the morning by visiting the ruins at Ephesus and ended the day wandering through the bazaars by the waterfront. Almost everything these days is a "knockoff," which is to say there are leather goods, watches and sunglasses that at first glance look exactly like their name-brand and expensive counterparts. These days even the Turkish carpets sold here are knockoffs of the real kilims that are prized by rug collectors around the world. The only pleasure left in markets where you wander through the same kinds of goods that can be found on many New York street corners these days is the charming patter of the tradesmen and hustlers: "How can I take your money?" "It's my turn now." This after you've stopped to look at a neighbor's stand. "Half price. Everything half price; then we bargain."

And today, up a narrow staircase between two jewelry shops, over-looking one of Asia Minor's oldest and most fabled harbors, where Saint Paul preached to the Ephesians and where, legend has it, Saint John brought the Virgin Mary after the death of Jesus, we once again check our E-mail at yet another Internet Café.

October 26 / Bodrum, Turkey

I have just finished William Martin's wonderful new novel, *Citizen Washington*. It has made me appreciate, perhaps more than any pure history could have done, what a remarkable man our first president was, and just how fortunate the thirteen colonies were to have him as the mortar that held them together in their struggle against Great Britain. I come away (as I believe Martin intended) less awed by Jefferson and Hamilton, more respectful of John Adams and much taken by Washington's injunction to "learn by doin' and do by finishin'."

I wonder how many of us today would have the courage and the tenacity to fight for so long and with such determination without adequate food, clothing or armaments. It is easy enough to recall Thomas Paine's reference to "summer soldiers and sunshine patriots," but I've rarely given much thought to the despair that must have surrounded General Washington as he watched the various militias melt away after they had fulfilled their terms of six months. To keep that despair hidden from others and to find the strength to lift himself and most of those around him back into action and on toward ultimate victory was truly heroic. Finally, as the first president, to have resisted the temptations of throne and all the vainglory that goes with it, to have resisted so much to which his contemporary Napoleon surrendered, was evidence of Washington's genuine greatness.

October 27 / Antalya, Turkey

The surroundings are spectacular—the Taurus mountain range behind, the Aegean in front of the city—but Antalya itself is rather drab and uninteresting. On its outskirts, however, lie the ancient cities of Perge and Aspendos. Perge goes back to the time of the Trojan Wars and was founded by Greeks. It is not as spectacular a site as Ephesus, but it boasts huge and splendid baths, with the heating chambers still to be seen and some of the original tilework still in place. There's also a fine *agora*, or marketplace, where goods and ideas were once traded, and an impressive esplanade of shop fronts. Roman chariots once rode along roads on either side of a fountain that poured water into a kilometer-long trough.

The city fathers of Aspendos, recognizing that they could not defeat Alexander the Great's army, purchased their survival (and saved Alexander the inconvenience of pillaging), and the city remained untouched. Nothing remains today, however, except the ruins of a magnificent aqueduct and the best-preserved Roman theater in the world. It was built during the reign of, and to honor, the emperor and philosopher Marcus Aurelius. There is much to admire in his stoicism and the directness of his ethical code. He laid it out simply and concisely in his book *Meditations*, and I have given away many copies to friends.

A couple of years ago *Nightline* was doing a series on "The Making of a Foreign Policy." We traveled with President Clinton to eastern Europe and Russia. The day we flew out of Andrews Air Force Base, the president had just returned from burying his mother in Arkansas. I bought a copy of *Meditations*, wrote an inscription (something to the effect that I had always found Marcus Aurelius a source of comfort during difficult times and hoped it would be for him, too) and gave it to him aboard Air Force One. He thanked me and observed that he hadn't read Marcus Aurelius in a long time.

A few days later, a quote from *Meditations* cropped up in a Clinton speech in Moscow. I was secretly pleased. A few weeks after that, the president was being interviewed and was asked what his all-time favorite book was. *Meditations*, he said.

I wondered about his failure to mention the book's unique standing in his esteem when I gave it to him. It seems to me that certainly would have been a natural reaction when someone hands you a copy of your all-time favorite book. Perhaps I've grown too cynical of our president.

October 28 / En route to Alexandria, Egypt

A group of armed men took over the parliament of Armenia yesterday. They shot the prime minister and a number of other parliamentarians. I was watching CNN when the news broke, and it was a perfect example of all that is wrong with television's electronic tail wagging the editorial dog. The anchor didn't have a clue as to what was happening, and neither, for that matter, did the Armenian journalist whom he had on a phone line. The name of the game these days, though, is, Since we're on the air anyway, keep talking until we can get a live picture up.

CNN killed off the poor prime minister in the first five minutes. Then, as fresh information became available, the network restored him to life and put him in some hospital in critical condition. Finally, CNN dispatched him to his eternal reward, once and for all. It is not altogether clear whether he was dead from the start and should not have been reported as taken to a hospital in "a critically wounded condition," or whether he had been critically wounded from the start and didn't die until some hours after CNN first reported him dead. In the long run, I suppose, it makes no particular difference; he is equally dead in either instance. But there is this dreadful rush to be first with the obvious.

In the old days we at least gave lip service to the notion that we would wait to report a story until we got most of the facts straight. The imperatives of "live" television, however, are different. They demand a constant patter of commentary and conversation on the story of the moment, even when nothing but the most basic information (i.e., there's been an outbreak of shooting inside the Armenian parliament) is known. For a television newsman to acknowledge, however briefly, that he is still in the process of trying to accumulate information and doesn't feel ready to report the story might be to give up control of the story to some other twenty-four-hour news operation, one less encumbered by a need to check its facts.

We of the television news industry have no greater fear than that of a viewer's finger on the remote control.

October 29 / Alexandria

There are heavily armed police on the pier. The tour bus that left for Cairo and the pyramids early this morning with a load of our fellow passengers on board was guarded front and rear by armored cars, as was a similar bus that took another group on a tour of Alexandria this morning.

In the various and sundry lectures with which passengers aboard our cruise ship are prepared for the next destination, nobody ever talks about "now"; "now" as in contemporaneous or recent events that might impinge on the carefree nature of our holiday; "now" as in Kurdish rebels or earthquakes in Turkey; "now" as in the attack on another crowd of tourists in Luxor a couple of years ago (that was the event that led the Egyptian government to start assigning armed police to large moving groups of tourists); "now" as in the nasty little confrontation between Israeli troops and Palestinian teenagers in Bethlehem earlier this week.

The ancient cultures and the antiquities are what we have come to see. We feel relatively safe in the past. The present is already too much with us.

October 30 / Port Said, Egypt

This is a grungy little city. It came into existence and achieved international importance only with the building of the Suez Canal in 1859. In 1956, the canal became the spark that nearly tore the Western alliance apart. Gamel Abdul Nasser, who had overthrown Farouk, the last king to sit on the Egyptian throne, tried to nationalize the canal. I need to check my history, but I believe it was Anthony Eden, the British prime minister, who immediately moved forces to prevent it. Eisenhower was furious. Nasser took several steps to the left, asked the Americans to leave Egypt and invited the Russians in.

So, here we are forty-three years later: The British are no longer a great international power. The United States gives more foreign aid to Egypt than any country in the world, save Israel. I saw a couple of old signs in Russian outside a quayside shop, but, beyond that, the Russians are completely out of the mix here. They, in fact, are up to their knees in Chechnya again. Much of the news this week has focused on the fact that the Russian army is surrounding the Chechen capital of Grozny. They have been bombing and shelling the hell out of it for days now. The military clearly wants to take Grozny on the ground and wipe out the Chechen guerrilla fighters once and for all. Russia's prime minister (Vladimir Putin, about whom little is known other than that he is a former KGB officer shuffled into the job by Boris Yeltsin) delivered a heartfelt eulogy for the recently murdered prime minister of Armenia yesterday. The thrust of his message was that Russians can empathize with such terrorist attacks. There was a series of unsolved terrorist bombings in Moscow last month, which in large part is why the Russian army is cracking down on the Chechens.

October 31 / Jerusalem

An EgyptAir Boeing 767 has crashed off the coast of Massachusetts and more than two hundred people are dead. No one has any idea at this point what caused the crash, although hypothesis and speculation can be had on CNN for 10 cents on the dollar. If, indeed, this was a terrorist act, however, no one has yet taken responsibility for it.

Grace Anne and I went over to the Church of the Holy Sepulcher this afternoon. It is a dizzying place to be. In one corner a group of Franciscan monks was leading pilgrims, most of them carrying burning candles, on Stations of the Cross. In another, a number of Armenian monks and novitiates, their leader wearing a black cowl, were prostrating themselves on either side of a long block of stone that shines with water. Tradition has it that this was the stone onto which Christ's lifeless body was lowered from the cross. The chanting of the Armenians intermingled with that of the Franciscans and yet another group of Greek Orthodox priests and pilgrims. At one point we found ourselves gathered at a shrine over the rocks of Golgotha. One of the Franciscans swung a censer beneath an altar erected over the spot where Christ was presumably crucified, waving the smoke in, around and over the hole that may have held the base of that infamous cross. No sooner did the Franciscans and their group of pilgrims vacate the area than a Greek Orthodox priest, who had been watching and glowering, arms folded over his chest, stepped in to remove a green altar cloth, revealing the Greek inscriptions on the marble.

The various Christian sects seem barely to tolerate one another, but care and control of the church are shared among them. If it is this difficult for them to share what is, after all, their common, holiest shrine, what hope is there for the ultimate disposition of Jerusalem itself, among the Jews, Christians and Muslims?

November

November 1 / Jerusalem

The followers of the three great religions that have so much of their history here are convinced of incompatible truths. The Jews and Muslims believe Christ was not the Messiah; the Christian pilgrims filling small plastic bags with dust and pebbles amid ancient olive trees in, what they are convinced, is the garden at Gethsemane, are absolutely convinced that these are the paths walked by the Son of God.

The Jews who lie buried on the Mount of Olives, their gravestones facing the eastern wall of the Old City, died believing they would be immediately admitted to heaven with the coming of the Messiah; not Jesus, but one who is yet to come. Virtue may have had something to do with their burial on the Mount of Olives, but placement is key. Even in death, there is the old real estate agent's admonition: location, location, location.

The Muslims expect Mohammed to return to the site from which he and his white steed ascended to heaven, under what is now the Dome of the Rock. It is the same place where, incidentally (in Jerusalem's wonderful euphemism for "Who really knows?"), "tradition has it that" Abraham raised his knife in obedience to God's command, in preparation for the sacrifice of his beloved son, Isaac.

Now, add to this heady mix the expectations of those already here, or preparing to come here for the dawn of the new millennium, for what they are convinced is the beginning of the Apocalypse, the Rapture, the end of the world as we have known it, and it should make for quite a New Year's celebration.

November 2 / Jerusalem

A little more on the subject of religious perspectives: Our guide today is an Orthodox rabbi. He has taught religion at Yale and frequently serves as an advisor to the Israeli government on religious matters. Grace Anne and I were somewhat startled, then, to hear him express the opinion that King Herod died before Christ was born. The book of Matthew in the New Testament is quite unambiguous on the subject, of course. Joseph and Mary fled into Egyptian exile with the baby Jesus because Herod had ordered the slaughter of all male babies under the age of two living in and around Bethlehem. Is it possible that the medieval monk who is presumed to have screwed up the calendar by placing Christ's birth after Herod's death actually got it right? Our rabbinical guide sent over an entry from the *Encyclopaedia Britannica* supporting his contention.

In any event, the Jewish perspective on Herod is something of a mixed bag. He was, on the one hand, altogether too tight with the Romans; on the other hand, he raised the most extraordinary and magnificent Temple. Solomon erected the first; Herod built the second—the one that was destroyed in A.D. 70 by the Romans. It is to the western wall of that ruined Temple that Jews from around the world have come ever since. From the construction point of view alone, it clearly was a breathtaking achievement. Some of the limestone blocks weighed as much as six hundred tons. How they were placed in position continues to mystify architects and builders to this day. The Swedish cranes that now dot the landscape of Jerusalem could not begin to handle those blocks.

The construction and destruction of the Second Temple are only of passing interest to most Christians, though. Herod is principally the architect of the slaughter of the innocents. Herod's role in building the Temple, however, is of surpassing interest to most Orthodox Jews who, like our rabbi/guide today, consider the Temple on the Mount to be the holiest spot on earth and are significantly less concerned with Herod's murderous obsession regarding the birth of the Messiah. A compelling case can be made, however, that if the Romans had not destroyed the Second Temple, the face of Judaism today would be totally different. The Levite priests, who succeeded one another according to the law of primogeniture, like a royal family, might still be in control of an essentially provincial religion. The role of the rabbis, which became important when Jerusalem was no longer the physical center of Judaism, when the religion had to become portable, would likely never have become what it is today.

In most parts of the world, these are interesting, even important matters of historical and religious concern. Here, they still seem to throb with contemporary importance.

November 3 / Jerusalem

Our appointment for lunch with Suha Arafat, wife of the Palestinian president, is set for 1:30 in Gaza. We are stuck at the border crossing, negotiating with a bunch of young Israeli soldiers, because the hotshot former foreign and diplomatic correspondent forgot to bring his and his wife's passports. My friend Ali Kadan Rabaia, a Palestinian Israeli of great personal charm, who is also a terrific reporter, is trying to pull rabbits out of a hat. It may or may not be helping that every second Palestinian passing through the checkpoint appears to be a huge *Nightline* fan. The Israeli kids with the M-16s have never heard of me and seem singularly unimpressed by my ABC News ID card. (These days, outside the borders of the United States and parts of Canada, the only news organization anyone has heard of is CNN.) Two attractive young Palestinian women recognize Ali and give him an effusive greeting. He introduces them to me, at which point attractive young woman number one cranks up the effusiveness to an even higher register. I'm prepared to be flattered on principle. When she passes through the checkpoint, Ali informs me she is the daughter of one of the PLO's most famous and effective hijackers. He was killed on the job, and Arafat himself formally adopted the daughter. She, dressed in Paris chic, has no trouble passing through Israeli security. Grace Anne and I remain stuck, waiting for a laissez-passer from the defense ministry in Jerusalem. One of the soldiers tells Ali that a fax is forthcoming. But it's already after 1 o'clock, so we just wander into Gaza, figuring that we'll deal with getting back into Israel later on.

Suha greets us in the living/dining room of a pleasant villa that she sometimes shares with the president of the Palestinian Authority on those rare occasions when he's in town. At the moment he is returning from Oslo, where he has been meeting with President Clinton and

Prime Minister Barak. The villa overlooks the Mediterranean, and the view is beautiful. The house itself would seem modest in Queens.

Suha, who is about thirty years younger than her husband, is smart, hospitable and charming. She laughs easily and frequently, says just a little more than the grim men around her husband appreciate. Today she tells us how her four-year-old daughter chilled Arafat just prior to a meeting with Clinton by repeatedly asking whether they would also be meeting "Monica."

When I express a passing interest in Gaza's new international airport, Suha insists on sending an escort with us to visit it. The airport sits on the Egyptian border and it takes a long time to get there. It's very new, quite handsome and absolutely empty. Very few airlines fly into Gaza, and those passengers who do still have to pass through Israeli security before they are free to enter Gaza. The region tends to be largely overlooked in discussions of what will happen next out here, but a few thousand Israeli settlers still sit on about 30 percent of the land. Gaza remains home to some 350,000 Palestinian refugees who continue to live in pretty dreadful camps and, while things are relatively quiet these days, it remains a seedbed for terrorism.

On our way out of Gaza (by now nobody seems to care that we have no passports) Ali introduces me to another young Palestinian woman and her two young children. She, it turns out, is the daughter of an even more notorious Palestinian hijacker and bomber of years gone by. She has no trouble passing through the checkpoint either.

November 4 / Jerusalem

It is our last day in Israel, and Ali picks us up and takes us to the Dome of the Rock, which seems unusually crowded. Ali (who, as a Muslim, probably should have known) learns that this is the anniversary of Mohammed's ascent to heaven from this very rock. In point of fact, it is a holiday for Muslims, which explains why we see so many women and children.

This rock has a lot of history. In addition to being the launching platform for the ascent of Mohammed and Abraham's binding of Isaac onto an altar, this may also have been the actual locus of the Holy of Holies, the place where the original Ark of the Covenant rested during the time of the First and Second Temples.

Stairs in the center of the mosque lead down into a cave in the heart of the rock. A hole has been carved into the ceiling of the cave and through it one can see the highest interior point of the Dome of the Rock. On this day at this time non-Muslims are forbidden to enter the cave. Ali engages a burly guard blocking our way, and, even though I speak no Arabic, it's clear that he's getting nowhere. Suddenly, the guard looks over in my direction and, in a clear, accent-free English, says: "Oh, my God, it's Ted Koppel." He is from Wisconsin, where he and his brother run a gas station. He tries to spend half of each year in Jerusalem.

The guard now insists that Grace Anne, Ali and I go down into the cave, even though about forty women and children are down there praying. We do. It's claustrophobic and stuffy, just like the tiny synagogue in the underground tunnel next to the western wall; just like Jesus' birthplace in Bethlehem; just like the tiny chapel in the bowels of the Church of the Holy Sepulchre.

We leave in order to attempt a last shopping sortie through the souk. I'm looking for small gifts to distribute in the office. Ali has a great suggestion: olive stone worry beads. I abandon my efforts when Ali learns from one of the shopkeepers that just about everything in his inventory has been imported from China. The old silk road is alive and prospering, although it has rarely seemed less exotic.

November 5 / Frankfurt, Germany

I spent a lot of time in this city when I was a boy. My father and mother had returned here from England, seeking restitution for all that the Nazis had taken. They lived here for the better part of three years. During those years I went to boarding school in England, but spent my vacations here. It was on the streets of Frankfurt, playing with eleven- and twelve-year-old German boys, that I learned my German that is, to this day, marked by an accent still immediately identifiable as "Frankfurter Deutsch."

When I first came here in 1950, much of the city was rubble. We were in the American zone, but a British passport gave me access to certain movie theaters and other facilities that were still closed to Germans. The other kids and I used to make extra spending money in those days by collecting newspapers and lead, which we stripped from the tops of empty wine bottles. We sold both paper and lead by the kilo at neighborhood collection points.

In those days, the iceman still delivered huge blocks of ice by horse-drawn cart. He would carry the ice from one floor of our apartment building to the next, and residents would stick it into lead-lined boxes that were the precursors of refrigerators. I would go to the store every morning to pick up that day's jug of milk and half a dozen fresh rolls.

Some of the old landmarks are still here but, for the most part, the Frankfurt of the early 1950s has been replaced by the thriving, bustling city that is today Germany's financial center.

I was delighted to find one randy landmark unchanged. At the Goethe Platz, there is a statue of three burghers, commissioned (my father told me nearly fifty years ago) but not paid for. The sculptor took his revenge in a particularly artistic fashion. Viewed head-on, the principal figure looks fine—elegantly dressed, with the end of a soft leather belt falling at his waist. Seen from the side, however, the belt becomes a large, flaccid penis, drooping for eternity.

November 6 / New York

We had a wonderful and memorable additional birthday celebration for Grace Anne. Over the past few weeks each member of the immediate family recorded his or her thoughts about Grace Anne on videotape. Those were skillfully woven together over photographs of Grace Anne that covered the time from her babyhood until now. Andrea did most of the heavy lifting on this project, and it came out beautifully. It always gives me pleasure to see her fine work on CNN; but this video, which will be seen by only a handful of people, is a real labor of love.

What strikes me most about the video is how breathtakingly beautiful Grace Anne was as a young woman. It has been almost forty years since we met at Stanford, but I could feel my heart in my throat again when I saw on the television screen the image that so captivated me as a young graduate student. There is in a mature relationship (and I suppose after forty years we can no longer deny the "mature" part) an evolution that takes place. Nature uses the perfection of young beauty as the lure that keeps the reproductive cycle going, but what Grace Anne and I have now is a far more complex romantic relationship. It is far deeper than what once drew us to each other. It is a love that allows us to look beyond the physical imperfections that age imposes, a love that now is based on the shared experiences of a lifetime together, and a knowledge of each other that is almost absolute.

The whole family went to dinner with some friends this evening, and, when it was over, the headwaiter, who immigrated to this country from Serbia thirty years ago, came over and congratulated us on our children. They are, indeed, a wonderful collection of human beings, and Grace Anne and I were glowing with pride this evening.

New York is in the middle of marathon fever. Tomorrow, literally thousands of men and women from all over the world will run in the New York Marathon. Andrea and I ran the Marine Corps Marathon in Washington fifteen years ago, and it remains one of our proudest achievements. What is so remarkable about running in a marathon is that you can feel the same sense of achievement finishing the race in five hours that the genuine athletes feel in completing more than twenty-six miles in two and a half hours or less. This is one of the only sports events in the world in which world champions and weekend warriors like me are competing, however briefly or unrealistically, on the same field. You could sense that pride and anticipation all over New York today. The competitors, many of them decked out in warm-ups adorned with the names of their home countries, were strolling and jogging through Central Park. It was unseasonably warm, with the temperature creeping up toward seventy. Too warm for the race (it will be much cooler tomorrow) but perfect for relishing the prospect.

November 7 / Potomac

We are home again. It has been a near perfect vacation, and I believe that all aspects of the birthday celebration for Grace Anne, from the holiday itself to the dinner last night, were all that the kids and I had planned. Nevertheless, as stimulating and enjoyable as travel can be, there is, as Dorothy noted in *The Wizard of Oz*, "no place like home." Indeed, these days, so many people are traveling to so many different places so much of the time that remaining stationary may soon become the most sought-after kind of relaxation.

November 8 / Potomac

I'm trying to catch up. In a few weeks I'm to moderate a "debate" among whichever Republican presidential candidates are left at that time, and another debate between Al Gore and Bill Bradley. Tom Bettag has sent me a videotape of two *Nightline* programs consisting of debates that took place while I was gone. I'm sure jet lag has something to do with it, but I fell asleep watching the tape of the Republicans. I woke up, rewound the tape and started to watch what I had missed, only to fall asleep again in the middle of the Gore-Bradley event.

As far as I could tell, what most animated the Republicans was the absence of George W. Bush. He had stayed in Texas, he said, in order to attend a dinner at Southern Methodist University in honor of his wife, Laura. Nobody quite believes that. Bush and his wife had to go to the extraordinary length of doing a satellite interview with one of the local stations in New Hampshire explaining how important the dinner really was and why George W. put his wife ahead of the opportunity to be a punching bag for his fellow Republicans McCain, Bauer, Forbes, Hatch and Keyes. The young woman conducting the interview asked Laura whether she would have understood if her husband had gone to New Hampshire rather than squiring her to the dinner. "Sure," said Laura, leaving George grinning uncomfortably next to her.

November 9 / Washington

Commercial television is like an overflowing bucket that has a small hole far below the waterline. The leak is not enough to empty the bucket anytime soon, but the water level is certainly going down at an alarmingly steady rate. What (momentarily, at least) seems to have plugged the leak is a tacky little quiz show, a throwback to one of the most embarrassing and devastating moments in television history; it has captured viewers big-time. There was a time, more than forty years ago, when quiz shows were all the rage on prime-time TV. *The 64,000 Dollar Question*, for example, made a national icon out of a mousy little psychologist whose expertise lay in boxing. Dr. Joyce Brothers later contended that she was simply blessed with a photographic memory, and had assumed (correctly) that the show's producers would be intrigued by a woman psychologist who knew everything there was to know about pugilism. So she memorized *The Encyclopedia of Boxing*. There was nothing wrong with that. Unfortunately, having developed a taste for broadcasting, she made a career out of it.

The other quiz show that dominated the ratings in the 1950s was called *Twenty-one*. It made a star of a Columbia University English professor by the name of Charles Van Doren—and then destroyed his reputation when it emerged that the program's producers had been feeding him the answers.

Fast forward to the summer of '99. Regis Philbin, a decent and genial man whose star flickered briefly when he played second banana to Joey Bishop on a failed ABC effort to match *The Tonight Show* many years ago, and who now dominates morning television together with his costar, Kathy Lee Gifford, emerged late last summer as the savior of ABC on a program called *Who Wants to Be a Millionaire?* It was on for ten or eleven days and was an instant smash. It's back now for the November "sweeps" and is an even bigger hit.

It has clearly struck a responsive chord with the American public, twenty-six million of them last Sunday alone. Why this harmless, slightly silly quiz program succeeds where almost every other attempt at network programming has failed is beyond me.

For the sake of full disclosure, I should admit that I haven't missed an episode yet.

November 10 / Washington

What, then, marks America as we come to the end of the century?

Television. We watch, on average (is it possible?) six or seven hours of it a day.

Political apathy. We drone on endlessly about the importance of the freedoms we enjoy, and the media wallows in covering campaigns, but we don't much bother going to the polls.

Dieting. We eat too much, we drink too much and we make millionaires of any half-wit with a notion of how we can lose the excess weight. Americans are on a gargantuan seesaw, teetering between fast-food establishments and diet centers.

Guns. There are more than two hundred million guns in America as we approach the end of the twentieth century—almost one gun per man, woman and child in the country. (The most lethal weapon in America, however, still appears to be the car. We kill each other on our highways at the rate of more than fifty thousand a year.)

Litigation. We sue at the drop of a hat, frequently on the assumption that if the target of our suit has deep enough pockets, some sort of financial settlement will be reached in preference to pursuing the lawsuit, with its attendant depositions, preliminary briefs and actual trial. Even the silliest little cases can cost hundreds of thousands of dollars to litigate and take up a great deal of your time.

Political correctness. This enforced brand of politeness has terrorized essentially decent people into adopting acceptable euphemisms in place of plain speaking. Most of the real cowering takes place among academics on our college campuses. The real bigots in our culture have done little or nothing to curb their racism, homophobia or antifeminism; they just don't talk about it in public as much anymore. I have a strong feeling, though, that one of these days there will be a gigantic eruption of pent-up hatred.

November 11 / Washington

This morning's *Washington Post* has a long feature piece on a tremendously expensive Japanese toy that the headline writer has called Y2K9. It's the puppy for the next millennium. Developed by the Sony Corporation, Y2K9 (his Japanese name is Aibo) carries a sixty-four-bit processor and sixteen megabytes of internal memory. Its personality is etched (I'm quoting liberally from the *Post*'s story) on an eight-megabyte "memory stick." Each Aibo will, according to Sony, "grow up" differently, according to the interaction between robo-pup and its owner. The toy is equipped with a 180,000-pixel color camera and has a distance sensor in its nose. (We're talking $2,500 worth of doggy here.) It does not, of course, require the attention and training of its real-life counterpart. It doesn't need to be walked, or fed. It doesn't require shots. It will never poop on your living room rug. All of which makes Aibo something of a paradigm for our time.

In so much of what we do these days, we seem to be looking for trouble-free, facile answers. We want to "have it all," preferably without having to pay for it. In real life, though, it is the act of working through the inconveniences, the troubles, the pain of a relationship, even with a dog, that invests that relationship with real meaning. What makes me mist up at the memory of our old lab, Damien, who passed on to his reward a couple of years ago, is not just the memory of his head nuzzling in the hollow of my knee when I took him for his last walk of the day after I got home from work. It is how frustrated I used to get in the winter, because Damien wanted to stay out and I didn't; he knew I couldn't take him in until after he'd done his business, and he regularly engaged in a deliberate and malicious act of bladder control.

Damien was a runaway who came to us when he was about one. He had clearly been abused, because at first he would cringe and bare his teeth whenever one of us put out a hand to pet him. It took a year to engage his trust and calm him down completely. The whole family invested in that process, and the fact that it was successful is what gave us such a sense of pride in Damien. I'm sure Sony's technicians spent a lot more time and effort creating Aibo, but that makes him their dog, not mine.

November 12 / Washington

As we were preparing to tape tonight's broadcast, one of the studio crew members was talking about the incredible quality of DVDs (I believe the initials stand for Digital Video Discs) compared to videotape. He was talking about the movies that are now available in this new format, and how the improved quality will soon make the videocassettes we've been renting and buying these last few years seem virtually primitive.

It got me to thinking about how many different technologies in this general area alone I've experienced in my lifetime. We have a really ancient record player at home that my father-in-law gave us some years ago. It's an original Edison and came with about twenty wax cylinders. These are items from 1906 or 1907. Granted, those were not a part of my personal experience, but the windup record player with the bullhorn speaker is. My first experience of listening to recorded music (other than on the radio) was with 78 r.p.m. records on one of those machines. My father's first tape recorder was actually a wire recorder. I have no idea how it worked, except that the audio was recorded on spools of thin, steel wire. If you got a kink in the wire, it was unusable.

Seventy-eight-r.p.m. records gave way to 45s, and then for years, of course, we listened to LPs, the long-playing records that spun at thirty-three and a third revolutions per minute. Those were replaced by eight-track cartridges that soon gave way to audiocassettes, which, in turn, were reduced to near obsolescence by CDs. Now it's all digital.

None of this takes into account the phenomenal advances in video cameras, nor does it begin to account for the role that the Internet is starting to play in terms of storing and processing audio and video information.

I hope I can keep up.

November 13 / St. Mary's County

I have often wondered what it must be like to have been born with the gift of optimism, to awaken each morning with a sense of promise and anticipation. I incline more toward a lingering aftertaste of some half-forgotten disaster, as though I had gambled away the house in some drunken poker game. Mind you, I find absolutely nothing admirable in pessimism, but it does have a certain practical application. We pessimists are less frequently disappointed than people with a sunnier disposition.

When I am unable to detect fiasco in my own immediate experience, I suspect that something terrible has befallen one of the kids. In point of fact, all those whom I love have given me far more reason to celebrate than to fear, and my own life has been a succession, if not an uninterrupted series, of hopes and dreams fulfilled.

I normally find it difficult to view the world through rose-colored lenses, but today it is almost impossible to do otherwise. It is a mid-autumn day of such perfection that my surroundings alone are a reproach to gloom. The sun is reflected as a blinding pillar of gold, trembling and shimmering where it has been flung onto St. Inigoes Creek. Defying the season, there are still a few white roses atop the arbor that we built on the occasion of Deirdre and Larry's wedding nine years ago. The lantana is ablaze with color and bursting with blackberry-like fruit. Our magnolia tree, one of the most magnificent I've ever seen, remains a deep, rich green, in stark contrast to the giant tulip poplar, on the other side of the house, which is almost totally bare of leaves. It has been an unexpectedly balmy day, but by late afternoon it was chilly enough to warrant the fire that is burning behind me now in the kitchen fireplace.

For the moment, at least, all of our lives appear to be in harmony and I am able, however briefly, to accept that perception as reality.

November 14 / St. Mary's County

As I mentioned earlier, every Saturday afternoon C-SPAN radio broadcasts approximately two hours' worth of audiotapes from the presidency of Lyndon Baines Johnson. They are truly remarkable, in that Johnson had authorized the taping of all telephone conversations conducted in the Oval Office, in his bedroom and at his ranch house in Texas. He obviously knew of the taping, but at least occasionally over the years he must have forgotten that the recorder was running. What emerges is a stunning portrait of the presidency. One moment Johnson is a president trying to convince a southern senator to lend his support to (or at least refrain from opposing) a piece of civil rights legislation. He is, simultaneously, a Texan talking as a southerner to a southerner. His drawl broadens so that "negroes" comes out "nigras," but the private Johnson is a more compelling and convincing advocate of civil rights than the public one ever was.

The next moment he is listening to one of his many foreign policy advisors, Dean Rusk or Robert McNamara or McGeorge Bundy, bring him up to date on the latest aspect of the expanding Vietnam conflict. There is never the slightest doubt as to who is in charge, but the listener is struck by the nature of these intelligent, businesslike exchanges. These men are neither fawning nor hesitant to lay out difficult options. One can be critical of the involvement in Vietnam and still come away from these tapes respecting the thoughtful and difficult process of decision making in which the president and his advisors engaged.

Some of Johnson's phone conversations are also hilariously trivial and profane, as when he bullies a hairdresser into coming to Washington and styling the coiffures of his wife and daughters for free. He leaves no doubt that he expects the stylist to tell the world that he has been summoned to the White House and that this form of free advertising should be ample compensation.

On another occasion he calls the president of Haggar slacks. Johnson clearly liked the slacks he'd been sent from the company on a previous occasion and wanted more; he also wanted some matching shirts. I was listening to this particular conversation while running along the towpath of the C&O Canal, and what nearly doubled me over was the president of the United States explaining that he needed a little more room in the crotch or, as Johnson put it, "along that seam between my balls and my bunghole."

I was never a particular Johnson fan, and yet I now find myself reassessing. It's difficult to believe that LBJ has been dead for twenty-six years already. Perhaps time has something to do with my changing perception of the man. Perhaps, also, it has something to do with the men who have occupied the Oval Office since Johnson. In every respect, though, he was a towering figure, and I'm inclined to believe that in another fifty years he'll be included among our great presidents.

November 15 / Potomac

Tuesdays with Morrie has been made into a television movie starring Jack Lemmon as my late friend Morrie Schwartz. The sequence of events leading to this film was as follows: The *Boston Globe* did a feature story on a retired sociology professor from Brandeis who was suffering from ALS, better known as Lou Gehrig's disease. The story caught the attention of Richard Harris, a *Nightline* senior producer. He was struck by the fact that the former teacher, though dying, was determined to celebrate his remaining life with as many of his friends, students and family members as possible. Morrie had actually insisted on some sort of a party cum memorial celebration at which those present would be able to tell the "dearly beloved" to his face how much they loved him.

One of our producers, Dan Morris, flew to Boston to meet with Morrie and to see whether he would agree to an interview with me. Thus began what would eventually become a series of three *Nightline* interviews and a regular exchange of phone calls between Morrie and me until shortly before his death.

Mitch Albom, a former student of Morrie's, saw the first program and was moved to call his old professor, as I mentioned earlier. Thus began his regular flights from Detroit to Boston and the conversations that would become the slim volume *Tuesdays with Morrie*. It has been at or near the top of the *New York Times* best-seller list for more than two years, and now Oprah Winfrey has turned it into a movie. I don't know how good the film will be, but I'm sure it will generate yet another round of interest in the book. Morrie would be delighted.

November 16 / Washington

Tonight we are reporting on a project run by successful African American men who believe that many black boys are failing in school because there are no positive male role models in their lives. In the course of researching the material, we found one statistic that just blew me away; in fact, I didn't believe it. Eight out of ten African American men are said to have spent time behind bars. That does not necessarily mean they have done time in prison; some were simply arrested and held, even if only for a few hours. Even so, I found that figure incredible. So I just spent a few minutes talking to five of my black colleagues here at *Nightline*, and they have *all* spent time behind bars. One of them, a videotape editor, was picked up by D.C. police on his way back to work from McDonald's. He apparently bore a resemblance to a suspect in some crime, and it took a phone call from his supervisor here at ABC to get him released from jail. One of our directors was repeatedly picked up driving to work, some years ago, because he had a new car. The first couple of times he was taken to jail and held. You would think that the police would have learned from their error, but my colleague assures me that he continued to be stopped by the police until he went to his news director (this was in another community) and suggested that the station do a story on what was happening to him.

What I find most astounding is the fact that none of the five men had even mentioned his arrest and incarceration until I raised the subject. In other words, it was a common enough occurrence that it never came up in the many conversations we have had about racism in America.

November 17 / Washington

The media is full of stories about EgyptAir 990, and the implication of all the stories is essentially that one of the pilots deliberately caused the airliner to crash. There are certain technical conclusions that have been reached on the basis of data found in one of the plane's two "black boxes." It seems the plane was taken off autopilot and subsequently, as the aircraft went into a dive, both engines were shut off. Questions are being raised about two elevators in the tail section that control whether the plane ascends or descends. One was found in a position that would have put the plane into a dive; the other was in position to allow the plane to gain altitude.

Taken by themselves each of these procedures could lend itself to a benign explanation, but collectively, together with a piece of information from the second black box, they have led sources from the National Transportation Safety Board to infer that the evidence points to a suicide-murder. That last item of information is the recording of a prayer (or at least a phrase invoking God) spoken in Arabic by one of the pilots just before the various procedures were set into motion. The inference is that he spoke those words in anticipation of what he was about to do.

The Egyptians are furious. They point out (correctly, according to a Muslim, Arabic-speaking intern of ours) that the prayer in question is the functional equivalent of a Catholic crossing himself. In other words, it could be spoken just before a man who knows he's going to die is shot; but it's just as likely to be said before a basketball player shoots an important foul. Some of the less responsible organs of the Egyptian press are claiming that U.S. authorities recovered the two black boxes, tampered with them and then put them back into the water before finally "recovering" them. Others blame a member of the crew of an Israeli airliner, charging that he planted a bomb in the hand luggage of the Egyptian crew.

There is almost a complete lack of understanding in Egypt of the kind of informed speculation that we tend to take for granted in the American media but which the Egyptians regard as a callous and totally unnecessary rush to judgment.

November 18 / Washington

Jake is two today.

Pam Kahn, who was one of the first producers on *Nightline* nearly twenty years ago, died today. She was only forty-five. Pam had a degenerative brain disease that afflicted her in a fashion similar to Alzheimer's. There was a lot she couldn't remember, and, for the last couple of years, she couldn't even talk. She married about ten years ago. Her widower is a sweet, mild-tempered accountant who never really got to enjoy his marriage. He stuck with, and by, Pam throughout all the bad times. "Through sickness," that reference in the marriage vows that we tend to take so casually, was in some respects the totality of his marriage to Pam.

She was a passionate civil libertarian. She felt very strongly about the injustices of the war in Central America during the 1980s and pushed us time and again to send her there. When she suspected at one time that Rick Kaplan (then our executive producer) and I were reluctant to send a woman into a war zone, she got justifiably furious. We never raised the issue again.

There are instances where life, truly, is not fair. The brevity of Pam's career, marriage and life is one such.

November 19 / Washington

Last week the president of the United States said the following: "The federal government is Y2K ready and leading by example. And the American people can have full faith that everything from air traffic control systems to Social Security payment systems will continue to work exactly as they should." This week, NBC has been broadcasting that statement exactly as delivered—after which the screen goes black and the words "What if he's wrong?" fill the space. That, in turn, is followed by scenes of panic, explosions and troops in the street. All of this is by way of a promotional device for a program appearing on NBC this coming Sunday: *Y2K: The Movie.*

Just when I was starting to think the level of network irresponsibility can't get much lower, NBC comes along to reassure me that we haven't reached rock bottom.

November 20 / New York

There will be a choral recital at the Madison Avenue Presbyterian Church tomorrow night. A bulletin board in front of the church advises passersby that the choir will be performing the works of W. A. Mozart. I wonder what quirk induced the author of that announcement to add the initials "W. A." Of all the composers who ever lived, perhaps only Beethoven is better known than Mozart; but assuming that someone did not know Mozart, would W. A. be much help?

In New York, having a familiar face such as mine produces a minor symphony of reactions. Couples dig each other in the ribs, tug on each other's sleeves and then stop and turn. I am not meant to have seen this. The simplest, easiest remark for me to react to is the robust, "Yo, Ted!" It is a frank, open recognition that requires nothing more in response than "How ya doin?" A surprising number of people regard the spotting of a familiar face as the opportunity for a quiz.

"Newsman, right?"

"Right."

"Channel 2!"

"No, Channel 7."

"Tom Brokaw?"

"No, Ted Koppel."

I have actually had one or two people look quizzically at me at this point and ask, "Are you sure?"

In a department store this afternoon I had a similar dialogue with a matron who was buying her son (he was certainly young enough to be her son) some shirts and ties. After we had established who I was, she informed me that her confusion had resulted from the fact that I used to have black hair. I assured her that I had never had black hair, that my hair used to be a reddish blond. No, she insisted, she was sure that it was once black. At this point the salesclerk, seeing that I needed help, voted for reddish blond and that settled the matter.

Tough town, New York.

November 21 / New York

Sometimes in life the best moments occur as a direct consequence of something you anticipate with less than enthusiasm.

My father-in-law is approaching the age of eighty-five. He has slipped significantly since we went to Notre Dame together back in September; indeed, that was clearly a high point for him. Still, he wanted to be present for his great-grandson's second birthday party on Saturday, so he and his wife, Penny, rented a car and driver to bring them to New York from Maryland. Today, we agreed that he would take all of us—Grace Anne and me, our four children, my daughter Deirdre's husband, Larry, and Jake—on a tour of historic Queens. That is, we would tour the places where he and my wife's late mother, Grace, went to school, went to church, were married and lived. He has done this before with our children, but somehow felt it needed to be done again with the entire family.

The outing had the potential for disaster. My father-in-law tires quickly these days. It is late November and the weather could have been awful. It meant coordinating the group for a reasonably early Sunday morning start, not normally their perkiest time of the week.

It was great. Everyone was on time. The weather was perfect, unseasonably warm. Larry and Deirdre drove their SUV and I rented a car. Larry brought a pair of walkie-talkies not only so we could stay in touch with one another but so that Pop could do a running commentary while we were driving. Tara videotaped while I drove, and then I videotaped at the various stops. The first destination, a church that had been attended by three generations of Gering women (my late mother-in-law's family), was also being visited today by a squad of New York City firemen, who arrived aboard their hook and ladder truck. While the Catholic members of the squad attended mass, Larry took Jake over to inspect the fire truck. Pop began by giving our kids the story of the family's connection with the church but then drifted over to the fire truck. I was able simultaneously to videotape Jake inspecting the interior of the truck and Pop filling in the remaining firemen on the background of the church.

But if that light and photogenic start to the morning put us all in a cheerful frame of mind, the next stop was heavenly. Outside the Church of the Ascension in Elmhurst, as Sunday morning worshipers filed in for the 11 o'clock mass, Pop began telling the kids how he and their "Nan," Grace Gering, had been married there sixty-one years ago last Friday. Just then, accompanied by two altar boys, one carrying a cross, the other a censer, Father Vito Buonanno emerged from the rectory on his way into the church.

Pop was blocking the door. As Father Vito listened to a retelling of the entire family connection, I could see him twitching, so I put the video camera down for a moment. He looked up, spotted me and now it was the group of us who had a difficult time extricating ourselves from his attention. Father Vito was just bubbling and insisted on giving Pop a special blessing, which of course made his day and ours.

We lunched at a diner on Queens Boulevard. There was a diner on that site when Pop was courting Nan sixty-five years ago, though the physical plant is not the same.

It was a genuinely joyful day, all the more so because when, in years to come, the kids look at the family collaboration that resulted in that videotape of their grandfather, it is destined to become one of their most precious keepsakes.

November 22 / Potomac

It's hard to believe that it has been thirty-six years since John F. Kennedy was assassinated. What makes it so difficult to believe is that it was only when I typed the date that I remembered the anniversary. Thirty-six years ago no one would have convinced me that the date could ever slip past me almost unnoticed.

I had only been working at ABC News for a few months. I was preparing a feature piece on Enrico Caruso. I no longer remember why. I was in the control room working with a radio engineer on cutting the piece when word came that Kennedy had been shot.

Grace Anne was pregnant at the time with our first child. Andrea was actually born five days later (coincidentally on Caroline Kennedy's birthday), but our great concern was that our first baby not be born on a day that we believed would, forever, carry that dreadful association.

I went to the dentist this morning to get a cavity filled. As I sat there in the reclining chair, I couldn't help but remember my mother's story of being rolled into the delivery room at the hospital in Nelson, England. My parents had married late in life, and my mother was almost forty-one years old when I was born. At one point, one of the nurses in the hospital held out her hand and asked my mother for her dental plates. Mom recalled laughing and telling the nurse that she had all her teeth. That was almost unthinkable in England in those days.

November 23 / En route to New York

I'm scheduled to present an award to Don Hewitt, the executive producer and creator of *60 Minutes*. The presentation is part of a celebratory fund-raising event put on by The Committee to Protect Journalists (CPJ), an organization that Grace Anne and I respect and support.

I got to the airport in plenty of time to catch the 5:30 Delta shuttle but forgot about Thanksgiving. The holiday is still two days off, but the number of people traveling is huge. The plane was already full when I got to the gate at 5:15. Customer relations did everything they could to be helpful, and finally a Delta captain who was deadheading this flight got off so that I could have his seat. One of the staffers told me the planes have been crammed since last Saturday. People seem to be taking off for Thanksgiving earlier and earlier each year—another sign of prosperity.

I am seated next to a woman with two small children. One daughter appears to be about three; the other is an infant no more than six months old. The infant is cuddled on her mother's lap. Cute but deadly. We have done a magnificent job of alerting parents to the danger of letting children sit in adult-sized car seats: The designs on car seats for children have become safer with each passing year. But we completely ignore the dangers of letting infants travel on their parents' laps aboard airliners. If, God forbid, this plane were to make an abrupt stop on the ground, or suddenly lose altitude once airborne, the baby next to me wouldn't have much of a chance of escaping injury. In this regard, the Europeans seem ahead of us. A mother and infant next to me aboard an Aer Lingus flight a couple of months ago were outfitted, by one of the flight attendants, with a small seat belt that could be attached to the mother's belt. It's not perfect but far better than what we're doing.

November 24 / En route to Washington

Last night's CPJ event was a breath of fresh air. The dinner itself was the typical Waldorf Astoria scene in which too many people are stuffed into a ballroom with altogether too many tables. Still, that's what enabled the organizers to announce with great pride that the event, for the first time, raised more than a million dollars.

CPJ has established itself as sort of an international 911 for battered journalists. Three of its awardees, decked out in ball gowns and tuxedos, spoke movingly last night of what they have personally endured in order to work as journalists under repressive governments. A fourth awardee could not attend because he is still being held in a Cuban prison.

I was especially moved by the words of a young Colombian reporter. She has risked her life many times covering the excesses of paramilitary groups and leftist guerrillas in her country. "The U.S. government keeps sending military aid to my country," she said. "We don't need any more guns; we need humanitarian aid."

I was sitting next to a Pakistani woman. She and her husband run a small weekly, the *Friday Times*, in Lahore. She told me how nine soldiers broke into her home last spring, literally dragged her husband off by his feet and kept her under house arrest for three days. Even though she didn't know what was happening to her husband, who was in a military prison, she put out the paper by herself, simultaneously organizing street protests demanding his release. She has an understandably jaundiced view of the "democratic" government that was overthrown by Gen. Pervez Musharraf in a military coup a few weeks ago.

What a treat it is to meet people like this. It reminds me why I love journalism so much and how far many of us in the American media have drifted from the idealism we had when we began in this business and before we got fat and happy.

November 25 / Potomac

It's Thanksgiving Day. Ken, the young man who has been dating our oldest daughter for most of the past year, called me at the office earlier this week and asked if we could get together. He wants to discuss something with me. There is always the remote possibility that he has something else on his mind—but I believe he is going to ask me for Andrea's hand in marriage. They are both in their thirties and he certainly doesn't need to put himself through this, but I'm delighted. It's a charming anachronism, and I'll try to make it as painless for him as possible. (Unless, of course, he's coming by to negotiate the dowry, in which case I'll tell him exactly what I think of these meaningless, old-fashioned customs.)

I've begun writing Chanukah cards because the festival of lights begins on December 4 this year. The Christmas and combo cards (for mixed marriages like ours) can still wait a while.

If, years from now, you wonder what one of the hallmarks of our culture was, check the Hallmarks. Hallmark is the biggest greeting card company in the country. It has built a multibillion-dollar industry on ersatz emotion and sentimentality. Greeting cards are to genuine emotions what powdered coffee is to the real thing. But as we spread our sentiments over an ever-expanding field of recipients, the chore of expressing our actual feelings has become too trying. Every year Americans send each other billions of cards, the sentiments conveyed actually those of the anonymous Cyranos who are getting rich writing their treacly poetry somewhere in Kansas City.

One of the reasons that ours is a less literate society than it used to be is that we have learned to substitute the prepackaged wit and sentimentality of others for the effort of generating our own.

November 26 / Potomac

There is a bird sanctuary abutting our property and a stream that winds through the glen. I suggested to Ken that we take a stroll down to the stream, and it was there that he asked for my permission to marry Andrea. He had clearly been anticipating the moment with some apprehension, but, as I said earlier, I'm grateful to him for the courtesy.

It made for a wonderful Thanksgiving weekend. My father-in-law seemed to derive fresh energy from the prospect of another wedding in the offing. The other kids were generous with their enthusiasm, and Grace Anne and I will be happy to welcome Ken into the family.

It's only after you've spent the bulk of your lifetime nursing and prodding and gentling your children through the inevitable problems that envelop every family that you can fully appreciate the prospect of seeing them established in their own careers, partnered with someone they love and who loves them in return and embarking on the journey of raising their own family.

In years to come, Thanksgiving will always be associated for us with the moment that Ken and Andrea committed to each other.

November 27 / Potomac

Today is Andrea's birthday. Ken formalized everything last night by popping the question and handing over the engagement ring.

There's some good news on the Irish front in that the Unionists voted yesterday to accept the agreement that will make Northern Ireland separate from England. They, the Protestants and the Catholic Sinn Fein will form a government, and only then will the IRA surrender its weapons. I find it difficult to believe that all of this will actually come to pass; there have been so many false starts and disappointments. Former senator George Mitchell deserves enormous credit for the patience and tenacity he has shown in shepherding this agreement to its present state.

In Chechnya, meanwhile, Russian troops seem to be on the verge of taking over the capital city of Grozny. The Russians have been bombing the city mercilessly for weeks now. I hear people analogizing between what the Russians are doing in Grozny and what the United States did in its bombing campaign over Belgrade. Clearly the Russians learned from the United States in terms of conducting a campaign that would be low in "friendly" casualties and therefore popular at home, but there is no similarity at all when you compare the pains taken by NATO bombers to avoid civilian casualties in Yugoslavia and the brutal Russian bombing campaign over Chechnya. President Clinton told Boris Yeltsin how much the United States disapproves of what is happening in Chechnya, but without the threat of any consequences, it was a meaningless bit of posturing.

The United States stands alone at the pinnacle of world power as we come to the end of this century. There is no real sense, however, that our foreign policy makers have any concerted idea of how or even where that power should be employed.

November 28 / Potomac

This morning's newspapers are filled with stories that illustrate the extremes on the economic scale here in the United States. There is ample evidence, on the one hand, of the vibrant economy, of the time and money available to be wasted. In the *New York Times* there is a silly little feature on Pink's Hot Dog Stand in Hollywood. A couple of excerpts: "The menu has grown to offer 21 kinds of hot dogs, and now, Pink's sells up to 2,000 of them a day—hot dogs with bacon, hot dogs with guacamole, hot dogs with sour cream, tomatoes, mustard relish and onions, hot dogs stuffed with jalapeno peppers." And this: "The wait for a chili dog, which normally costs $2.40 [celebrating its sixtieth anniversary, Pink's was, for two days, selling its hot dogs for 60 cents], stretched for up to four hours near the corner of Melrose and La Brea Avenues."

There is also in the *Times* a more substantive article on valet parking in Los Angeles: "Here you can leave the keys with Jeeves at hospitals and mini-malls, movie theaters and grocery stores, the occasional Starbucks and at least one gym, not to mention practically every fancy private party for twenty people or more." One of the larger valet parking companies has sixteen hundred employees and pays its valets, most of them Hispanic, between six and seven dollars an hour.

By contrast the dominant story on the front page of the *Washington Post* is headlined "On Chicken's Front Line." Featured in the story is a worker by the name of Walt Frazier who has spent twenty years on the line. He is now largely crippled by the debilitating and repetitive nature of the work. At the peak of his career he was one of the best "chicken hangers" in the business. "He could grab a reluctant chicken off a conveyer belt and hoist it overhead at a pace of one bird every two seconds." Depending on whether he worked the day shift or the night shift, Frazier earned $8.80 or $8.90 an hour.

> The slaughterhouse challenges the senses. The plant smells like wet feathers. Temperatures range from below freezing—in what is known as the 28-degree room, where packages await shipping—to 120 degrees by the scalder, which loosens feathers. In the summer, live hang (where Frazier worked) becomes so unbearably hot that chickens can suffocate in less than a minute.
>
> The din is such that yearly hearing tests are necessary. Water from high-pressure hoses soaks the concrete floor. Fat turns surfaces slick. Blood drips from gutted chickens.

At age forty-one Frazier is no longer able to operate as a "chicken hanger." After two rounds of surgery to repair his damaged wrists, he filed a workman's compensation claim seeking expenses and lost wages for the seven months he says he was too hurt to work. The Delaware Workers Compensation Board awarded him $711.

Considering that the valet parking employees in Los Angeles are making tips on top of their six dollars or so an hour, and that their work is conducted in a far more pleasant environment than the slaughter-house, even they are worlds apart from Frazier and his fellow workers.

Those of us who routinely employ the services of valet parking, who will, without a thought, spend on parking what Frazier, on his best day, earned in an hour by hanging three hundred flailing chickens by their feet from a hook, inhabit a different universe. The world of manual labor is, no doubt, much improved over what it was at the beginning of this century, but the price of a poor or inadequate education remains a life of hardship, struggle and inequity that can surely be overcome if only it ever rises near the top of our list of national priorities.

November 29 / En route to New York

I have agreed to moderate a panel on AIDS/HIV at the United Nations tomorrow morning. The organizers have asked that I come to New York this evening so that the panelists and I will have a chance to focus on the material and decide on how best to present it.

There is always a certain cringe factor inherent in sessions like these. The panelists are all well-intentioned people (in this case, doctors, health-care specialists and economists) and there is no quarreling with the basic premise of their thesis. They are convinced that business must take a lead in developing public relations campaigns to alert people to the precautions they must take to avoid becoming infected with HIV. They also believe that businesses will come to realize that the worldwide spread of AIDS is so inherently damaging to their own economic interests that they will do whatever is necessary to inhibit it. Still, these sessions so often turn into instances of preaching to the choir. Actually, it's worse than that. Activists frequently attend these sessions with their own agenda, and then it becomes (a) an exchange between those already in agreement with one another, and (b) speeches from the floor by those who don't think the topic of the day goes far enough.

November 30 / En route to Washington

I don't know if anyone in the audience learned much from our panel discussion. They were, as I expected, an extremely knowledgeable bunch. I learned a lot, though.

Every twentieth person who died in sub–Saharan Africa this past year died of AIDS. Fifty-six percent of all people in that same region will die before they reach the age of sixty. In South Africa alone, 750,000 to a million people will die of AIDS this year. Since the AIDS epidemic began roughly twenty years ago, fifty million people world-wide have been infected. And while advances have been made in delaying the transition from HIV positive to full-blown AIDS, not a single cure has been registered. Those who have been infected will die from the disease, and the projection is that it will take only half as long (that is, ten years) for the next fifty million people to be infected. And it is no longer true that more men than women are being infected—certainly not in Africa, where 20 percent more women than men are becoming infected these days.

It's certainly time for *Nightline* to do another town meeting on the subject. I think the belief is growing among the general public that the danger of AIDS is diminishing. In this country, it may be; but internationally, it is growing, and disease does not respect international boundaries.

December

December 1 / Washington

I remember flying to Tokyo a few years ago. One of the other passengers, an entrepreneur, recognized me and came over to talk for a while. He was, he told me, going to Japan in order to set up what he described as a "virtual" shopping mall. People would be using their computer screens to scroll from floor to floor and from shop to shop. They would be able to examine goods on-screen, order them with the tap of a key and have the amounts automatically subtracted from their bank or credit card accounts.

It would, he acknowledged, be a difficult sell in Japan, because tradition plays such an important role in that country. Still, he was confident that the astronomical real estate prices in downtown Tokyo would convince some of the merchants he was visiting to try a different "virtual" approach.

I was intrigued by the picture he sketched but unconvinced that it would ever get off the ground. Amazon.com and eBay have made a believer out of me. It is astonishing how little time it has taken for vast segments of the American public to latch on to the convenience of Internet shopping. It may prove to be one of those pivotal developments that changes the very nature of how we live. Just as air-conditioning made states like Arizona and Nevada accessible and desirable to millions of new residents; just as interstate highways, beltways and shopping malls siphoned millions of Americans out of the cities and into previously isolated farm country on the outskirts of those cities; so, too, will the Internet simultaneously make us instantly accessible to one another and more isolated in terms of direct, personal contact.

We are moving toward societies in which children can be educated at home, people can conduct their businesses from home, we can all be entertained at home and all necessary transactions can be completed from home—all of us, that is, who are computer-literate and wealthy enough to afford the technology and the sorts of homes in which such quasi-isolationism can be considered desirable.

December 2 / Washington

It is after midnight and we have just finished doing our *Nightline* program on the first Republican presidential "debate" involving all of the candidates. The event was sponsored by our ABC affiliate WMUR in New Hampshire, and, initially, I was supposed to comoderate the event. The structure of the format, though, was so restrictive (and, it seemed to us, so tilted in favor of the front-runner, George W. Bush) that Tom Bettag and I suggested to ABC News president David Westin that we pull out. He was totally supportive. I hope he's as pleased with that decision tonight as I am.

It is a joke to call an event like the one that transpired tonight a debate. Two reporters sat and asked questions of one candidate after another. Each man was supposed to answer only the question he was asked, and was given a minute and thirty seconds in which to do so. Since the next candidate would then be asked another question altogether, it was an act of rhetorical contortion for one man to address himself to what one of his rivals had said.

Senator Orrin Hatch used the opportunity of his two-minute closing statement (during which he was free to say whatever he wanted) to decry the format, but then Hatch doesn't have a snowball's chance in hell of winning the nomination. Gary Bauer and Alan Keyes don't either, but they are obliged to be treated like the three candidates who do have a chance. It clogs up the process that, ultimately, decrees that only those candidates with an enormous war chest have any chance at victory. That's the way the system is set up. So, this time around, only Bush, McCain and Forbes can hope to stay in the race. But as far as the "debates" are concerned, we pretend that it's a level playing field.

Because we were able to pull the best three or four minutes out of the ninety-minute event, *Nightline* made the whole thing look pretty good. That's the ultimate irony.

December 3 / Washington

The Polar Lander is scheduled to make a "soft" landing on Mars sometime today, after which it is expected to begin sending back both sound and pictures. The achievement, if it works, is mind-boggling, but we have become so apathetic to the general subject of space exploration that the event is attracting only a moderate amount of attention.

Mankind has been dreaming of moments like this throughout the millennia, but now we are so preoccupied with our own well-being here on Earth that the implications of a successful soft landing on Mars causes hardly a ripple. I'm hard-pressed to explain it, but I feel it. We may mention it at the end of our broadcast tonight but I'm certainly not pressing to change the subject of our program.

We have, in the course of less than fifty years, realized the first important steps of space travel, and, almost immediately, lost interest. It will probably take some extraordinary discovery in space or a genuine calamity here on Earth to reignite the passion we once had.

December 4 / Potomac

Perhaps the Mars Polar Lander has crashed, perhaps its antenna is simply misdirected, but nothing has been heard or seen of it since it entered the Martian atmosphere sometime yesterday afternoon. The possibility of failure has actually attracted more attention than did the prospect of success. There is still hope at the Jet Propulsion Laboratory in Pasadena that contact will be reestablished.

The big story of this past week was, surprisingly, the meeting of international delegates to the World Trade Organization in Seattle, Washington. What attracted attention was a sixties-like series of demonstrations opposing the WTO. Opposition covers a wide political spectrum. There are far-right-wingers who perceive the organization as an international cabal that will undermine U.S. sovereignty. There are left-wingers who also see a cabal, but one between the member governments and the world's leading corporations. There are environmentalists and AIDS activists convinced that big business puts profit over human concerns. And there is big labor, equally convinced that international corporations will drain jobs out of first-world countries like the United States and transfer them to the cheap labor of the developing world.

This strange coalition of unlikely bedfellows was aided and abetted by a bunch of young anarchists who shocked the sensibilities of law-abiding residents in Seattle by smashing the windows of a Nordstrom's department store and a Starbucks coffeehouse. When the police responded with pepper spray, tear gas and a few rubber bullets, television discovered an unsuspected interest in the WTO.

Whatever the reason (and it may be nothing loftier than President Clinton's unwillingness to undermine Al Gore's support among labor unions), the Seattle round broke up without reaching any sort of agreement on international trade. The chances for progress will be greatly enhanced after the presidential elections.

December 5 / Potomac

I still have a hard time believing that this is true, but I am told that the commercial rate for the next Super Bowl (which is being carried by ABC in January) is a staggering $2 million per thirty-second commercial. The alleged reason for this windfall is the frantic level of competitiveness between and among the practitioners of e-commerce, who have been bidding up the price of airtime to hawk their services.

I can't help but feel we are in the middle of the biggest Ponzi scheme or business pyramid since investors a few hundred years ago went bonkers about tulips. A great deal of money was paid then for the rarer examples; and, I believe, a Turkish sultan offered an incredible sum to anyone who could breed a pure black tulip.

By this I don't mean to suggest that e-commerce is not here to stay, nor even that it won't come to dominate the marketplace even more than it already does. Still, there appears to be a total lack of discrimination these days about what will and will not work on the Internet. Almost everyone, it seems to me, is buying on the come. I understand the general principle of "frictionless" commerce, in which buyer and seller can, easily and instantly, generate the exchange of goods and services for money regardless of time or location. But there has rarely been a greater opportunity for both intellectual and financial thievery. The Internet makes information, products and services available in greater quantities than ever before. Quality control in each remains the problem. A lot of people will lose their fortunes and reputations in the gold rush mentality of e-commerce before we find and exercise the proper controls.

December 6 / Los Angeles

Tom Bettag and I flew out here to Disney headquarters for some meetings about the future of *Nightline* and the Internet. We were early, so we ate lunch at the Disney cafeteria. I'm sure there were some people there over the age of thirty-five, but we didn't see many. Entertainment is very much a young person's business these days.

We are at a point in the development of our industry very similar to the transition point from radio to television in the late forties or early fifties. Back then the stars of radio were reluctant to shift from one medium to the other. It was easy to understand why. There were millions of radio sets in the country and only a few thousand television sets. It would have been difficult to comprehend how totally television would displace radio as the country's principal source of entertainment and news. Were it not for the portability of radio, which became possible only with the development of the transistor, radio might have been wiped out altogether. Now, we are trying to understand and anticipate what the impact of complete interactivity on the Internet will mean as it relates to the development of television.

December 7 / Washington

I doubt that the name TiVo, or even the device itself, will be remembered long, but it is, I believe, the first generation of a technology that will revolutionize the way we watch and interact with our television sets.

At its most basic level, TiVo is simply a quicker, better videotape recorder. Except that there is no tape, there is a hard disk and the viewer can make an instant decision (phone rings, hit the remote control) to "pause" the program he's watching, automatically recording from that moment on until the viewer is free to begin watching again. Neat, but simply the beginning. TiVo is also capable of "remembering" what you watch and of then "asking" you if you would like to have that program recorded on a regular basis, or if you would like it to record other, similar programs. That's the revolutionary part.

Soon, I believe, viewers will, either through their viewing habits or by virtue of filling out a profile, be able to tell their recorders what kinds of material should be gathered on hard disk while they are off pursuing their daily activities. As that technology becomes more sophisticated, "search engines" will track down medical material for people suffering from a certain disease, business background on a particular client—anything and everything, to fill the customized viewing needs of that person.

We may not like every aspect of where this is leading. As this technology intuitively mines our likes and dislikes, it is simultaneously stripping away the last vestiges of our privacy. But there is no question that it has already begun happening.

December 8 / Washington

It has been more than forty years since Fidel Castro overthrew Fulgencio Batista in Cuba. During that period Cuban troops and agents have supported leftist opposition movements throughout Central and Latin America and throughout much of Africa. And during that time a succession of U.S. administrations has authorized operations against Cuba in general, Castro in particular and Cuban-backed guerrillas all over. Castro's survival has been nothing short of miraculous. The lack of political freedom inside Cuba remains oppressive, and the level of animus toward Castro within the huge and hugely influential Cuban-American community in southern Florida is as vitriolic as ever.

Into this combustible mixture comes the story of a six-year-old boy, Elian Gonzalez, whose mother joined her boyfriend and eight or nine other Cubans in trying to make their escape from the island aboard a small boat. The mother and boyfriend drowned. The child survived by hanging on to an inner tube for two days and nights.

The boy was immediately taken in by relatives of his natural father, who remains behind in Havana. The father has demanded the return of his child; the relatives in Miami are saying no. Castro, to no one's surprise, has decided to make an international scandal of the issue. International (and, for that matter, U.S.) law is probably on the side of the natural father. Political pressure in southern Florida has been mobilized against returning the boy. Daily demonstrations and rallies are surging through the streets of Havana, demanding the return of the child.

This situation is, in so many respects, a throwback to the Cold War between capitalism and communism. What Castro seems to know intuitively is that this is an acutely embarrassing case for the U.S. government. Washington is in the awkward position of seeming to put the boy's economic welfare ahead of his father's right to raise his own child. No one, incidentally, has suggested that the man was a bad father. If the child is sent back, though, there will be political repercussions in Florida. Thus far, there has been no overt display of conscience or courage.

December 9 / Washington

In rolling toward the slam-bang, once-in-a-millennium finale of this year, we have begun looking at some of the visions of the future that have accumulated on film and elsewhere over the past sixty or seventy years. It's mostly predictable stuff: Women in evening gowns dancing through futuristic kitchens, aided and abetted in their newly carefree lives by a variety of "thinking" appliances. Mom, Dad and the kids sipping sodas and coffee (Dad puffing on a cigar) while the family automobile zips along on autopilot under the benign eye of a distant traffic controller. Boy and girl "spooning" (this was before crass sex in its current incarnation was acknowledged openly in the media) in a hovering aircraft, only to be told to "move along now" by an airborne cop with an Irish accent.

What is so extraordinary about all these ancient and largely innocent visions of the future is how much they reveal of our past. If you would understand how lily-white America really was in the forties and fifties, you have only to scan its contemporaneous dreams for the future. African Americans do not exist, neither do Hispanics—at least not in anything but the most subservient roles. There's certainly no such thing as homosexuality. As for women, those pert little creatures have no greater ambition than to preside over the kitchen, mother their children and be an ornament to their husbands.

What also leaps out at the viewer of these old films and industrial promotions is how truly mundane most visions of the future really are. The true visionaries are rarely understood and therefore almost never consulted.

December 10 / Washington

Years ago, cartoonists used to mock the image of self-important Central and Latin American dictators and generals, sashes slung over their shoulders, chests decorated with gigantic medals. We have outdone them.

I remember how desperately I yearned for an Emmy when I was a young reporter. My thirty-first and thirty-second such awards arrived in the mail earlier this week. The "academy" that awards them is a pompous, useless organization that feeds upon our vanity. Networks like to brag about how many Emmys they have won because it seems to bestow legitimacy on what we do. It doesn't.

We have more damned awards than programs. If you've been on the air for a season or two and haven't won somebody's award for something, you probably deserve a special award for originality.

One of *Nightline*'s correspondents, John Donvan, won an Emmy a few weeks back and confessed on our morning conference call how pointless he had always thought they were, but that he never felt he could fairly say so until he had won one.

Exactly!

December 11 / Potomac

The nation is pregnant with lists. In our frenzy to get a grip on the millennium, or at least the twentieth century, we are madly prioritizing events, people, accomplishments. There does seem to be a vague acknowledgment that not all of the greatest men and women were born in or emigrated to the United States. Gandhi and Churchill manage to elbow onto lists between Babe Ruth and Frank Sinatra. But most American lists appear to be heavily weighted in favor of the United States.

One of the most interesting lists that I glimpsed the other day has been assembled by The Learning Channel, a cable network. In the top

one hundred greatest accomplishments, the building of the Panama
Canal cropped up somewhere around fifty-seventh. Television was
about fifteen. I'm curious to know what will be deemed the greatest
single accomplishment of the past hundred years.

I note in this morning's newspapers that Franjo Tudjman, the president of Croatia, died yesterday. It was Tudjman who ordered the
expulsion of about six hundred thousand Serbs over a very short period
of time, setting the pattern for much of the ethnic cleansing that has
taken place in the Balkans over this past decade. Tudjman was widely
quoted during the 1990 campaign in which he was elected president as
thanking God that "my wife is not a Serb or a Jew." He began his professional life as a Marxist but ended it by reviving the sort of fascism
that was popular in Croatia during World War II. Still, he was useful to
the Clinton administration in mounting a military offensive against
the Serbs in 1995, when the United States was trying to pressure Belgrade into signing the Dayton Accords.

Tudjman was a racist and a bully, but in the current spirit of assigning everyone a place on a list, Franjo Tudjman doesn't even make the
top ten in this century.

December 12 / Potomac

Hillary Rodham Clinton, who has to all intents and purposes
announced her candidacy for a U.S. Senate seat for New York,
declared last week that she doesn't believe the U.S. military's policy of
"don't ask, don't tell" is working. The policy was established during
the early months of the Clinton administration as a compromise
between gay activists, who wanted a more tolerant policy toward
homosexuals in the services, and the Pentagon, which did not.

Hillary is certainly right about this one. The policy hasn't worked.
It has merely driven more gays out of the military than ever before.
Non-coms and officers who, technically, are not allowed to ask subordinates if they are gay are doing so anyway. Harassment of gays has
hardly abated; it appears to be worse than ever.

Last summer a gay soldier who had been taunted unmercifully by
other troops finally beat up one of his tormentors. The tormentor, in
turn, was taunted by other soldiers for having been beaten up by a
"faggot." Thus provoked, he took a baseball bat and clubbed the gay

soldier to death while he slept. What emerged from the trial was a clear pattern of uncontrolled harassment from which there appears to be no escape. For a gay soldier to complain formally would require him to address questions about his own sexuality. He would have the option of lying or confirming his homosexuality, which, under the current rules, would give the military the right to discharge him.

President Clinton conceded, during a radio interview, that he, too, believes the policy is not working. I don't think he can get it turned around; he has too few allies in the Pentagon. Maybe John McCain could do it.

December 13 / Potomac

I'm sitting in my office at home, surrounded by photographs and mementos of events I've covered over the past thirty-seven years that I've been with ABC News. On one wall there's a photograph of our son, Andrew, aged about four, with Henry Kissinger at Andrews Air Force Base. We had just come back from a round of shuttle diplomacy in the Middle East. Andrew is now about to turn thirty. There's also a photograph of Kissinger with Andrea and Deirdre as children, supplemented by a recent picture of Andrea and Kissinger, following a CNN interview, with Andrea holding up the old photograph. There's a photograph, in which I'm interviewing Yassir Arafat, that was taken in Beirut in the mid-seventies. I was picked up at my hotel in the middle of the night, blindfolded and driven to meet with the PLO leader. Underneath that photograph is one taken in a California prison with Bobby Kennedy's assassin, Sirhan Sirhan. We were not allowed to film or videotape, so we shot hundreds of stills and I did a radio interview. It was, in some respects, much more dramatic than a filmed interview would have been. Ethel Kennedy didn't talk to me for years thereafter. We were thinking only of our "get" (Sirhan had not previously been interviewed), but in that Sirhan believed the interview might help his application for parole, I can understand her anger.

There's one photograph of a walking interview I did with Maurice Chevalier, the great French music hall singer, in Central Park on the occasion of his farewell tour through the United States. It was one of the longest reports ever run on the ABC evening news program—almost nine minutes.

Two of my most precious photographs hang on opposite sides of the room. On one wall I'm shaking hands with Zhouenli during the burial of Edgar Snow's ashes in Beijing in 1973. My ABC colleagues and I were the only Americans in Beijing at the time, so we were invited to attend the ceremony honoring the author of *Red Star Over China*. Snow spent years traveling and living with Mao Zedong and the early Communist leaders before they came to power, and, for many years thereafter, his book provided the only real insight into their background by an English-speaking journalist and writer. On the other wall I'm pictured standing next to Harry Truman in 1968, a few years before his death. I was Miami bureau chief and had driven down to Key West, where Truman liked to winter.

There are photographs with Governor George Wallace in his prime, and Richard Nixon in 1964. There is one with South Vietnamese president Nguyen Van Thieu, in the garden of his presidential palace in Saigon. I think the picture was taken in 1973, a couple of years before the fall of Saigon. As I recall the occasion Thieu had asked me about the mood in Washington, and I had just told him that there was absolutely no more appetite for fighting in Vietnam. He wanted to know whether Nixon would resume the bombing if the North Vietnamese continued filtering troops into the South. "No," I told him. "Nixon is all wrapped up in the Watergate affair." Thieu insisted that Nixon had promised to resume the bombing. He refused to believe it wouldn't happen.

Above the picture with Thieu, there are photographs taken in Moscow with Mikhail Gorbachev during his last few weeks in office. In the background you can see Boris Yeltsin. The two men had just come out of a meeting in which Yeltsin had told Gorbachev that his time in power was over. I learned later that Yeltsin was angry that I had spent so much time talking to Gorbachev; he felt I should have recognized that the power had already transferred to him.

So many memories, so much faded power.

December 14 / En route to Washington

I spent the afternoon in New York watching William F. Buckley Jr. record the last two episodes of his interview program, *Firing Line*. Then he and I sat together and recorded this evening's *Nightline*. We had pulled together a setup piece that was largely a celebration of Bill's thirty-three years on the air, interwoven with a scanty profile that gives a limited sense of his extraordinary background. He had hosted his own television program longer than any other person has hosted a program.

Buckley, however, is one of the very few people of our time whom it is fair to describe as a Renaissance Man—gifted pianist, prolific author of both fiction and nonfiction, world-class sailor who developed his own method of celestial navigation. Most of all, though, Bill will be remembered as the popularizer of modern American conservatism. He has done this largely through his newspaper columns, the conservative journal, *National Review*, that he created and, of course, the television program.

I think it's fair to say that in the 1960s the word "conservative" was used in the mass media as a term of disapproval. Most conservatives of that time were routinely dismissed as right-wing nuts or cranks. Barry Goldwater, the Arizona senator who was the Republican nominee for president in 1964, was adored by his supporters, but he was dismissed by much of the media. He was painted as an extremist of dangerous proportions by the Lyndon Johnson campaign, and it wasn't until Ronald Reagan became president in 1980 that a conservative could be seen as both rational and likable. Buckley deserves much of the credit.

He could be mean, dismissive and cantankerous, but he is so prodigiously bright and researched his opponents so carefully that he was rarely defeated in debate. Indeed, it can be fairly said that Buckley helped make conservatism part of the American political mainstream.

December 15 / Mount Sunapee, New Hampshire

You know it has been a long day when you have to check the hotel menu to see where you are. It appears that I am in Mount Sunapee. We are a mere half-hour ride away from Claremont where, tomorrow morning at 9:30, Senator John McCain, one of the leading Republican candidates for president, and former senator Bill Bradley, who, next to Al Gore, is the only other Democratic candidate for president, will make an unusual joint pledge not to accept "soft" money contributions to their campaigns, if nominated. ("Soft," as distinct from "hard," campaign contributions are made to the party, rather than to the candidate directly. Direct contributions to a candidate cannot exceed $1,000 per donor. "Soft" money, which is not supposed to benefit an individual candidate, theoretically can be unlimited.)

Bradley's position is a little mushier than McCain's. He promises not to accept "soft" money if the Republican nominee makes the same promise, no sure thing by a long shot. The two of them have chosen to make this announcement in Claremont for at least three reasons: (1) because each man thinks it will play well among New Hampshire voters (notoriously independent, if not ornery); (2) because they know it will piss off their opponents; and (3) because Bradley is scheduled to appear with Vice President Al Gore at a town meeting that I'm moderating on Friday, and his campaign aides clearly believe it will give him a leg up.

There is cold fury within both the Gore and Bush campaigns directed at *Nightline* and me because they believe we have allowed ourselves to be used in devoting a show to McCain and Bradley. (There was a long, snippy editorial in the *Wall Street Journal* to that effect this morning.) In a sense we have been mousetrapped. It's a good news story, and I can think of no reason why we should have refused to cover it. But it does give Bradley some significant momentum going into his Friday meeting with Gore.

What can never be predicted by anyone, of course, is how well either McCain or Bradley will do tomorrow in the face of some challenging questions.

December 16 / Manchester, New Hampshire

There is, at times, an Alice-in-Wonderland quality to these presidential campaigns. I'm thinking in particular of the advance people, that is, the men and women who are charged with seeing to it that transportation is available to get their candidates where they're going at the time they're supposed to be there; that the candidate will meet and appropriately fuss over potentially helpful local VIPs; that the traveling media will be able to eat, sleep, relieve themselves and, most important, file stories about the candidate. The advance people are the dedicated staffers who will take care of those and a thousand other details that must be dealt with constantly.

The advance people for McCain and Bradley were adamant that

this morning's event take place outdoors, at precisely the same place where President Clinton and House Speaker Newt Gingrich promised, four and a half years ago, to address the issue of campaign finance reform. We pointed out that on December 16 it would be freezing cold. In order to erect a tent around the event, it was necessary to cut down a venerable apple tree, for which the owners demanded that ABC News pay them $4,000. I'm not sure what the space heaters we rented cost, but whatever it was, it was too much—they didn't work, and all of us, candidates, moderator and audience, were freezing.

Still, McCain and Bradley wanted to sit out there for an hour, without coats. Apparently no one on their advance teams had paid attention to that little detail of weather. I told the candidates I would follow their lead, if they insisted—since I was leaving on Saturday for a Florida vacation and could recover from whatever cold or flu I contracted at my leisure; they, however, would still be campaigning throughout the country.

We all wore coats.

December 17 / Nashua, New Hampshire

Today is our daughter Deirdre's birthday. Clearly the main event of the day, which she conveyed to me this morning, is that she is pregnant with her second child. What a joy!

The town meeting at which Vice President Gore and Senator Bradley were given chance after chance to offer succinct answers to questions from a gathering of local citizens was like nothing so much as putting a couple of starving men into a cafeteria. Again and again I asked them to keep their answers relatively short, or at least related to the questions being asked. Both of them appeared afraid that if they relinquished control of the microphone they would never be given another chance to speak. During the first fifty minutes of the town meeting they addressed a mere five questions. They just can't help themselves.

It got better as the program went along, but they seem to forget that *Nightline* goes on the air at 11:35 at night. If viewers aren't captivated by the first half hour, they are certainly not going to hang around past midnight for the remaining hour. The debate had the potential of being special, but it was mostly mundane and predictable.

I wonder what would happen to our political process if someone with genuine political support also showed a genuine flair for rhetoric and a willingness to be concise and straightforward. *The Candidate*, a wonderful film that starred Robert Redford as a plain-talking senatorial candidate, dealt with that proposition back in the seventies. What happened in the movie would probably happen in reality. The candidate gained immediate and enormous public attention and, ultimately, support because of his refreshing candor. Then, when it became apparent that he might actually win the election, his handlers toned him down, until he became just as cautious and mundane as any other politician in a close race.

Earlier in the day, the producers and I met with Bradley and his aides, then with Gore and his. Precisely half an hour had been set aside for each campaign (at their insistence, not ours) to discuss technical details of the forum. Bradley and his advisors were fifteen minutes late and then spent their remaining fifteen minutes (Gore was coming to the theater at 12:30, by which time the Bradley people had to be gone) arguing over my insistence that both candidates remain seated. My concern was that if either or both of them started roaming the stage and "interacting" with the audience, all semblance of control would be lost. Bradley finally resolved the matter for his team by snatching off his microphone and pretending to walk out in a huff. He was grinning broadly, and it nicely defused the growing acrimony between his staff and me. The end result, though, was that no one on his staff had learned anything. Gore, by contrast, immediately agreed to remain seated and then spent the full half hour pumping me, the producers and the director on everything from camera angles to how the audience was selected.

If this was any reflection of how the respective campaigns are being run, Bradley is not well served.

Ironically, at the end of last night's town meeting, Bradley leaned over and said, "It was better sitting down."

December 18 / En route to Captiva

For me, the year will end where it began, in Captiva. But this trip has me grousing once again about the airlines. I was approached at Dulles Airport by a man who runs a public interest operation for airline passengers. He would like to see *Nightline* do another program on airline deregulation. It was an easy sale. I don't have to look beyond my own family, several of whom had their flights canceled days before departure, without explanation, to recognize that airline service is deteriorating. Nonstop flights are routinely being replaced with so-called "direct" flights. For us that means stopping in the Carolinas or Atlanta on the way to Fort Myers. Our daughter Tara found herself rebooked onto a flight that leaves at 6 a.m. and detours through Pittsburgh. My own nonstop return flight to Washington was canceled and replaced with a six-hour marathon connecting through Chicago.

My new friend, who keeps his jaundiced eye fixed on the industry, explained it takes twice as long to get from one point to another in the United States in 1999 as it did in 1980. When I return from vacation I'll see how much of that charge is hyperbole. The airlines have focused all their energies on business customers and (as he put it) bribe them with bonus mileage plans. The ordinary passenger, the tourist, the occasional flyer, pays inflated prices and gets little in return. The establishment of "hubs," where one airline (Delta in Atlanta, US Air in Pittsburgh or Northwest in Minneapolis) houses its fleet of aircraft, has been economically useful for the airlines but has led to a profusion of roundabout flights, the diversion of a great many flights and an exorbitant consumption of fuel. Those additional costs are simply passed on to the passengers. Other flights, like the ones to and from Fort Myers, which service tourists more than businesspeople, are being canceled altogether.

I can't pretend to understand the issue yet, but my own anecdotal experience and the inability of the nice customer relations lady at Dulles this morning to explain why flights that are routinely full are being canceled, leads me to believe that this is a story worth exploring.

December 19 / Captiva

On the recommendation of friends, I have begun reading *The Deptford Trilogy* by Robertson Davies. It's quite wonderful. The narrator finds himself passionately interested in saints, miracles, and, although he himself is a somewhat dour Scots Protestant, he is fascinated by the manner in which the Catholic Church determines just which miracles contribute to the process of canonizing which saints. In the course of his own research, the narrator stumbles across a group of Jesuits, the Bollandists, whose task it is to assemble and record all available information about saints. One of their leading scholars is a Spanish Jesuit, Padre Ignacio Blazon, who is also fluent in Greek, Latin, Hebrew, French and English. Blazon loves fine food and promises to entertain and inform the hero of our book in exchange for good and bountiful meals. In the course of a train trip and fortified by a sumptuous picnic basket, Blazon offers these intriguing reflections on the nature of miracles.

> Oh, miracles! They happen everywhere. They are conditional. If I take a photograph of you, it is a compliment and perhaps rather a bore. If I go into the South African jungle and take a photograph of a primitive, he probably thinks it a miracle and he may be afraid I have stolen a part of his soul. If I take a picture of a dog and show it to him, he does not even know what he looks like, so he is not impressed; he is lost in a collective of dogginess. Miracles are things people cannot explain. . . . Life itself is too great a miracle for us to make so much fuss about potty little reversals of what we pompously assume to be the natural order.

Just so!

The fact is that this has been a century of pseudomiracles. That is, when we first achieved the capacity to fly, to communicate from one continent to another by telephone, to record movement and sound on celluloid, to witness events as they are happening thousands of miles away, to cram entire libraries of information onto silicone chips, to cure diseases that have ravaged mankind for thousands of years, we regarded each of these achievements as miraculous. And so they were to our conventional way of thinking when we first observed them. Except that, as we became accustomed to these various inventions, they have all come to seem quite normal to us. The story of the Red Sea parting remains miraculous to us because it is supposed to have happened only once. Similarly, the story of Jesus raising Lazarus from the dead—he never repeated the feat or passed the ability on to anyone else, so the miracle never became ordinary.

Man continues to achieve the most extraordinary things, to expand the boundaries of knowledge beyond anything that could reasonably have been anticipated even a hundred years ago. Any one of a thousand current devices or procedures would have been deemed a miracle two or three thousand years ago. And yet, we are left with the same mystery that stymied mankind since our ancestors began to reason: Does God exist? You would think that our extraordinary accumulation of knowledge, over this past century in particular, would have brought us somewhat closer to an answer. Yet it seems as elusive as ever.

Many of our past predictions about where we would be at the end of the twentieth century have proved flawed. And it is only when we read the words of the great philosophers and prophets who spoke and wrote about the nature of Man that we realize how fundamentally unchanged we are. It is in our struggle to conquer our base instincts and reach for our best that we are most likely to be recognizable to the generations yet to come.

December 20 / Captiva

The State Department is in a silly battle with ABC News. A few days ago, one of our correspondents, Sheila MacVicar, followed up on a worldwide State Department notice to American travelers. The essence of the notice is that there is intelligence suggesting terrorists have targeted American tourists and businessmen. The State Department's travel advisory is one of these typically vacuous alerts that provides no real information of any value: "Stay away from crowded places," that sort of thing.

Sheila placed several telephone calls to U.S. embassies in Europe and the Middle East, identifying herself as an American citizen and asking whether there was anything in particular she could do to mitigate the risk; what specifically she should do or not do. In each case, the U.S. official answering the phone had essentially nothing to offer. Indeed, in most cases the official claimed not even to know what Sheila was talking about. She recorded the voices of each person at each embassy and used that material in a report she prepared for *World News Tonight.*

The State Department raised holy hell, claiming that this was irresponsible. Frankly, I think it was a brilliant way of illuminating the idiocy of these travel alerts. They are essentially useless, except insofar as they give the department a little cover in the event that Americans are killed in a terrorist attack. I'm told that today some deputy spokesman informed ABC News that no one at the State Department will be providing information or interviews to our news division until some official statement from ABC has been released indicating that we will never do this sort of thing again.

What a draconian threat! No more interviews from the State Department. How will we ever survive that?

December 21 / Captiva

This morning's *Wall Street Journal* reports that "News footage will be shared by ABC, CBS and Fox under a cooperative that will send common video to affiliates of all three networks in a bid to cut costs. The three broadcasters already swap footage informally, and executives say editorial content won't be shared."

Well, that's a relief.

Am I the only one who finds something totally bizarre in this "push me pull you" logic? The world of communications is fracturing and splintering in a thousand different directions, while megacorporations like Disney, Viacom and General Electric have acquired the old networks, ABC, CBS and NBC. Now the news divisions of ABC and CBS have joined with Fox and are going to pool their video to cut costs, coalescing even further. Does this mean the megacorporations made an economic error in acquiring the networks? Are the big, traditional news operations no longer perceived as financially viable on their own? Or are all the small companies, focusing on special-interest audiences, the ones embarked on a mistaken mission?

Well, I never was a businessman. What may prove to have been the undoing of all network news organizations was the initial profitability of *60 Minutes* some thirty or so years ago. Ever since then, the networks have simply regarded their news divisions as profit centers, just like a refrigerator division. I have been a newsman for forty years, though, and the idea of sharing facilities with CBS and Fox feels all wrong. The only quality guarantee the consumers of our product ever had was the fact that we were all in competition with one another. That has, it is true, also driven us in the direction of producing and airing more trash than we ever did before. But somewhere, buried in the bowels of each network news division, there still lives the small flame of hard news competition, which drives us to cover important events as thoroughly and as well as we can, in part because we fear that one of the other news divisions will do it better.

In the world of television news, competition extends to the video that our camera crews shoot. Pools were created for static events like a White House press conference, or in cases where the president, for example, would not permit more than one camera crew to join him on Air Force One. Now, it seems to me, the line is being erased altogether. I predict that before too many years have passed, one or more of the news divisions will expire.

December 22 / Captiva

There is a natural tendency during this time of year for much of the country to shut down. Christmas, while still celebrated by many Christians around the country as a time of reverence, has over the years evolved into a broader, more commercial event that overshadows all else. Department stores begin decorating (or marketing) shortly after Halloween. TV commercials start turning Christmasy at that time as well. Radio stations begin playing Christmas songs right after Thanksgiving. Most original television broadcasting ends during the second week of December, for reasons I don't quite understand, since you would think a lot of people watch television at that time of year.

The period between Christmas and New Year's is sort of a Bermuda Triangle, into which all other events fall and disappear. This year, of course, there is the additional fuss being made over the new millennium. There is a rising chorus of warnings from the government about the danger of terrorist attacks, and attention is now beginning to focus with some seriousness on the assorted problems presented by Y2K. There is something of a pro forma concern attached to both these threats, however, as though the authorities were most concerned that if, indeed, something were to happen, they could at least point to all their warnings as evidence that they knew it was coming.

There seems to be some sort of general agreement not to press anything of any real importance until the old year has passed and we have come face-to-face with what this particular new year has in store for us.

December 23 / Captiva

A friend has been confiding some of his problems to me. They are, unfortunately, very common these days. His brother and his oldest son have drug and alcohol problems. He is also terribly worried about one of his younger sons, in his early teens; it is all but impossible to keep the youngster away from others his own age who drink too much and who experiment with drugs. My friend and his wife would like the family to move, but the two of them are stymied as to where in the United States they could move without confronting similar problems.

It is easy enough to explain away the high drug use in our inner cities. Life is so difficult and violent there that anything that numbs the pain makes some tragic sense. How then to explain the same epidemic in our affluent neighborhoods? More and more, the example of society's religious conservatives, be they Christian, Jewish or Muslim, demands to be taken seriously. One can only infer that a life spent adhering to rigorous strictures and religious discipline provides an equilibrium that is missing in the lives of most of our children. This is not to suggest that orthodoxy does not produce its own unhappiness, or that some of the most freewheeling homes cannot be among the happiest. We shortchange ourselves, though, when we regard religious teachings as little more than codified superstition. Those that have withstood the test of time have much accumulated practical wisdom to impart. Some parents are simply afraid to raise their children with a firm hand, thinking themselves to be out of step. Families that operate within the influence of a church, temple or mosque are able to gain contemporary support for traditional values.

I believe that most American children these days are too coddled and that far too much attention is paid to the wishes and opinions of youngsters who haven't lived enough or learned enough to be treated as the equals of the adults who should be molding them.

December 24 / Captiva

I wonder if there has been a time when more citizens of a nation are, simultaneously, affluent and depressed. The America of 1999 is living proof of the cliché that money does not bring happiness.

The unemployment level has rarely been lower over a more sustained period. Inflation continues to be all but nonexistent. There is, of course, a massive chasm between the very wealthy and the very poor, but I doubt that there has ever been such a massive middle class in any culture or society throughout history. America has come close to becoming the functioning meritocracy it has always claimed to be. It remains more difficult to achieve success if you are a woman, or an African American or an Hispanic, or openly gay in some places; but even those hurdles are tumbling. There is a danger that the very poor, whose education and health care are tragically far behind the rest of the country, will become a permanent afterthought, all but precluded from ever catching up.

Still, so many people are, on paper, indisputably fortunate to live in such an unbelievably rich and blessed nation, and yet these Americans do not strike me, by and large, as a happy people. There is a sullen edge to our satisfaction. Our toys don't do it. Our houses and vacation condos don't do it. Two cars are not enough. The ability to travel wherever we wish is neutralized by the inconvenience of traveling under such crowded conditions. The richest people I know tend by and large also to be the unhappiest. More people are under psychiatric care and taking antidepressants than ever. Arguably, they might be even worse off without such care, but why do we seem under such unprecedented pressure when times are so good? I'm generalizing far too much, but this is not a happy country as we prepare for our millennial celebration. And the worst part is that we don't seem altogether sure of what we're missing.

December 25 / Captiva

The *New York Times* has returned once again, on its editorial page, to the subject of the new millennium. This time, the *Times* is musing about "This Millennial Christmas." They have come back to the Scythian-born monk who, in the sixth century, calculated (or, so it would seem, miscalculated) the time of Jesus' birth. "The scholarly judgment," notes the *Times*, "is that the historical Jesus [an interesting phrase that; suggesting, perhaps, a less gifted Jesus than the one of religious origin] was probably born around 4 or 6 B.C."

But nobody ever addresses the question of why, if the Christian calendar purports to begin at the time of Jesus' birth, it didn't start on December 25 (setting aside for a moment the question of whether that would have been December 25 of the year zero or of the year one). I guess we'll have to wait for another editorial to address that issue.

I want to add a postscript to my concern of the other day relating to a sharing of news video among the news divisions of CBS, ABC and Fox:

I was watching the NBC evening news tonight and saw a gripping report on the impending collapse of the Chechen capital of Grozny. There was lots of combat footage, shot from the vantage points of both the Russian army and the Chechen rebels. The reporter, however, showed up comfortably at the end of the piece reporting from Red Square in Moscow. Who the hell shot the video? The Russians? The Chechens? Some intrepid British cameraman who didn't get credit? It makes a difference. Since the young man who narrated the story quite clearly did not report it, who did? There is a world of difference between a team of newspeople—reporter, cameraperson and sound person—gathering raw material together on site and then collaborating to turn it into a television report and, alternatively, having an anonymous camera team ship the video to Moscow, London or New York so that it can be voiced by someone who had nothing whatsoever to do with gathering the material.

December 26 / Captiva

There are now, according to the Sunday *Times*, about eight million people in this country worth more than $1 million. There are 275,000 worth $10 million or more. Those figures, however, do not (cannot) explain the examples of wretched excess cited in Monique Yazigi's article: the anonymous woman of means, if not brains, who paid $3,000 to have her preferred eyebrow plucker flown across the country for an emergency pluck, cut and wax; the Park Avenue ladies who have their linens flown to Paris to be dry-cleaned (the monthly tab for that is said to run in excess of $6,000). One couple, writes Yazigi, flies their palm trees from the Hamptons down to Palm Beach in the winter in order to keep them warm. More such idiocies are no doubt being hatched among the ten-year-olds also described by Yazigi, standing outside their exclusive Upper East Side school, summoning their individual town cars with their individual cellular phones.

At the same time we learn that individual and corporate charitable gifts are down across the board. If all of this, in combination, doesn't warrant a good, old-fashioned apocalypse, I don't know what does.

December 27 / Captiva

In some respects, *People* magazine, which began life as an offshoot of a small, but popular page in *Time* magazine, has become emblematic of our age. The focus of its attention is, for the most part, people whose names will baffle the players of trivia contests ten years from now. Accomplishment plays little role. These are young, attractive people who star in television programs or in films, or are supermodels. They look great and, if they know anything, they have made a virtue of concealing it.

But this oxymoronic notion of transitory fame seems to be what the American public craves. Perhaps this is because Andy Warhol's famous observation about "fifteen minutes of fame" has taken root nationally. We may regard it as part of our national patrimony, an entitlement. The fleeting fame of each additional loser is further confirmation that "my" moment in the spotlight awaits. We seem unable to generate any enthusiasm for real accomplishment, unless, of course, it has led to the acquisition of huge sums of money; we are prepared to make exceptions for the very rich.

For the most part, though, the nature of fame these days is such that it burns out in just a few years. One of the most active industries of this last decade has been the creative replacement of one set of famous people with the next. They are famous because they are well known, and they are well known because they are famous. That has always been an element of American life during this twentieth century, but the recycling of fame has never been more ruthless, nor has it happened more quickly.

December 28 / Captiva

I once believed that if only the world had known what was happening in the concentration camps of Europe during World War II, or in the gulags of the Soviet Union during Stalin's bloody reign, or during Mao's Great Leap Forward when perhaps as many as thirty million Chinese starved to death, it would have made a difference. I no longer hold to that view. Television has given us the capacity to see and hear what is happening in otherwise inaccessible places (although more and more, American television is shirking its responsibility in this respect). It has simply made us more callous. We could not, as a nation, be less concerned or involved in what the Russians are doing in Chechnya. There are said to be fifty thousand civilians trapped in the capital of Grozny. The Russian army is methodically taking the city apart, and we are worried whether the planes will fly on time on New Year's Day.

The war between the Ethiopians and Eritreans has dragged on for years, and I am ashamed to admit I don't know how many years, or how many tens of thousands have died in the fighting. The same can be said of Sudan, where I believe close to two million have died as a consequence of the war.

Surely, as we revel in our unprecedented ability to communicate with one another by fax and mobile phone, as we are newly able to distribute to, and receive information from, myriad sources on the Internet, there ought to be some commensurate level of concern and response.

After World War II, good people around the world were able to take some refuge in the phrase: "We never knew." We know.

December 29 / Captiva

The year began with Monica, and so it ends. She has signed a contract with Jenny Craig, the weight-loss people. To prove her worthiness, Monica has reportedly lost thirty-one pounds. That is a hefty load of avoirdupois and should qualify almost anyone to be a spokesperson for a diet plan. But it does raise certain questions about what, in a spokesperson, a corporation is looking for to flog its product. Monica makes it in the "pounds lost" category. She has a lovely smile and, as evidenced on Barbara Walters's program, a bubbly personality. Still, skeptic that I am, I don't think that's what the Jenny Craig folk found so appealing. They are, after all, in this for the money, and must believe that having Monica promote their diet is going to cause millions of other women to try the program. But why do they think that? Is there some subtle undercurrent at work here? *If the woman who performed fellatio on the president can lose thirty-one pounds on this diet, surely it will work for me.* Or is it just as crass as it seems, that anybody with name recognition, no matter its source, is a useful tool of merchandising?

There are, I suppose, obvious limits. No one would want a pederast or serial killer pushing his product. But it strikes me that the line is becoming more blurred than ever before, and if, say, a potential spokesman were a serial killer with a nice smile—another Ted Bundy—and if the product identification were not too crass, perhaps a mobile phone service . . .

Well, that's conjecture for a new millennium.

December 30 / Captiva

That gentle murmur in the background may be the surf, although I'm coming to believe that it is more likely the sound of everyone straining to say something profound as we whip this millennial donkey to the finish line.

The recent techno-achievements have been awe-inspiring. My son and son-in-law are trying to teach me how to use my new Palm Pilot. I keep looking at that tiny, hand-sized rectangle of computer power and wondering how it does what it does. (It holds thousands of names and addresses, calendar entries, memos and, I'm sure, much more that I have yet to learn.) This is, in a sense, an echo of my entry a few days ago on the subject of miracles. Or perhaps it comes closer to approaching the essence of faith. I can blithely refer to the power of the silicone chip with the same slippery ease that permits reference to the power of the Almighty. The comparison is, I understand, irreverent, but we have only two options when it comes to dealing with those things we cannot hope to understand: We either deny their existence or accept their accomplishments on faith. I see the works of the Almighty every day and am swept along by the rhythm of His divine plan, but I haven't a clue as to how or why these things are. The prophets and psalmists of our great religions have suggested that lack of faith is a dangerous thing, which can lead to all manner of discomfort in the hereafter. And so, I suspect, many of us profess belief out of superstitious fear. I wonder how much faith there would be in the world without the cloud of divine disappointment hanging over our heads.

As for the minor miracles of computers and video cameras, it is laziness rather than fear that makes believers of us. We can't be bothered to learn how they work and so we simply accept them on faith.

It may be that the greatest miracle of the twentieth century rests in the paradox that even as we have harnessed the power of the atom, learned to send messages across the universe, travel at several times the speed of sound and encapsulate entire libraries of information on a chip the size of a fingernail, God's size and power remain, proportionately to our own, as great or greater than ever.

December 31 / Captiva

I am grateful to be sitting in the same lovely room overlooking the Gulf of Mexico in which I began this enterprise 365 days ago. I know now that there are both advantages and pitfalls inherent in keeping a journal. It is a useful discipline, although one that is uninterested in the peevishness of an uninspired muse. When you commit to making daily entries, lack of inspiration is a shortcoming but not an excuse. There have obviously been days when my only motive has been "to get the damned thing done." And then, in scanning a few of the entries I'm struck by how easily events of evident importance evaporate into relative insignificance. There is also little objectivity in the way we view the world. Kosovo was of no importance to most of us as the year began, despite the brutal campaign of ethnic cleansing initiated by Milošević. It rose to occupy a position of huge significance when the United States led NATO forces in an air war against the Serb military and infrastructure. Now it has all but disappeared again from our awareness. That won't make the harsh Balkan winter any easier to bear for Serbs or Kosovar Albanians without shelter, but we have lost interest, most of us, even in the roles of our own young men and women serving in the NATO peacekeeping force.

Boris Yeltsin resigned as president of Russia today, to be replaced by that faceless functionary from the KGB, Vladimir Putin. It is an event of real importance, but we've apparently decided it can wait until after the new millennium is launched by a global string of fireworks displays and rock concerts. The various networks deployed ground stations and correspondents around the world, but more or less ignored the news out of Russia in favor of the celebration.

This was the year that Microsoft lost a major court battle with the Justice Department. It may, ultimately, lead to the breakup of the software giant. Still, Microsoft's stock closed the year near its all-time high, and that could stand as a metaphor for our time. There may be trouble ahead, but there's probably a lot more profit to be made before it happens.

As I write, our own new year is still six hours off. It remains possible that Y2K will wreak some kind of havoc. But where the clock has already struck midnight, in the far Pacific and in Asia and in Russia, there is no evidence of anything untoward, and all of those countries were far less prepared, I suspect, than the United States. The new year has also arrived in Jerusalem, and if the apocalypse accompanied it in any guise, CNN has not yet heard the news, nor has Peter Jennings. We can begin to focus our attention once again on the more mundane things in life.

Nineteen ninety-nine is over. It ends, for me, more or less as it began. I would have been tempted to say precisely as it began, but Elie Wiesel, who has cast an eye over the first and last words of this journal, believes that there is importance in emphasis and that optimism is an essential ingredient.

Foreboding and hope, then.

Ted Koppel, a thirty-seven-year veteran of ABC News, has been anchor of *Nightline* since March 1980. He has won every major broadcasting award, including thirty-two Emmys, six Peabodys, nine Overseas Press Club awards, two George Polk Awards and two Sigma Delta Chi Awards. Before *Nightline*, he was a foreign, domestic and war correspondent, a bureau chief and ABC's chief diplomatic correspondent.

He is the author, with Marvin Kalb, of *In the National Interest* and, with Kyle Gibson, of *Nightline: History in the Making and the Making of Television*. Koppel was born in England but came to America at age thirteen. He is married, has four children and lives in Potomac, Maryland.

A NOTE ABOUT THE TYPE

This book was set in Janson, a typeface long thought to have
been made by the Dutchman Anton Janson, who was a practic-
ing typefounder in Leipzig during the years 1668–1687. However, it has been conclusively demonstrated that these types are
actually the work of Nicholas Kis (1650–1702), a Hungarian,
who most probably learned his trade from the master Dutch
typefounder Dirk Voskens. The type is an excellent example of
the influential and sturdy Dutch types that prevailed in England
up to the time William Caslon (1692–1766) developed his own
incomparable designs from them.

Composed by North Market Street Graphics
Printed and bound by Berryville Graphics
Designed by Virginia Tan